Sanctions against South Africa

The Peaceful Alternative to Violent Change

United Nations, New York, 1988

UNITED NATIONS PUBLICATION

Sales No. E.88.I.5

02900
ISBN 92-1-100324-5

I.   SOUTH AFRICA: THE CASE FOR MANDATORY ECONOMIC SANCTIONS

[This paper was prepared as part of the documentation for the World
Conference on Sanctions against Racist South Africa held in Paris from 16 to
20 June 1986.]

INTRODUCTION

The Paris Declaration on Sanctions Against South Africa 1/ is a succinct analysis of the case for the imposition of mandatory economic sanctions under Chapter VII of the Charter of the United Nations. The Declaration identifies clearly and pragmatically the purpose of sanctions; it appraises the oil and arms embargoes and notes the strengths and weaknesses of these measures; it underlines the potential implications of its proposed course of action for the other States of the region and suggests a concrete programme of international assistance; finally, the Declaration recognizes that the process of fighting for full mandatory sanctions will be long and difficult and pragmatically suggests measures that Member States should adopt in the interim.

The suggestion contained in the Paris Declaration of urging national action by Member States whilst continuing to advocate comprehensive mandatory sanctions has found favour in the General Assembly and the Security Council. Paragraph 7 of General Assembly resolution 39/72 G of 13 December 1984 proposes specific national measures, pending mandatory sanctions by the Security Council. The measures proposed include a cessation of further investments in and loans to South Africa. The resolution also advocates an end to all promotion of trade with South Africa. In the wake of the declaration of the state of emergency by the régime, Security Council resolution 569 (1985), adopted on 26 July 1985, urged Member States, inter alia, to suspend new investments in South Africa, to prohibit the sale of krugerrands and to suspend guaranteed export loans.

Encouraged by the growing acceptance of sanctions within the international community, and pressurized by a growing tide of public opinion in favour of such action, many Western States have instituted economic measures against the régime. In addition, a wide variety of non-governmental institutions and local government bodies have effectively instituted limited sanctions.

The case for mandatory economic sanctions is clear and urgent. It has been articulated by the various organs of the United Nations, by the leaders of the neighbouring States, and by black South African leaders in the liberation movements, the trade unions and the churches. President Kenneth Kuanda of Zambia justified his country's support for sanctions thus: "A catastrophic explosion which will engulf all of us in the region is imminent. If you don't apply sanctions hundreds of thousands of people will die and your investments will go up in flames." In 1981, the Paris Declaration characterized the apartheid régime as constituting "no longer a threat to, but a manifest breach of international peace and security". In short, mandatory economic sanctions are perceived as the only peaceful means remaining with which to eliminate apartheid.

Section I of the present report gives a general overview of arguments against economic sanctions in the current period, many of which have not altered over the years. Hence, it is still argued that South African blacks and neighbouring States will be most sorely burdened by the imposition of sanctions; that South Africa is a supplier of strategic minerals and hence that its trading partners cannot afford to jeopardize this vital source by a policy of sanctions; and that sanctions will harden the obduracy of the régime's rulers and hence reduce the likelihood of peaceful change.

Section II examines the impact of sanctions already introduced. It begins with a brief outline of the various economic measures in force against South Africa, then examines the major consequences of these measures, documenting in particular the withdrawals of major corporations from South Africa and assessing future possibilities and obstacles in this regard. It then examines the response of the international banking sector. Third, it assesses the political response of the South African and international business communities. This shows that the sanctions already introduced are beginning to bear fruit. As such it argues for an intensification of the campaign for mandatory economic sanctions and underlines the importance of interim measures by Member States pending Security Council action.

In summary, the present paper argues that nothing has occurred in the recent past to undermine the case for sanctions: white minority rule continues in South Africa and is increasingly dependent on massive internal repression; Namibia is still occupied; and aggression perpetrated by the racist régime against the independent States of southern Africa has escalated alarmingly.

There have been important developments in recent years, however, developments that exercise a considerable impact on the question of sanctions. These developments are of a twofold nature: first, as suggested above, they reinforce the underlying reasons for imposing economic sanctions on the <u>apartheid</u> régime. That <u>apartheid</u> constitutes a "manifest breach of international peace and security" is increasingly evident. Second, selective measures have been imposed and their ability to exert pressure and influence events in South Africa is manifest. An assessment of this latter development constitutes a primary focus of this paper.

I. GENERAL OVERVIEW OF ARGUMENTS AGAINST ECONOMIC SANCTIONS

The outstanding characteristic of South Africa in the present decade has been the marked escalation of internal repression and regional aggression by the régime, matched by resolute resistance internally and regionally. Between September 1984 and March 1986 official estimates of the number of black South Africans killed by the police and military exceeded 1,450. In an unsuccessful attempt to contain the resistance, troops occupied most of the major black residential areas, and in July 1984 a state of emergency was declared in many areas to bolster the already Draconian security laws. The state of emergency was lifted in March 1986, but in April the régime introduced in Parliament the Public Safety Amendment Bill, which, if enacted, will empower the Minister of Law and Order to declare any area an "unrest area", a decision not subject to inquiry by the courts. This means that a <u>de facto</u> state of emergency may be imposed any time the Minister so orders.

The intensified repression has been met with resolute and organized resistance by the oppressed people of South Africa. The increased popularity of the liberation movement is one measure of this resistance. The rise of internal political and civic organization is another. The rapid growth of the trade union movement and the recent formation of the 550,000-strong Congress of South African Trade Unions (COSATU) is further evidence of a deep-seated resistance to <u>apartheid</u>.

The resistance has taken varied forms. An avowed aim of the anti-apartheid forces has been to render the townships "ungovernable". To this end, community councillors - widely perceived as apartheid's representatives in the black townships - have been forced to resign their positions. Black policemen have been driven from their homes in the townships. In addition, thousands of residents of many of the major black townships have refused to pay housing rent to the township authorities. In the townships of the Vaal triangle area, where the current phase of resistance was sparked in September 1984, the residents have not paid rent for some 18 months. In many areas, street and area committees have emerged to give organizational form to the spontaneous popular resistance in several townships, such organizations having assumed some of the functions of the defunct community councils, thus providing a form of alternative local government.

Two other forms of resistance have been widely adopted in the current phase. They are, first, work stayaways which have generated unprecedented support. In November 1984, an estimated 500,000 workers responded to a trade union call for a one-day work stoppage. In addition, there have been numerous, powerfully supported, local stoppages. Second, consumer boycotts by the black residents of particular cities and towns have met with great success. These boycotts, characteristically of all white-owned stores, although sometimes of particular stores or products, have constituted a powerful pressure on local traders whose dependence on the custom of black residents has been sharply demonstrated.

In the region, Angola, Botswana, Lesotho and Mozambique have all been invaded by the régime's military forces. In Angola, Mozambique and Lesotho the South African régime has supported, and in some cases created, armed opposition to these independent States. In Mozambique the régime supports an armed opposition despite the existence of a non-aggression pact between the respective Governments. Lesotho, surrounded by South Africa and, as such, particularly vulnerable, has on numerous occasions, been blockaded by the régime's customs officials on the pretext of performing regular customs duties. This has meant that vital food and medical supplies as well as other essential commodities have been prevented from reaching Lesotho. Lesotho's exports have effectively been denied access to their markets in South Africa and abroad. This action generated considerable political instability in Lesotho, culminating in a military coup in early 1986.

These developments have led to a growing recognition that sanctions offer the final alternative to full-scale civil war in South Africa and the military conflagration of the entire region. This recognition is reflected at a number of levels.

A. Support for sanctions from the international community, black South African leaders and neighbouring States

In the international community there has been a marked escalation in the number of measures aimed at the economic isolation of the régime. To this end, popular pressure has been directed at transnational corporations, international banks and institutional investors to sever their links with South Africa. Local governments and other public institutions have been urged to withdraw investments from, and use their purchasing power against, corporations active in South Africa. Trade unions and student bodies have taken action against corporations and colleges with South African linked investments. There has been pressure on national Governments to impose sanctions on South Africa and most have responded to local and international pressure by taking some form of economic action against the régime. In an unexpected development, such action has emanated also from the international banking sector. This will be discussed in the following section of the paper.

Second, black South African leaders and organizations have responded to the current crisis by strongly supporting the campaign for economic sanctions. This takes on added significance in the light of the heavy penalties which the régime is empowered to impose on those advocating sanctions. Prominent amongst those calling for sanctions are leading clergy - notably Bishop Desmond Tutu and the Reverend Alan Boesak - and clerical organizations. The motivation of the churches is similar to that of the international community. Hence, on 28 June 1985, the National Conference of the South African Council of Churches concluded that "... disinvestment and similar economic measures are now called for as a peaceful and effective means of putting pressure on the South African Government to bring about the fundamental changes this country needs". The Council describes the situation as "... now so serious that economic action must be taken to strengthen political and diplomatic pressures on South Africa". Bishop Tutu expressed it thus: "Our land is burning and bleeding, and I call on the international community to apply punitive sanctions against the Government. I have no hope of real change from the Government unless it is forced." He added that "... the more concerted and united, the more likely it is going to be that [sanctions] will be effective and immediate". On 2 May, a declaration of the Catholic Bishops Conference stated that "sanctions should be intensified if no fundamental change in apartheid takes place".

Particularly significant in this regard are the views of COSATU. Opponents of economic sanctions frequently rely on the argument that black workers would bear the brunt of the burden imposed by sanctions. However, in December 1985, COSATU, a powerfully representative voice of black workers, resolved to support disinvestment as "an essential and effective form of pressure on the South African régime". This view is shared by the United Democratic Front, an organization with considerable black popular support. At its 1985 annual conference, the United Democratic Front demanded "an end to the exploitation of the people and the natural wealth of our country by foreign investors".

Given the widespread support from black South African leaders and organizations for sanctions, it appears patronizing and self-serving to argue that black interests would be most severely retarded by sanctions - particularly as this argument is most frequently used by the business sector and the South African Government. Sanctions will generate economic hardships and these will, in part, be experienced by black workers. It should be noted though that detailed research indicates that, partly because of the relatively marginal role that a great many blacks play in the money economy, the impact of sanctions on overall black welfare would not be as great as is sometimes suggested. This latter is, however, not the central argument. The point at issue is that, in order to eliminate the acute suffering generated by <u>apartheid</u>, black South Africans are prepared to endure additional hardship. Accordingly, there is widespread black support for the imposition of sanctions and this was manifested in various polls carried out by respectable newspapers in which an overwhelming majority came out for sanctions.

Third, in the recent period, the support by neighbouring southern African States for sanctions has also intensified. The régime loses no opportunity to underline the potential consequences of sanctions for these States and warns of retaliation against them. In November 1985 a South African cabinet minister threatened to repatriate 1.2 million migrant workers in the event of intensified economic pressure. The neighbouring States are frequently reminded by South African government officials of their dependence on South Africa's transport infrastructure. These threats notwithstanding, in September 1985, the front-line States - Angola, Botswana, Mozambique, the United Republic of Tanzania, Zambia and Zimbabwe - called for increased economic pressure on South Africa, including sanctions.

It is undeniable that the neighbouring States are in fact extremely vulnerable to retaliatory action by the régime. However, each of these States is already experiencing the dire consequences of their proximity to <u>apartheid</u> South Africa. At the 1985 meeting of the Southern African Development Co-ordination Conference (SADCC), it was estimated that South African destabilization had cost these States $10 billion over a four-year period. Quite clearly the economic and political stability of each of these States rests on the elimination of <u>apartheid</u>, and the imposition of sanctions is perceived by their Governments as an important weapon in securing the eradication of <u>apartheid</u>. Such sanctions should be accompanied by a co-ordinated international programme of assistance to these States in the likely event of South African retaliation. The structure necessary for co-ordinating an assistance programme exists in the shape of SADCC, which achieved remarkable stability despite the hostility of the racist régime.

B.   <u>Response of the business community and the régime</u>

The movement in favour of sanctions has indeed made broad gains, and the actions taken so far have proved the potential power of sanctions to bring about change. This perception is particularly strong in business circles, as is evident from the statements of the Chief Executive Officer of the Associated Chambers of Commerce (ASSOCOM), representing powerful South African business interests in the commercial and trading sector. In 1981 this gentleman said that South Africa was in a stronger position than ever to resist sanctions which, in any event, he did not believe could be successfully implemented. He also noted South Africa's bounty of strategic minerals and warned of the possibility of retaliation concluding that, "... in such an economic war, South Africa would probably be the winner". However, in March 1985, ASSOCOM urged the business sector to "take immediate steps to counter the threat of disinvestment". ASSOCOM warned that the supporters of sanctions constituted "a lobby gaining strength and which could do tremendous damage to this country ... time was running out fast. Events were moving against South Africa and once decisions to disinvest or apply sanctions had been made, they would be almost impossible to reverse".

The response of the South African and international business community to the imposition of sanctions (which is examined in greater detail in section II) is particularly important. It is a testimony of the campaign's success and of the power of economic pressure. Moreover, it strongly underlines the importance of interim action by States and non-governmental organizations pending mandatory sanctions. Already business has responded to the pressure by attempting to distance itself from the régime and by taking up a position in opposition to apartheid. Now indeed the anti-apartheid stance of the business community has become the most loudly proclaimed reason for opposing sanctions, whereas, in previous years, the traditional business response to threats of economic action was to assert that economic growth would of its own accord erode apartheid and measures such as sanctions that inhibit economic growth would thereby reinforce apartheid. This essentially passive argument has, in the main, been replaced by the assertion that the business community is a specific and aggressive force for change in South Africa. It is important that these claims be examined in detail.

Finally, the reaction of the South African régime to the increasingly successful sanctions campaign must also be considered.

There are, in general, five arguments advanced by the régime in opposition to the sanctions campaign. Two of these have already been dealt with above, namely, the argument that sanctions will impact most harmfully on black South African workers and on the neighbouring States.

The third argument utilized by the régime asserts that its trading partners are dependent on South Africa for the supply of certain strategic minerals. The minerals in question are chromium, manganese, vanadium and the platinum group minerals, all deemed essential to Western defence and industrial interests. There has been considerable research into this question and most studies conclude that the United States of America and the member countries of the Organization for Economic Co-operation and Development (OECD) could all take steps to reduce their vulnerability. The arguments are summarized in a recent book, 2/ and the conclusions strongly debunk the notion that the West could not afford, because of South Africa's mineral bounty, to impose sanctions. For example, the author shows that, although South Africa accounts for a substantial proportion of world chrome production and reserves, South African chrome is low-grade and substitutable from other sources. Furthermore, a large proportion of the chrome used in the West is used for decorative purposes and could be significantly curtailed. Manganese and vanadium are both obtainable from other sources. South Africa has by far the largest known reserves of platinum, although there are unassessed reserves in Canada and high-grade deposits in Zimbabwe. Furthermore, there is considerable capacity for recycling platinum. The author concludes, in fact, that the civil disruption generated by apartheid and unforeseen by South Africa's trading partners, is a more serious threat to mineral supplies than the sanctions. An article entitled "Don't Lose Sleep over Strategic Metals" in the 30 September 1985 issue of the well-known business magazine Fortune argued that United States fear of losing supplies of strategic minerals was misplaced.

The argument that the South African régime would withhold mineral supplies in the event of selective economic pressures does not warrant serious consideration. A recent threat by President Botha to withhold chromium supplies was hastily withdrawn after adverse market reaction.

Fourth, the régime frequently argues that sanctions will not harm the strong and sophisticated South African economy, that externally imposed self-reliance will be of benefit and that sanctions could not be effectively implemented. These arguments are, it is claimed, supported by the Southern Rhodesian case and by South Africa's experience with the arms and oil embargoes.

The argument that the Southern Rhodesian economy benefited from sanctions is little more than wishful thinking and is debunked by every serious analysis of the period. Whilst there are undoubtedly important lessons to be drawn from the Southern Rhodesian experience, it is not possible to compare the impact on the Southern Rhodesian economy with the potential impact on the South African economy. The South African economy is likely to be more adversely affected precisely because of its size and sophistication. The South African economy requires trade, investment and technology transfers to a far greater extent than does a smaller economy. Hence, whilst Southern Rhodesia may have been capable of limited and temporary autarkic growth, the same cannot be said of the South African economy.

It is frequently argued that the development of a local armaments industry and the coal-to-oil process (both supposedly fueled by the embargoes in force) demonstrate the counter-productive effect of imposing sanctions. A closer examination shows matters to be otherwise. First, South Africa is not self-reliant. It is estimated that after completion of the costly oil-to-coal programme (itself heavily dependent on imported know-how) South Africa will still have to import approximately 50 per cent of its oil requirements. With respect to arms, it is estimated that in 1984, 30 per cent of the weapons used by the military and 80 per cent of the components of locally manufactured arms were imported. Second, petroleum and arms produced by South Africa are considerably more expensive than comparable purchases on the international market - the output of the coal-to-oil process was 20 per cent above the international market price before the recent price decline; it is estimated that in 1984, the arms embargo added $2.1 billion to the military budget.

Thus the Southern Rhodesian experience and the oil and arms embargoes do not establish the impossibility of implementing sanctions. The violations in the Southern Rhodesian case were by and large perpetrated with the assistance of South Africa itself. In the case of the arms and oil embargoes, the violations establish a case for a more vigorous campaign against the transnational corporations responsible. But, principally, they establish the case for comprehensive, mandatory sanctions, which are considerably more difficult to violate than selective sanctions.

Finally, the South African régime argues, in the blunt words of President Botha, that "outside interference will retard social change", a statement made in response to President Ronald Reagan's executive order imposing limited sanctions by the United States. It is an argument sometimes voiced in the international community, the notion that further pressure will drive South Africa's rulers into the laager - a still more intransigent position. However, what is at issue is not the psychology of the régime's rulers, but rather social change. The piecemeal changes introduced thus far have been rejected as irrelevant and cosmetic by the vast majority of South Africans. Botha has stated emphatically that his reformist plans do not even include integrated schools and residential areas; he has repeatedly refused to release political prisoners and legalize the liberation movements. Under these circumstances, serious consideration cannot be given to a plea for "more time". The limits of the régime's reformism have been laid out. They exclude the all-important question of the political rights of blacks as the majority.

C. Summary

In summary, international opposition to apartheid is increasingly bringing economic pressure to the fore. Many Governments have introduced varying forms of economic sanctions; the response of major corporations and banks to anti-apartheid pressure frequently constitutes itself as another form of economic sanction; and there is increasing support for mandatory economic sanctions under Chapter VII of the Charter.

Internal political developments coupled with international support for sanctions has had a considerable impact at all levels of southern African society. Black South African leaders have been vocal in support of sanctions as have the leaders of other States of the region.

This section has briefly examined conventional responses to sanctions against the background of recent developments. In the following section, the impact of sanctions on the business sector will be examined. It will be shown that the impact of sanctions introduced thus far reinforces the case for mandatory economic sanctions, and underlines the necessity for Member States and non-governmental institutions to pursue and expand selective measures in the interim.

II. IMPACT OF SANCTIONS ON THE BUSINESS SECTOR

This section examines the impact of the campaign for mandatory economic sanctions. In particular, it analyses the impact of the interim measures already imposed by Member States and non-governmental institutions.

Several important qualifications must be borne in mind, however. Sanctions are not, in the first instance, designed to undermine or to destroy the national economy. Rather, they are designed to pressurize and undermine the strength of those groups that either hold power in society or are responsible for creating, implementing or bolstering apartheid. Accordingly, the success of the campaign thus far is measured by its impact on the business sector.

In focusing on the business sector, it is possible to examine the responses of a group that has benefited handsomely from apartheid and whose interests are directly threatened by a campaign that utilizes economic pressure as its primary weapon. The yardsticks used to measure the success of the campaign are, first, the extent of corporate withdrawal from South Africa; second, the impact on the international banking sector; and third, the impact on the political activities of the business sector.

When utilizing the above-mentioned criteria, an additional qualification must be noted. Shifts in the behaviour and activities of the business sector are, in part, attributable to the sanctions campaign, but there are other, equally important, sources of pressure. These are first, the uncertainty generated by the violence of the régime and the resistance of the black majority - the "unrest" - which has had a marked impact on business confidence and its political decisions; and second, the deep economic recession that obviously influenced the business sector. Fortune magazine reports that the average annual after-tax return from United States corporations with direct investments in South Africa shrank from 31 per cent in 1980 to 7 per cent in 1983. Business Week reports a figure of 5 per cent for 1985. The variables are also, of course, not mutually independent; hence, for example, the economic recession and the "unrest" react upon and exacerbate one another.

It is important to understand this complex interplay of factors because, if not borne in mind, it would be possible either to exaggerate or to understate the impact of sanctions. However, whilst it is difficult to establish the precise impact of sanctions, it can be easily established that it is a powerful and much feared weapon in the widespread resistance to apartheid.

A. Intensification of the sanctions campaign

The range of sanction measures in force against South Africa are not described in detail in the present paper. However, some general points must be made. By way of example, references are made to evidence mainly from the United States, partly because of the strength of the campaign there in the recent past, and partly because of the relatively detailed information available. It does not suggest that similar efforts are not being made elsewhere.

The most striking features of the sanctions campaign are, first, its extent and international character, underpinned by countless, small local campaigns; and second, the ingenuity employed by the campaigners and the diverse demands made of those in economic collaboration with the apartheid régime. In essence, the campaign reflects widespread abhorrence of apartheid, as well as support for the notion that economic sanctions against apartheid and those associated with it are a powerful and legitimate weapon.

The objective of the campaigners is clearly that economic links with apartheid be severed. To this end pressure has been placed on national Governments to impose binding sanctions on the apartheid régime and this is reflected in the rapid escalation of measures being imposed at the central government level. It is also

reflected in growing support in the United Nations for comprehensive, mandatory
sanctions. However, the campaign is not focused single-mindedly at the national
level. Consequently, an analysis that equates the success of the campaign on
sanctions with the passing of national legislation only would be grossly
inadequate. The pattern of pressure has evolved to one directed at the most
accessible level of authority - the college administrator, the employer, the local
bank manager, the pension fund trustee, the local government officer - and one that
presses the authority to modify its economic link with apartheid. The degree of
modification agreed to by the authorities and acceptable to the campaigners varies
widely. Hence, certain of the authorities in question have modified their links
with apartheid by remaining active in South Africa yet have, for example, accepted
codified employment standards, or have agreed to sever any links with the military
and other apartheid enforcing agencies. In other circumstances, total severance
has been demanded and, frequently, has been attained.

Refusal to accept the demands has, where possible, resulted in economic action
by the campaigners against the institutions that remain active in South Africa.
The boycott of Shell products is one example of this economic pressure. The
widespread sale of stocks in corporations that remain active in South Africa is
another.

In addition to national and international actions, it is also important to
consider some of the more localized forms of pressure - trade unionists refusing to
handle South African products; local consumers boycotting South African products;
and withdrawal of funds from banks active in South Africa. The importance of these
small contributions should not be underestimated. Mr. John Chettle, the
Washington, D.C. representative of the South African Foundation and an aggressive
opponent of sanctions, writes that, "each action can be represented as a limited
and largely symbolical one ... but these actions cumulatively have very serious
implications on the reform programme in South Africa, on the relations between two
historically friendly countries and on United States foreign policy generally".

Not all the campaigns are small and local in character. The campaign waged by
the Interfaith Center on Corporate Responsibility (ICCR) of New York, a
church-backed organization, exemplifies a sophisticated, nationally co-ordinated
campaign. The ICCR campaign has targeted 12 major United States corporations with
the avowed aim of "breaking the bonds of economic oppression that make United
States corporations partners in apartheid". The 12 corporations are all designated
"key investors in apartheid" by virtue of the size of their investment, the crucial
nature of the product they produce and/or their links with the régime. ICCR
demands withdrawal and lists progressively escalating measures that will be taken
in order to secure compliance with this demand.

The intensity of the locally based campaigns and the seriousness of the
threats made by the campaigners is underlined in a March 1986 report of the
American Committee on Africa, a leading anti-apartheid campaigner in the United
States. The report notes that "... since 1976, divestment and/or selective
purchasing legislation has been enacted in 17 states, 60 cities, nine counties and
one United States territory. These measures mandate a total of approximately
$5 billion on divestment from United States corporations and banks involved in

South Africa". Seventeen of the states and 37 of the cities and counties mentioned enacted these measures in 1985, indicating the growing acceptability of this form of action. Divestment legislation was being debated in 24 United States states and many more cities in 1986. In addition, many of the states that previously approved divestment measures are now following this up with selective purchasing legislation prohibiting purchases of South African produced goods or even prohibiting purchases of goods from United States corporations with South African links.

This locally based activity is increasingly reflected at the national level. Most Western States have in the recent past taken economic action against South Africa, although much of it remains symbolic. Some of the common features are prohibition on the importation of krugerrands; cessation of government financing of, tax credits for, trade with and investment in South Africa; the withdrawal of trade attachés and government support for trade missions; restrictions on the export of particular commodities - computers for example - that have a military function. There is limited action inhibiting investment, ranging from the strong prohibitions on new investment in Swedish and French law, to considerably weaker steps in other Western States. There is limited action against trade although the prohibitions in several countries on the importation of South African agricultural products and coal are significant.

For the purpose of assessing the impact of the sanctions campaign, certain general observations are necessary. The evidence points conclusively to a rapid escalation of sanctions activity, which, however, has been characterized by its unevenness. This is predictable in the event of unilateral action by Member States responding to different local pressures and circumstances. However, the very unevenness of the campaign subjects it to abuse and creates loopholes. Moreover, the fact that resolute anti-apartheid action in one country is being exploited by another country that continues to trade with and invest in South Africa will weaken the campaign in the former.

The evidence of the nationally pursued measures points in two directions. It establishes the potency of the national measures and, at the same time, underlines the essentially interim nature of these measures. In other words, it underlines the importance of comprehensive and mandatory international sanctions. Accordingly, the process whereby many of the recent sanctions decisions are being taken or ratified by intergovernmental bodies - the Nordic States, the Commonwealth, the European Economic Community (EEC) - is to be welcomed. The possibility of consolidating those commonly accepted sanctions measures into a mandatory Security Council resolution should also be considered.

B. Impact on transnational corporations

Much of the sanctions campaign currently being waged in the West is directed at transnational corporations active in South Africa. The campaign is predicated on an understanding of the crucial role played by direct foreign investment in the apartheid economy and society. This role is extensively documented in papers prepared by and for the Centre against Apartheid. Suffice it to say that foreign investment is estimated to account for roughly one third of the economic growth in South Africa. Recent estimates by the South African Reserve Bank of direct foreign investment placed the total figure at approximately $8.5 billion. The largest direct foreign investment in South Africa is British based, amounting to approximately 50 per cent of the total. The United States share has declined in recent years and is now estimated to stand at approximately $1.8 billion. The exact size of direct foreign investment by companies in the Federal Republic of Germany is not known but is conservatively estimated at $1.1 billion.

Furthermore, the quality of direct investment is as significant as its quantity. Whilst the United States share has declined somewhat in the recent past, in early 1985, United States corporations controlled 70 per cent of the computer industry, 50 per cent of the petroleum industry and 30 per cent of the automobile industry. In other major industrial sectors - electronics and chemicals for example - foreign investment is similarly prominent. In short, foreign corporations are not only valuable providers of capital, but they are also essential providers of technology and skills.

The table below outlines the position with respect to United States corporations, the country for which the most comprehensive data are available.

United States firms in South Africa

Year	Numbers leaving country	Numbers starting new business
1983	6	3
1984	7	2
1985	28	-

The table speaks for itself, although it is important to note that the corporations that have withdrawn from South Africa generally represent those with relatively small holdings in South Africa. However, several of the more prominent United States corporations, such as Coca Cola, Ford and Union Carbide, have reduced their stake in recent years.

Few corporations cite political pressure as the reason for their departure. It is clear, nevertheless, that those corporations susceptible to consumer boycotts or selective purchasing legislation in the United States are particularly sensitive to the sanctions campaign. Bell and Howell, the educational products manufacturer, and Motorola both withdrew, citing selective purchasing legislation, and Eastman Kodak ceased sales to the police and military in order to meet the same demands. American Telephone and Telegraph Company, faced by the threat of a shareholder resolution calling for withdrawal, agreed to sever all ties with South Africa, including ceasing company purchases of platinum and palladium from South African mines.

These may be counted as successes for the sanctions campaign, but they should also serve to indicate the refusal of large United States corporations with more substantial interests in South Africa to cease their collaboration with that country. Hence, the 12 corporations targeted by ICCR have until recently given no indication that they intend bowing to withdrawal pressure. In April 1986, however, the Chief Executive of International Business Machines (IBM) - one of the major targets of the sanctions campaign - indicated that the company was reassessing its position in South Africa. He stated that "the economic activity there is worse than it was a year ago, the economic pressure in the United States is heightened, and Mr. Botha is too slow".

A handful of United Kingdom companies have recently sold their portfolio interests in South African companies. Both Barclays and Standard Banks have reduced their holdings in their subsidiaries. In general, though, there is little evidence that United Kingdom companies are reconsidering their position in any substantial sense. Direct investment in South Africa by firms in the Federal Republic of Germany has indeed increased substantially - by approximately 40 per cent over the past five years - and now stands at roughly $1.1 billion. Both BMW and Mercedes Benz have recently invested in additional plants in South Africa. The Chief Executive of the Chamber of Trade and Industry of the Federal Republic in South Africa explains this development thus: "So far we have not encountered much pressure from inside Germany, except from some church groups."

It appears that the successes of the sanctions campaign in the United States is rebounding to the advantage of the Federal Republic, Japanese and Italian competitors of United States corporations. Apart from the actual withdrawals, the rising tide of sanctions in the United States has turned South African purchasers away from United States corporations to their competitors. This trend is particularly apparent in the computer industry where the greatest beneficiaries of a decline in the IBM market share are Japan's Hitachi and Italy's Olivetti. The latter has recently established an assembly plant in South Africa and is the largest supplier of personal computers to the régime.

In general, the position of Japanese corporations demands closer examination. In 1968, the Japanese Government prohibited direct investments in South Africa and Namibia by Japanese nationals and corporations. However, Japanese products and factories are an increasingly prominent feature of South Africa, a position achieved, it appears, through a variety of licensing and marketing arrangements. The importance of Hitachi in the computer market has already been mentioned. Japanese motor vehicles account for 40 per cent of the South African market, substantially higher than that of United States corporations. The Managing Director of Nissan South Africa characterizes the Japanese business sector as "very supportive of South Africa".

When measured in terms of corporate withdrawals, the success of the campaign in the United States is small but tangible. However, Japanese and European corporations have clearly perceived the advantages of the pressure applied to United States corporations and have systematically increased their stake in South Africa. The danger of this process undermining future successes in the United States cannot be overemphasized. In view of this, co-ordinated actions among groups of countries, especially trade competitors, are of primary importance in order to carry out effectively specific programmes of sanctions.

The successes achieved thus far, though small in number, nevertheless constitute a powerful vote of no confidence in apartheid South Africa and are a strong discouragement to other would-be investors. This is one of the reasons why the campaign that focuses on major, high profile investors is important. Moreover, burgeoning divestment in the United States and the growing emphasis on selective purchasing will undoubtedly bear fruit.

C. The banking crisis

On 31 July 1985 the Chase Manhattan Bank in the United States decided to freeze its unused credit lines available to South Africa and to withdraw outstanding credits as they matured. Chase's action was quickly followed by other major United States banks. On 27 August, the régime closed the foreign currency and stock exchange markets. On 2 September, South Africa became the first sovereign debtor to renege on its short-term interbank debt when, on that day, its Central Bank froze all repayment of principal on its foreign debt for a period of four months.

South Africa's acute dependence on the international banking sector has been extensively documented. 3/ Suffice it to say that South Africa's industrial sector - particularly the large and strategic state corporations - and the growth of the régime's military machine were all critically dependent on a ballooning international debt. The South African banking sector itself is dominated by the subsidiaries of two British banks, Barclays and Standard Chartered. At the time the crisis broke, South Africa's debt to foreign banks stood at $24 billion, of which $14 billion was in short-term debt. Given the role of the United States banks in precipitating the crisis, it should be noted that between 1981 and 1984, United States private bank loans to South Africa increased from $2.7 billion to $4.9 billion.

The general circumstances underlying South Africa's acute dependence on foreign loan capital are not analysed here, though they are to be found in a combination of acute dependence on gold, failed economic policies and the cost of apartheid. These factors, compounded by serious mismanagement on the part of the Central Bank and major private banks, also accounted for the skewed maturity structure of the South African debt.

These circumstances do not explain the reluctance of the banks to assist South Africa. Debt problems are, after all, not uniquely South African. In essence, the banks were making a judgement on the state of apartheid South Africa and its future prospects; the assessment by the international banks of the strength of the anti-apartheid forces, coupled with the intransigence of the régime, led to the decision to withdraw. It is this assessment that caused such panic in South African business circles.

Whilst Chase Manhattan's decision was decisive, there were earlier indications of considerable nervousness on the part of the banks. An article in Euromoney of December 1985 entitled "The Banks Abandon South Africa", reveals that one of the reasons for the reliance on short-term debt was the refusal of the lenders to provide large medium-term loans to South African borrowers. In the wake of successive landmarks in the current phase of resistance - the Vaal uprising in September 1984 and the Langa massacre in March 1985 - the banks raised their rates or shortened their maturities. According to Euromoney, Chase's decision to withdraw was predicated on the French Government's ban on new investments and the South African Government's declaration of the state of emergency on 20 July 1984.

The international banks - particularly the United States and British banks - have experienced considerable pressure from the sanctions campaigners. Citibank, the most aggressively anti-sanctions of United States banks, has been targeted as one of the "key investors" by ICCR and, as a consequence, United States churches have withdrawn $100 million from the bank. Harvard University has withdrawn a further $51 million. Similarly, in the United Kingdom, Barclays in particular has been a target of anti-apartheid pressure. Barclays, with approximately $1.2 billion in outstanding loans, has said that it would not commit any new money to South Africa "until there are changes which confirm an end to the bankrupt policy of institutionalized racial discrimination".

In February 1986, the international banks nevertheless reached an interim accommodation with South Africa. Whilst the régime's negotiators have described the terms of the accommodation as "onerous", ASSOCOM has described it as "good for business confidence". The international banks, for their part, have been at pains to deny that they have reached a "rescheduling agreement", describing it as an "interim and short-term compromise" designed to ensure that money already on loan is returned. The bankers are emphatic that the South Africans are not being allowed to return to the market.

The debt crisis has established once again the power of selective measures. In this instance, a powerful interest group was targeted, one that is particularly unwilling to allow "political" or "moral" factors to interfere with its business decisions. In the event, a combination of the resistance in South Africa and the pressure of the sanctions campaign in the international arena has obliged the banks to distance themselves from apartheid. In so doing, they have generated a severe crisis for the régime and the South African business community.

All commentators agreed, however, that lack of access to the money market will severely constrain the economy. Accordingly, it is to be expected that the régime will make every effort to re-enter the money markets and the interim arrangement with the banks is evidence of limited success already achieved. The only secure way of preventing further steps is by the imposition of mandatory economic sanctions.

This conclusion is borne out by the evident differences between the bankers themselves, differences that in part reflect the varying strengths of the sanctions campaign. Hence, the Governor of the South African Reserve Bank told Euromoney that, at the outbreak of the crisis, he was particularly "concerned about the German and Swiss banks, they were loyally standing by us". When the interim agreement was concluded, an international banker commented that "there will be no new money from most foreign banks, especially the American and British banks". A South African banker commented that "the Europeans were willing to roll over

credit. We had to accept tough measures to keep the door open for the Americans".
If the European banks are allowed to re-enter the South African market, the
strength of the campaign in the United Kingdom and the United States will be
undermined. This can be prevented by resolute action in particular European
countries, but ultimately the problem points to the necessity for comprehensive
mandatory sanctions.

Above all, the debt crisis must surely explode any remaining myths about South
Africa's "self-sufficiency" or "invulnerability". Euromoney concludes its analysis
of the crisis thus: "Political events brought South Africa's debt mountain
tumbling down and it cannot be put back together again without further political
change."

D. Political response of the business sector

Despite the deteriorating economic situation and the pressure exerted by the
sanctions campaign, transnational corporations are extremely reluctant to withdraw
from South Africa. This reluctance is particularly marked in the case of
corporations with large plant and capital equipment committed to South Africa.
South African-owned business, despite a recent spate of large overseas acquisitions
by major South African corporations, is obviously constrained in its ability to
relocate elsewhere.

The business sector has accordingly developed a set of responses designed to
eliminate or at least deflect the pressure imposed upon it.

The dominant response within the international business community has been to
assert that, within its sphere of influence, apartheid is being eliminated, and,
moreover, that this process was initiated at the behest of the corporations. In
other words, it is argued that transnational corporations treat their workers
equally with respect to wages and working conditions, that they even pay wages
above the legal minimum and above the national average. In addition, the
corporations assert that their integrity is demonstrated by their willingness to
sign one or the other of the employment codes of conduct - the Sullivan Code and
the EEC Code are the most prominent. This is said to constitute a public
commitment to the elimination of apartheid.

These claims will not be examined in any detail here. It has been
persuasively argued that many of the relatively small number of transnational
corporations that have signed the codes do not implement them. It has also been
pointed out that concepts such as "equal pay for equal work" have little
significance in the South African context because of the racial make-up of job
categories and unequal educational opportunities. Powerful though these arguments
are, the rejection of the codes does not stem from their record of achievement in
the workplace.

The codes are rejected by anti-apartheid campaigners because they do not
address the problem at hand. This is particularly apparent when the application of
the codes is counterposed as an anti-apartheid weapon with the sanctions campaign.

The latter is designed as a weapon to eliminate apartheid in the society generally. The codes focus on the factory only and, even if successful in their stated aim, would not reduce the necessity for the pressure applied by sanctions. In addition it may be argued that the codes have become - indeed that they were devised as - the means by the TNCs to assert anti-apartheid principles, engage in limited reforms on the factory floor, and simultaneously remain "good corporate citizens" of racist South Africa.

There are recent signs of a substantial, albeit reluctant, re-evaluation by leading South African and international corporations and business figures. These have been inspired by a growing perception that apartheid is, in the view of the anti-apartheid forces, inextricably linked with the business sector - the sanctions campaign, the consumer boycotts and the frequent work stayaways support this perception - and accordingly that the inevitable demise of apartheid may spell the demise of those corporations' activities in a liberated South Africa. The business sector is also beginning to realize that the elimination of apartheid is a pre-condition for economic prosperity and that local resistance and international pressure will not be satisfied with the cosmetic or, at best, partial reforms offered by the employment codes.

This re-evaluation accounts for the amplification in November 1984 of the Sullivan Code. Signatories are now urged to support the right of black-owned businesses to operate in the main urban areas; they are expected to support freedom of mobility and provide family accommodation for African workers and, in general, are urged to support the rescission of apartheid.

The new-found opposition to apartheid on the part of the business community takes two predominant forms. The first is the mushrooming of philanthropic foundations ostensibly designed to promote black advancement, usually in education, but also in housing and general welfare. Major United States corporations - Mobil, IBM and Coca Cola to name three - have provided multi-million dollar grants for this purpose. Leading South African corporations are pursuing a similar course through institutions like the Urban Foundation.

Second, leading representatives of the business community have publicly opposed repressive aspects of apartheid such as detention without trial, forced removals and the pass laws. Several corporations - notably Coca Cola and Barclays Bank - have called for the release of political prisoners and negotiations with the African National Congress of South Africa (ANC). A delegation of leading South African businessmen recently held a highly publicized meeting with ANC in Zambia. In a move harshly criticized by representatives of the régime, the Chief Executive of General Motors in South Africa publicly offered to pay legal expenses and fines incurred by any black General Motors workers who broke the law segregating the beaches of Port Elizabeth, the city where the company's plant is located. This was interpreted by the régime to be in conflict with "good corporate citizenship" and to be an incitement to civil disobedience.

These activities on the part of the business community do not constitute grounds for relaxing the pressure imposed by the sanctions campaign. It should be noted that the response of the business sector is vacillating. Leading business representatives supported the imposition of the state of emergency as a means of restoring "law and order". In addition, the depth of business disaffection with apartheid is open to question. There are previous instances in South African history - during the Defiance Campaign of the 1950s and the 1976 Soweto uprising - when business loudly opposed apartheid only to fall back into a comfortable relationship with the régime once the police and the military had restored "law and order".

It is the persistent and sustained pressure of the current period that accounts for the reluctant and as yet half-hearted decision of business to oppose the worst excesses of apartheid. In particular, the widespread acceptance of the sanctions weapon has persuaded business. To the extent that this changed perception on its part represents an advance for the anti-apartheid struggle, it also represents an argument for the intensification of the sanctions campaign. Past experience indicates that the business community is, at best, a fickle participant in opposing the régime. It also indicates that business responds most strongly when its material interests are directly threatened. This is why the sanctions campaign is such a powerful weapon with respect to the business community.

III. CONCLUSION

This paper has examined the case for economic sanctions against apartheid South Africa in the light of recent developments.

The arguments against sanctions - characteristically articulated by the régime and the business community - have been examined and have been rejected. In general, the major reason for imposing sanctions still maintains. Apartheid constitutes an increasingly manifest breach of international peace and security. The view that sanctions offers the final remaining peaceful means of eliminating apartheid is widely supported in South Africa itself, in the region and in the international community.

There is growing support for the imposition of sanctions. Locally based actions against institutions economically linked with South Africa have succeeded in establishing a selective form of sanctions despite the frequent reluctance of some national Governments to pursue this course. However, as a result of the strength of popular opinion, many Governments have imposed varying sanctions measures.

Sanctions introduced thus far have had a powerful impact on the business community. Faced with opposition in their home countries and a deteriorating situation in South Africa, corporations have started to withdraw. This has been expressed most dramatically by the actions of the international banks. Corporations reluctant to withdraw have attempted in a variety of ways to distance themselves from the régime, so as to deflect growing anti-apartheid pressure.

We have established the power of these interim measures and every effort must be made to facilitate their intensification. There is, however, danger in the uneven development of this pressure, a danger that could be averted by mandatory comprehensive sanctions. Moreover, having established the power of these interim measures, the myth of "invulnerability" has been conclusively exploded. Comprehensive mandatory sanctions imposed by the Security Council under Chapter VII of the Charter will surely have a demonstrably greater impact than the measures thus far introduced and will hasten the demise of the apartheid system.

Notes

1/   Report of the International Conference on Sanctions against South Africa, Paris, 20-27 May 1981 (A/CONF.107/8), sect. X.A.

2/   Kevin Danaher, In Whose Interest? - A Guide to U.S.-South Africa Relations (Institute of Policy Studies), 1984.

3/   See, for example, Chris Child, "Apartheid, economic collaboration and the case for United Nations comprehensive mandatory sanctions against South Africa", Notes and Documents No. 6/84.

II. UNITED NATIONS SANCTIONS AND SOUTH AFRICA:
LESSONS FROM THE CASE OF SOUTHERN RHODESIA

by

Elizabeth S. Schmidt

[Ms. Schmidt has written extensively on southern Africa and conducted
research in Zimbabwe in 1985 and 1986.]

I. THE CASE FOR UNITED NATIONS SANCTIONS AGAINST SOUTH AFRICA

For nearly three decades opponents of apartheid have advocated the imposition of comprehensive mandatory economic sanctions against South Africa. Under international law, sanctions are defined as punitive measures - economic, diplomatic, cultural, and others - imposed against a State that has violated international law. Their purpose is to pressure the violator to return to compliance with the law. If sanctions are abandoned as a means to achieve this end, military action is the only alternative. Therefore, sanctions are considered to be a non-violent substitute for war. 1/

The United Nations is the only organization that can mandate sanctions that are virtually universal - that is, sanctions that must be applied by all United Nations Member States. Under Chapter VII of the Charter of the United Nations, the Security Council may apply sanctions in order "to maintain or restore international peace and security". Such sanctions may be imposed against a Member State when that State is deemed a "threat to the peace", commits a "breach of the peace" or an "act of aggression" (Article 39). Acceptable measures of non-military coercion include: "complete or partial interruption of economic relations and of rail, sea, air, postal, telegraphic, radio, and other means of communication, and the severance of diplomatic relations" (Article 41). The Security Council may also authorize other actions to be undertaken by air, sea, or land forces, including naval blockades (Article 42).

In the case of South Africa, there are several grounds upon which United Nations sanctions should be imposed. Firstly, the system of apartheid, with its features of institutionalized racism, white minority rule, and the denial of fundamental human rights to the African majority and to other black South Africans, has long been considered by United Nations Member States to be a "threat to the peace". Thus, perpetuation of the status quo is reason enough for sanctions. 2/

Secondly, South Africa's refusal to relinquish the Territory of Namibia, granting it independence under internationally acceptable terms, is a breach of the peace, an act of aggression, and a violation of international law. In 1966, the United Nations General Assembly voted to terminate the League of Nations mandate that had permitted South Africa to govern Namibia and ordered Pretoria to place the Territory under United Nations administration. 3/ Subsequent Security Council resolutions upheld the General Assembly's action. 4/ In June 1971, an Advisory Opinion of the International Court of Justice declared South Africa's continued presence in Namibia to be illegal. 5/ In spite of these actions by the General Assembly, the Security Council and the International Court of Justice, South Africa has refused to grant independence to Namibia and has persisted in its illegal occupation of that Territory.

The South African policy of regional destabilization is the third ground upon which United Nations sanctions should be imposed. Since the mid-1970s, South Africa has routinely violated the territorial sovereignty of its neighbours through aerial bombardments, cross-border raids, the training and equipping of rebel armies and full-scale military invasions. Although Angola and Mozambique have suffered most severely at the hands of South Africa and its proxies, Botswana, Lesotho, Zambia and Zimbabwe have also been regular victims of South African attacks. It is estimated that South African destabilization and sanctions against the region have cost the nine southern African States approximately $20 billion since 1980. 6/ South African activities in the region clearly qualify as "acts of aggression" under the Charter of the United Nations.

Having established the legitimacy of imposing economic sanctions against South Africa, it is important to clarify the objectives of such action. No one who has seriously considered the question argues that sanctions alone will bring about the destruction of apartheid. Rather, sanctions are regarded as a means of weakening the South African economy, thereby rendering the system more vulnerable to pressure from within. Faced with a rapidly disintegrating economy, South Africa will be less able to finance a war against its own people, as well as against Namibia, and the neighboring States. Ultimately, the combined pressures of the internal political struggle and the constraints of economic sanctions will force Pretoria to negotiate a transfer of power from the minority to the majority. In such a context, the implementation of comprehensive mandatory economic sanctions would be, in the words of Chris Child, "the most effective and single most important contribution those outside South Africa can make to the cause of freedom". 7/

A. Sanctions imposed by the General Assembly

The issue of South African sanctions has been on the agenda of the United Nations for nearly 30 years. In 1959, the African National Congress of South Africa appealed to the General Assembly to request that all Member States sever trade links with South Africa. 8/ Acting upon this request in 1962, the General Assembly called upon all members to:

(a) Break diplomatic relations with South Africa or refrain from establishing them;

(b) Close ports to ships flying the South African flag;

(c) Forbid their ships to enter South African ports;

(d) Boycott South African trade;

(e) Refuse landing or passage facilities to aircraft belonging to the Government of South Africa or companies registered in that country.

The same resolution established the Special Committee against Apartheid to monitor South African policies and requested the Security Council to take action, including sanctions, to ensure South African compliance with United Nations resolutions. 9/

In subsequent years, the General Assembly passed numerous resolutions condemning Pretoria's continued application of apartheid and its failure to observe international law. Most notably, in 1963 it called for an oil embargo against South Africa, and in 1976, in the aftermath of the Soweto uprising, the General Assembly called for mandatory sanctions against South Africa under Chapter VII of the Charter. The 1976 resolution maintained that the internal situation in South Africa was a grave threat to the peace, as were South Africa's "repeated acts of aggression against Angola and Zambia" and "the continuing massacres and other atrocities by the racist régime of South Africa against schoolchildren and other peaceful demonstrators against apartheid and racial discrimination". 10/

The major weakness in the anti-apartheid efforts of the General Assembly was not the result of deficient political will. Rather, the flaw was a structural one, stemming from the limits imposed upon its authority under the Charter. The General Assembly can only recommend measures; it cannot force compliance with its resolutions. As noted above, only the Security Council can impose mandatory sanctions.

B. Sanctions imposed by the Security Council

Any permanent member of the Security Council can thwart the imposition of mandatory sanctions against South Africa with a simple veto. 11/ Over the years, South Africa's major economic partners in trade, investment, credit and banking, most importantly the United Kingdom of Great Britain and Northern Ireland and the United States of America, have consistently vetoed comprehensive mandatory economic sanctions. However, after two particularly grave crises in South Africa, the Security Council was able to impose limited sanctions against South Africa, the first set voluntary, the second mandatory.

The first instance, in 1963, followed the extended aftermath of the 1960 Sharpeville massacre. In August 1963, the Security Council described the situation in South Africa as "seriously disturbing international peace and security" and called upon all Member States "to cease forthwith the sale and shipment of arms, ammunition of all types and military vehicles to South Africa". 12/ A proposal for a total trade boycott was defeated, and those sanctions that were passed were completely voluntary. 13/

In December 1963, the Security Council again called for a voluntary ban on arms sales to South Africa, this time adding equipment and materials for the manufacture of arms to the list of prohibited items. 14/ In 1970, in an attempt to strengthen the arms embargo even further, the Security Council called upon Member States to withhold spare parts for vehicles and military equipment used by South African military and police forces. 15/

The second major invocation of Chapter VII occurred in 1977, following the enormous loss of life at the hands of South African security forces during the Soweto uprising; the death in detention of the black leader Steve Biko; the banning and detention of scores of black leaders; and the outlawing of their organizations. Contributing factors were South Africa's massive military build-up, its persistent aggression against neighbouring States, and the fact that Pretoria was deemed by many experts to be on the threshold of producing nuclear weapons. Thus, in November 1977, the Security Council declared the policies and acts of the South African Government to be a danger to international peace and security. It further determined that South Africa's procurement of arms was a "threat to the peace" and imposed a mandatory arms embargo. The sale of arms to South Africa by any State Member of the United Nations was now illegal. 16/

In July 1985, soon after Pretoria imposed a state of emergency, the culmination of the bloodiest year in South Africa since 1976, the Security Council urged United Nations Member States voluntarily to impose sanctions against South Africa. This time, the United States and the United Kingdom did not veto the resolution; they merely abstained from voting. The result was the passage of the strongest anti-apartheid measure taken by the Security Council since it imposed a mandatory arms embargo in 1977. The resolution called for a voluntary cessation of new investment in South Africa; a ban on the sale of krugerrands; the suspension of export loan guarantees; a ban on new nuclear contracts; and an end to the sale of computer equipment that could be used by South African security forces. 17/

In May 1986, a few weeks before the imposition of the second state of emergency in less than a year, South African commandos launched a series of cross-border raids into neighbouring countries - this time into the capital cities of Botswana, Zambia and Zimbabwe. The Security Council convened an urgent meeting to debate yet another resolution calling for mandatory economic sanctions against South Africa. Again, the United States and the United Kingdom vetoed the resolution, delaying once more the imposition of mandatory United Nations sanctions against South Africa. 18/

II. SANCTIONS IMPOSED BY INTERNATIONAL ORGANIZATIONS AND GOVERNMENTS

From its inception in 1963, the Organization of African Unity (OAU) has consistently urged its members to impose sanctions against South Africa. Member nations that had diplomatic relations with South Africa severed them, and those that did not have diplomatic relations refused to establish them. In accordance with OAU policy, many African countries officially boycott trade with South Africa and deny overflying rights to South African aircraft. 19/

Since November 1973, Arab oil producing countries have officially refused to sell oil to South Africa. In 1979, after the fall of the Shah, Iran joined the boycott, rendering complete the embargo of South Africa by the Organization of Petroleum Exporting Countries (OPEC). 20/

More recently, the Southern African Development Co-ordination Conference (SADCC), the front-line States, and the Non-Aligned Movement have made repeated calls for sanctions. Since the beginning of 1985, the European Economic Community (EEC), a group of nations within the Commonwealth, and an increasing number of individual countries have imposed some form of limited sanctions against South Africa. Among the latter are: Australia, Brazil, Canada, Denmark, France, Japan, New Zealand, Norway, Panama, Sweden, the United Kingdom and the United States.

The nature and scope of the sanctions imposed by these countries vary considerably. The United Kingdom, for instance, has merely banned the import of South African gold coins. It agreed to this limited measure only under tremendous pressure from the Commonwealth, the parliamentary opposition, and the British Anti-Apartheid Movement. In October 1986, the United States Congress approved a sanctions package that was a significantly watered down version of the original House bill. Yet it was enacted only over President Reagan's veto. In contrast, Sweden and Norway not only ban new investment in South Africa, they also prohibit the transfer of patent and manufacturing rights, a measure that goes far beyond that of most countries in preventing the technology flow to South Africa. Denmark has instituted an almost total boycott on South African trade. Norway and Sweden are expected soon to follow suit.

III. ARE SANCTIONS PRODUCTIVE? AN ASSESSMENT OF THE SOUTHERN RHODESIAN CASE

Opponents of economic sanctions against South Africa frequently claim that such measures would be counter-productive, increasing intransigence among the white minority instead of pushing them over the threshold to majority rule. In an effort to bolster their position, such critics often cite the embargo of white minority-ruled Southern Rhodesia, now Zimbabwe, as a case in point.

Those who claim that sanctions failed in Southern Rhodesia tend to base their argument on three erroneous assumptions: firstly, they consider only the short-term effects of sanctions instead of studying their impact over the long term; secondly, they consider sanctions in a vacuum, whereas proponents of sanctions speak of their effectiveness in conjunction with other forces; thirdly, they fail to recognize that South Africa is not Southern Rhodesia and that many experts believe the former to be even more vulnerable to economic sanctions than the latter.

Significantly, prominent white businessmen interviewed recently in Zimbabwe maintained that sanctions were a major factor in forcing the Smith régime to negotiate a final settlement. 21/ Assessing their 14-year battle to keep the Southern Rhodesian economy from succumbing to the effects of international economic sanctions, the businessmen concluded that in the end they lost.

"Some people feel that sanctions failed", claimed a former employee of the Association of Rhodesian Industries, noting that sanctions did not force an immediate transition to majority rule. "I think they failed initially", he added. "But in the long term they exercised a very important element - maybe not even admitted at the time by the Government. Certainly they did not help". 22/

"Sanctions by themselves would sooner or later have forced a political decision," affirmed a colleague employed by the Associated Chambers of Commerce of Rhodesia during the sanctions period. "No economy anywhere in the world can exist under a sanctions-type situation for a long period of time ... Sooner or later something had to give". 23/ If Southern Rhodesia's petroleum lifeline had been severed and if South Africa had not served as a back door to international trade, the businessmen agreed that the country could not have survived for more than a matter of months.

A. Southern Rhodesian sanctions chronology

The application of United Nations sanctions against Southern Rhodesia between 1965 and 1979 constituted the most far reaching and ambitious attempt to date to implement economic sanctions under international auspices. 24/ A significant weakness in the endeavour was the gradual way in which sanctions were imposed, moving from partial to comprehensive, from voluntary to mandatory. 25/ The lag time of two and one-half years between the initiation of sanctions and the imposition of comprehensive mandatory sanctions by the Security Council gave Southern Rhodesia time to restructure its economy, to develop new markets, and to devise sophisticated means of disposing of its products clandestinely.

The Southern Rhodesian sanctions saga began on 11 November 1965, when Prime Minister Ian Smith announced a unilateral declaration of independence

(UDI), severing the colony's relationship with the United Kingdom. The
British Government refused to recognize Southern Rhodesia as independent so
long as the white minority régime refused to accept the possibility of
eventual majority rule. In a decade characterized by militant African
nationalism and rapid decolonization, Southern Rhodesian-style "independence"
could never be defended to the Commonwealth or to the world at large. 26/ The
day after UDI, the Security Council called upon all Member States of the
United Nations to withhold recognition of Southern Rhodesia and to provide it
no assistance.

From the outset the United Kingdom rejected the use of force and all-out
economic warfare in the effort to bring Southern Rhodesia back to legality.
Instead, it proposed a limited set of economic sanctions, the purpose of which
was not to bring Smith to his knees, but to make him "reasonable". 27/ The
day UDI was declared, the United Kingdom imposed selective sanctions against
Southern Rhodesia and urged the world community to do likewise. The first
wave of British sanctions included a ban on the purchase of Southern Rhodesian
sugar and tobacco - which constituted 71 per cent of the value of Southern
Rhodesian exports to the United Kingdom - a cessation of British aid and
export credit guarantees, and the removal of Southern Rhodesia from the
sterling area and the Commonwealth preference system. 28/ The United Kingdom
also banned the export of arms to Southern Rhodesia, including spare parts.
The export of British capital to the rebel country was outlawed, and Southern
Rhodesia was prohibited access to the London capital market, its major source
of financing. 29/

On 20 November 1965, the Security Council voted to impose voluntary
sanctions on Southern Rhodesia, requesting all Member States to break economic
relations with that country. In particular, the Security Council emphasized
the need for an embargo on the sale of arms, military matériel, petroleum and
petroleum products. 30/ At this time, the United Kingdom still refused to
concede that the Southern Rhodesian situation constituted "a threat to
international peace and security", and thus, that the rebel country should be
subject to mandatory economic sanctions under Chapter VII of the United
Nations Charter. 31/

In December 1965, the United Kingdom expanded its embargo list, adding
Southern Rhodesian copper, chrome, asbestos, iron and steel, corn and beef to
the array of prohibited items. The ban on Southern Rhodesian goods now
encompassed 95 per cent of the value of Southern Rhodesian exports to the
United Kingdom. The sale of petroleum and petroleum products to Southern
Rhodesia was also prohibited. 32/ The assets of the Southern Rhodesian
Reserve Bank in London, worth approximately 10 million pounds sterling, were
frozen, and the payment of dividends, interest and pensions to Southern
Rhodesian citizens was blocked in London accounts. 33/ By the end of January
1966, the United Kingdom had effectively banned all exports to Southern
Rhodesia, with the exception of food, medical supplies and educational
materials. By the end of February 1966, the remaining 5 per cent of the United
Kingdom's customary imports from Southern Rhodesia were banned. 34/

It was not until 16 December 1966, more than a year after UDI, that the
Security Council imposed selective mandatory sanctions against Southern
Rhodesia, recognizing that the state of affairs in that country was "a threat
to the peace". The selective mandatory sanctions barred the purchase of
Southern Rhodesian asbestos, iron ore, chrome, pig iron, sugar, tobacco,
copper, meat, meat products, hides, skins and leather. Also prohibited was

the sale to Southern Rhodesia of arms, ammunition, military equipment and equipment for arms manufacture, aircraft, motor vehicles and equipment, petroleum, and petroleum products. Member States of the United Nations were also barred from aiding in the transport of oil to Southern Rhodesia and from rendering financial assistance to the rebel country. 35/ These sanctions effected approximately 60 per cent, by value, of Southern Rhodesia's exports and 15 per cent, by value, of its imports. 36/ Failure of any Member State to implement the mandatory sanctions constituted a violation of Article 25 of the Charter.

Two and one-half years after UDI, in the face of the continued intransigence by the minority régime, the Security Council imposed comprehensive mandatory economic sanctions against Southern Rhodesia. As of 29 May 1968, citizens, entities, and the Governments of United Nations Member States were prohibited from importing any item that originated in Southern Rhodesia. Nor could they export any item to Southern Rhodesia, with the exception of medical and educational supplies, publications, news material and, in special humanitarian circumstances, foodstuffs. The transport of Southern Rhodesian goods was prohibited. Investments in, and the provision of loans or other financial resources to, Southern Rhodesia were also off-limits. The promotion of emigration to Southern Rhodesia was banned. Airline companies were prohibited from operating flights to or from Southern Rhodesia and from connecting with any airline company constituted in Southern Rhodesia. Southern Rhodesian passports were no longer to be recognized. United Nations Member States were required to break diplomatic relations with Southern Rhodesia and to withdraw all trade representatives from that country. 37/

B. Short-term effects of sanctions

When the first sanctions were imposed on Southern Rhodesia in 1965, its economy was extremely dependent upon foreign trade and investment. Exports earned 40 per cent of Southern Rhodesia's national income, of which 34 per cent was in turn spent on imports. 38/ The country was essentially an exporter of primary products, the most important being tobacco, which constituted nearly one third of total export value, and minerals, which comprised another 22 per cent. In terms of imports, Southern Rhodesia relied on the outside world for virtually all of its machinery, transport equipment, chemicals, and spare parts - and for all of its petroleum. 39/ According to Southern Rhodesia's National Development Plan of 1965, the inflow from abroad of capital, technical skills, and management capability was absolutely crucial to the country's economic growth. 40/

In spite of massive sanctions busting by Western countries and corporations, the immediate impact of sanctions on the Southern Rhodesian economy was absolutely devastating. Between 1965 and 1966, the total value of Southern Rhodesian exports fell by 38 per cent. By 1968 total exports were worth slightly more than half their 1965 value. 41/ Minister of Finance John Wrathall told the Legislative Assembly in July 1966 that "Exports are Southern Rhodesia's lifeblood. Our success or failure as a nation depends on our ability to make good, by whatever means possible, the loss of the export markets which have been closed by sanctions". 42/

Sanctions reduced not only the volume of Southern Rhodesian exports, but also their value. The régime's covert trading partners were not willing to

risk the purchase of contraband products unless they could strike a good
bargain. Thus, in order to circumvent sanctions, Southern Rhodesia had to
sell cheap and buy dear. Moreover, sanctions-induced costs were added to the
basic price every step of the way. Southern Rhodesia had to pay the extra
expenses incurred as a result of rerouting through third parties, the fees of
numerous middlemen, and for the paperwork that disguised the products'
origin. Since Southern Rhodesia was selling at a discount and buying at a
premium, it was paying the extra charges at both ends of the deal. Over the
14-year sanctions period, the discount alone was estimated to have cost
Southern Rhodesia $R 1.1 billion. 43/

The rapid deterioration in Southern Rhodesia's terms of trade caused
serious problems for the country. By 1973 even Prime Minister Ian Smith was
forced to concede in parliament that:

> "The imposition of sanctions created many trading problems for us.
> We find that we are compelled to export at a discount and import at a
> premium. The result is that we lose out on both transactions. This has
> the effect of reducing profit margins internally, and at the national
> level, it has an adverse effect on our balance of payments and foreign
> reserves. Because our foreign reserves are depleted artificially, our
> natural development is prejudiced." 44/

As a result of drastically reduced export values, Southern Rhodesia's
foreign exchange earnings declined dramatically. Thus, the Smith régime
imposed stringent import controls. Between 1965 and 1966, imports declined by
30 per cent, affecting agricultural and industrial inputs, new machinery and
spare parts. 45/

Tobacco, the most vital export, was most severely damaged by the trade
embargo. Between 1965 and 1966, the volume of tobacco produced fell by one
half and its value declined by two thirds. 46/ "Sanctions disrupted our
tobacco industry terribly," asserted John Graylin, who in 1965 was chairman of
the Tobacco Export Promotion Council. "The prices fell alarmingly. We could
not sell it. We had a big stockpile ... Then we started to have to sell it
under the counter" - but at a tremendous discount. The covert process "was
not very profitable," Graylin concluded, adding that sanctions "did knock our
tobacco industry for a six". 47/ At tremendous cost to the national budget,
the Government was forced to subsidize tobacco growers in order to keep them
afloat, paying out some $R 16 million per year. By the time independence came
in 1980, the tobacco industry had lost billions of dollars. 48/

Writing for the South African Financial Mail in 1968, Ruth Weiss described
the plight of Southern Rhodesian farmers under sanctions. "Agriculture is the
real casualty of the sanctions war", she wrote. "The tobacco industry has
suffered and will take years to recover ... Agriculture's ills are the
country's ills. When the tobacco cheque shrinks, as it will do in the coming
sales season ... commerce and industry will feel the effects as well".
Although the Government was giving massive subsidies to tobacco farmers to
help them diversify, Weiss maintained that "it will take diversification
years, not months, to offset the loss of tobacco revenues". 49/

While many of the big growers survived the sanctions years, many of the
smaller farmers did not. Before sanctions were imposed there were
approximately 3,600 white tobacco farmers in Southern Rhodesia. By 1975 only
1,600 remained. 50/

Agriculture, although hardest hit, was by no means the only sector of the economy affected by sanctions. The motor vehicles industry was also severely damaged. Shortly after the imposition of sanctions, the Southern Rhodesian Government instituted gasoline rationing. As gasoline sales declined, so did automobile sales and repairs. By June 1966 new car sales had diminished by more than 40 per cent since December 1965. As a result of government controls, the number of imported vehicle kits to be assembled in Southern Rhodesia was cut back severely. The price of imported spare parts increased sharply. 51/ At the end of 1966, BMC and Ford, the two largest assembly plants, were producing at a rate of seven to eight units a day, compared to 21 to 24 units a day in 1965. Both companies had lost their export markets overnight, that is, one quarter of their total sales. By early 1967 both plants were forced to shut down. 52/

Meanwhile, the commercial sector was also incurring heavy losses. The strict import controls imposed by the Government served to stimulate local industry, but to the detriment of both quality and variety. Although they accepted government protection of local industry as a necessary evil, merchants maintained that such measures must be only temporary. Because local industry was not keeping up with local demand, stocks were running down. Thus, over the long term, the stringent import control measures would force smaller entrepreneurs out of business. 53/ In June 1966 John Hughes, president of the Associated Chambers of Commerce of Southern Rhodesia, declared that "many firms are struggling for their continued existence ... They cannot continue this holding operation indefinitely". 54/

Southern Rhodesian railways were also running at a serious deficit. In 1967 the Financial Mail described the "slow death" of the rail system, attributing it to the "sanctions war". With the operating deficit growing daily, the railways were in the red to the tune of eight million pounds sterling by June 1967. In late 1966, Zambia had declared the entry of all but essential goods illegal if they had been transported at any point on Southern Rhodesian railways. South African goods were thus stalled in Southern Rhodesia, awaiting slow and cumbersome transport by Zambian trucks. By far the largest decline in railway revenue was due to the loss of Zambian copper exports and petroleum imports. Meanwhile, British investment in the rail system was frozen and revenue transfers between Zambia and Southern Rhodesia ceased. Southern Rhodesia faced a severe shortage of railway cars as well as supplies normally ordered from the United Kingdom. In consequence, equipment and rolling stock fell into disrepair. 55/

As a result of transport snarl-ups, Southern Rhodesian coal sales suffered. There were simply too few rail trucks to carry the coal north to Zambia and Zaire. From July to September 1966, an average of 56,000 tons of coal per month were shipped from Southern Rhodesia to its two northern neighbours, compared to 130,000 tons per month during the same period in 1965. Sales declined even further when Zambia opened new coal deposits of its own. By November 1966 Zambia was purchasing only half the volume of coal it had absorbed prior to the imposition of sanctions. 56/

After the first few years of hardship and readjustment, the Southern Rhodesian economy began to regain its strength. Commercial farmers were forced to diversify - away from reliance on tobacco to large-scale production of maize, cotton, soybeans and beef. The enhanced production of these crops in turn stimulated food processing, textiles, clothing and footwear manufacturing, as well as other import substitution industries. The consequent industrial boom of 1966 to 1974 focused almost exclusively on the production of consumer goods. Southern Rhodesia continued to be dependent upon the outside world for most of its capital goods and many of its raw materials, imported with great difficulty and expense.

C. Sanctions busting: oil and chrome

Southern Rhodesia would not have been able to survive 14 years of economic sanctions had there not been massive gaps in sanctions enforcement. From the outset South Africa and Portugal, the colonial power in Mozambique until June 1975, refused to implement sanctions against Southern Rhodesia. It was common knowledge that oil was Southern Rhodesia's lifeline and that Southern Rhodesian oil had to be transported through either South Africa or Mozambique. Therefore, for sanctions to be effective, it was imperative that Portugal and South Africa enforce them. The United Kingdom, however, refused to consider any action that could result in a confrontation with South Africa or Portugal. 57/

In April 1966 the Security Council authorized the United Kingdom to intercept oil tankers bound for the Mozambican port of Beira if it was believed that they were carrying Southern Rhodesian-bound oil. 58/ For the next 10 years, at a cost of some 100 million pounds sterling, a British naval blockade effectively cut off the flow of oil through Beira, forcing the shutdown of the Beira to Umtali (Southern Rhodesia) pipeline. 59/ The British Government, however, refused to extend the patrol to the southern port of Lourenço Marques (now Maputo), claiming that a blockade so close to South African waters would be unnecessarily provocative. 60/ As a result, for the first 10 years of sanctions the bulk of Southern Rhodesian oil was processed in South African refineries, transported by ship to Lourenço Marques, and then by rail to Southern Rhodesia. When the newly independent Government in Mozambique closed its border with Southern Rhodesia in March 1976, South Africa took over the transport network, supplying oil to Southern Rhodesia by way of a rail link hastily built between the two countries. 61/

While the United Kingdom and other Western Powers were not eager to embroil themselves in a conflict with South Africa and Portugal, the refusal of Pretoria and Lisbon to impose mandatory sanctions against Southern Rhodesia was itself grounds for punitive United Nations action. The failure of any Member State to implement measures ordered by the Security Council for the maintenance of international peace and security constitutes a violation of Article 25 of the Charter of the United Nations. Member States must also refrain from giving assistance to any State being subjected to preventive or enforcement action by the Security Council. 62/ The proposal to extend economic sanctions to South Africa and Portugal, in order to force their compliance with mandatory sanctions against Southern Rhodesia, was rejected outright by the United Kingdom and its allies on the Security Council. 63/

When sanctions were imposed against Southern Rhodesia in 1966, the need for oil was its primary area of vulnerability. The country had no oil supplies of its own, and its stockpile was only sufficient for a few weeks' requirements. When Southern Rhodesia's transport system continued to function and its industries did not grind to a halt, it became clear to all observers that somehow, some way, Southern Rhodesia was getting its oil. Yet, it was not until the late 1970s that serious investigations into the leakage were made. It was subsequently revealed that the five transnational companies that were marketing oil in Southern Rhodesia before UDI continued to do so afterwards. The South African subsidiaries of Mobil, Caltex, BP, Shell and Total, in collaboration with the South African, Portuguese and British Governments, ensured Southern Rhodesia a continuous supply of oil and other petroleum products throughout the sanctions period. Fueling both the economy and the war machine, these corporations and Governments added years to the life of the white minority régime. 65/

The rail link from Lourenço Marques and South Africa passed through the ranch of Garfield Todd, the Prime Minister of Southern Rhodesia from 1953 to 1958. An ardent opponent of the Smith régime, Todd was placed under severe restrictions for five and one-half years of the UDI period. Confined to his ranch in 1972, he was not only prohibited from leaving it, but also from receiving visitors, speaking on the telephone, writing for publication, or even being mentioned in the newspapers. During the 14 years of sanctions, Mr. Todd kept track of the oil tankers that passed through his ranch, bringing the illicit oil to Southern Rhodesia. In a recent interview Mr. Todd recalled:

"I was restricted on my ranch, but the trains from the south passed through it for 11 miles. So no train ... could get past without us seeing it. And you cannot camouflage oil tankers. I would stand on the house where I had a grandstand view of the trains coming in. I would keep daily a record of the number of these oil tankers that passed through the ranch. So when people were saying that no oil was coming in, I could keep records - and I did - and handed them on the correct [figures]."

Mr. Todd claims that the tankers were coming into Southern Rhodesia "in droves", the normal train carrying from 18 to 30 tankers. 66/ Other sources indicate that Southern Rhodesia was consuming some 15,000 barrels of oil a day, the carrying capacity of 70 railway tank cars. Thus, Southern Rhodesia required several train loads of oil each day to meet its requirements. 67/

Despite the fact that it was a capital offence to divulge such information, Mr. Todd smuggled his documentation to the British Government. "But of course", he recalled,

"I did not realize until some time later that the British Government was really co-operating with the sanctions busting. They knew. I think they could probably have given me much more accurate information than I was giving them."

As it transpired, Mr. Todd was witness to more than simply the passage of oil tankers through his ranch. From 1975 the guerrilla war began to escalate. "When the war was at its height", Mr. Todd maintained:

"the area in which we live was really a focal point, because through our ranch is the only area where the rail line goes through hills ... And so there was plenty of protection for the people who were laying the land mines. But once the trains got through our ranch, they were up onto open country, from there right down to Rutenga. And so our ranch - and that did not make us any more popular either - was where the trains were continually being blown up. We could see it from the roof."

Other violations of sanctions were not as covert. In November 1971, the
so-called Byrd Amendment became United States law, enabling the United States
to import Southern Rhodesian chrome ore in contravention of United Nations
sanctions. The Byrd Amendment (section 503 of the Military Procurement Act)
amended the Strategic and Critical Materials Stock Piling Act to outlaw any
prohibition on the importation into the United States of any strategic and
critical material from any non-communist country so long as the importation of
such material from communist countries was not prohibited. 68/ Although
Southern Rhodesian chrome ore was not mentioned in the law, Senator Harry Byrd
of Virginia, a long-time opponent of United States and United Nations policy
toward Southern Rhodesia, made no secret of the fact that his amendment was
specifically intended to make way for its importation. 69/

Although Southern Rhodesian chrome ore was the mineral of greatest
concern to supporters of the Byrd Amendment, other Southern Rhodesian minerals
also found their way through the Byrd loophole. In 1972, Southern Rhodesia
produced 22 of the 72 minerals and mineral products listed by the United
States as "strategic and critical". Between 1972 and 1977, when the Byrd
Amendment was repealed, the United States imported $212 million worth of
Southern Rhodesian ferrochrome, chrome ore and nickel, as well as asbestos,
copper and other ores and alloys. 70/

Soon after the Byrd Amendment was signed into law by President Nixon, Ian
Smith told U.S. News and World Report that the reopening of the United States
chrome market would help Southern Rhodesia to surmount its foreign exchange
problems. 71/ Editorials in the Rhodesian Herald called the move "a wonderful
boost for Southern Rhodesian morale" and forecast "the accelerated erosion of
sanctions". 72/ The Herald predicted an increase in business confidence; the
Byrd Amendment meant that buyers could be assured of an uninterrupted supply
of Southern Rhodesian mineral products. Once again competitive, Southern
Rhodesia would be able to demand higher prices for its products, bringing in
greater amounts of much needed foreign exchange. One editorial concluded that:

" ... the American move is at the least a signal to the world that
sanctions are not important enough to warrant serious sacrifices; and at
the most that their usefulness has lost its credibility in American eyes."

Judith Todd Acton, an outspoken opponent of the Smith régime who was
forced into exile in 1972, maintained that the passage of the Byrd Amendment
was a significant victory for the Smith forces. The renewed export of large
quantities of chrome "was very important in keeping the Smith régime going".
The chrome sales brought in "the foreign currency that enabled Southern
Rhodesia to keep on buying oil ... possibly arms. And oil was the fuel of
the war ...". 73/

In a recent interview, a prominent white businessman still living in
Zimbabwe scoffed at the idea that the loss of Southern Rhodesian chrome and
ferrochrome had damaged Western security. While speaking freely of his own
vital role in the covert sale of Southern Rhodesian minerals during the
sanctions period he remarked that:

"The essentiality of Southern Rhodesian chrome ore and ferrochrome
was always greatly exaggerated. We encouraged the exaggeration,
obviously, because it was to our advantage to do so ... We did encourage
the rumours that if we were excluded the world would go to hell in a boat,

and the United States would become wholly dependent on the Soviet Union. But as I say, that was to some extent blarney - to safeguard our position." 74/

The passage of the Byrd Amendment was very advantageous, he added, because Southern Rhodesian minerals had been "blotted out of the United States market by sanctions". Until 1972, there were few loopholes in the United States enforcement that Southern Rhodesian mineral exporters could exploit:

"The United States was one of the markets where, when it was imposing sanctions, we did not find it either possible or convenient to try to break those sanctions. The United States, funnily enough, for the period in which it had sanctions on imports into the United States, administered them fairly efficiently. In consequence, we had to supply other markets in the world and leave the United States to our competitors." 74/

The Byrd Amendment was finally repealed in March 1977, at the urging of the recently elected president, Jimmy Carter, and the United States State Department. 75/ According to the minerals exporter quoted above, the consequences for Southern Rhodesia were absolutely devastating:

"What happened when the Byrd Amendment was repealed was the thing which in fact sank us in ferrochrome and chrome ore. The United States ... decided it was going to make sanctions on chrome work, and they did it, in my view, very cleverly. They not only stopped the import of the goods into the United States; they also introduced a regulation ... which said that the United States would not allow stainless steel into the United States unless the exporting country had, in effect, taken measures against chrome from Southern Rhodesia. This meant that the United States found a means of extending its own domestic actions to most other countries ...

"There are very few large stainless steel producers in the world who can do without the United States market ... or can do without their ambitions to penetrate the United States market. They and their Governments were confronted with the position that if they or their Governments did not take measures against Southern Rhodesian ferrochrome, their stainless would be excluded from the United States, which meant that they, in turn, suddenly felt obliged for commercial - and not political - reasons to back off Southern Rhodesian ferrochrome." 74/

The United States was not satisfied with a certificate simply stating that the chrome ore or ferrochrome had originated in South Africa - which, outside of Southern Rhodesia and the Soviet Union, possessed some of the world's largest chrome ore deposits. Rather, the businessman maintained, the chrome ore and ferrochrome had to be analyzed upon receipt. Since the chrome ore mined in Southern Rhodesia was of much higher quality than that mined in South Africa, a scientific test could easily distinguish between the two. Any chrome ore or ferrochrome that failed the scientific test of origin was rejected. In the same manner, all stainless steel imports had to be accompanied by the results of similar tests conducted in the country where the steel was produced - as proof that the ferrochrome contained in the steel was not of Southern Rhodesian origin. The businessman continued:

"This was very neatly done. Whoever thought it up in the United States was probably the first person to engage in the enforcement of sanctions who knew what he was doing, because it was done with a certain amount of elegance and accuracy. Now the net result was that we found ourselves blotted out of most significant markets.

"We responded with a desperate effort to downgrade our ferrochrome - which we managed to do in one furnace out of four. But it was uneconomic, and because of raw material availability in one thing or another, it could not be done for a significant part of our production." 74/

While ferrochrome continued to be produced, the ability of the Southern Rhodesian industry to manufacture lower grade ferrochrome was limited by technical considerations. Consequently, the bulk of the ferrochrome, which was of a quality higher than the South African product, had to be put into stock. As a result, the businessman concluded, "We did continue a dribble to the outside world, but it was a dribble". One decisive move was sufficient to eliminate effectively Southern Rhodesia from the international chrome market.

Soon after the repeal of the Byrd Amendment, the businessman went to Prime Minister Smith and his ministers with the admission that "After ten years, we have lost. There is nothing more I can do about it". His predictions had been correct, he claimed:

"For the remaining period of sanctions our production had to be reduced. Everything we produced, with the exception of this small dribble which we could produce below that figure of chrome content, just went into stock. And you know, things ground slowly, but slowly to a halt. One could dribble out small quantities of the better grade, but very small quantities to odd, remote markets. ... It was peanut trade - nothing to keep the industry going on." 74/

Once the United States acquired the political will to make sanctions effective, it found the technical means to close the loopholes. Because it represented an extremely large market for stainless steel and related products, the United States was able to make other countries comply with its stringent enforcement demands. According to the minerals exporter, political appeals from Washington would have resulted in no more than lip-service. Economic pressures, on the other hand, ensured ready co-operation:

"The American measures attacked the commercial interests of those countries, and one reached the position for the first time in the history of sanctions where it was not only the Governments of these countries which were trying to enforce sanctions, but the individual firms. ... They told us 'Our own commercial interests dictate that we no longer buy from you'." 74/

The subsequent elimination of Southern Rhodesia from the world chrome market had far reaching ramifications. "The surrender of the Southern Rhodesian Government resulted from two things", asserted the minerals exporter. "First, its inability to win the war; second, its growing inability to finance the war". 74/ The loss of such major foreign exchange earners as chrome ore and ferrochrome, he concluded, "would certainly have been a contributing factor in the growing inability of the Southern Rhodesian Government to finance the war - internally and externally". 74/

While oil and chrome were by no means the only products sold under the counter during the sanctions period, they were among the most significant. The sale of chrome and the acquisition of oil enabled Southern Rhodesia to keep its economy, and later, its war machine running. Those countries and corporations that assisted Southern Rhodesia in these vital areas were largely responsible for the ineffectiveness of sanctions in the short run and the consequent degeneration into civil war.

D. Collaboration of foreign Governments

"Sanctions must be backed by political will to the very end - including the use of force", asserted Nathan Shamuyarira, the Zimbabwean Minister of Information, Posts, and Telecommunications. Otherwise, he maintained, they would not be effective. "The target State", he continued, "must feel that it has to compromise or the army will be sent in". 76/ In the case of Southern Rhodesia, that possibility was rejected even before sanctions were imposed. In his recent book, King Solomon's Mines Revisited, William Minter wrote:

> "Many observers ... argued that a quick, decisive blow against Smith might have established British authority in Salisbury. But success would have required British willingness to use force, to go immediately to all-out economic warfare, or to appeal to Africans and other loyal British citizens in Southern Rhodesia to rebel. All these measures were ruled out in advance."

According to William Minter, the Labour Government of Harold Wilson "repeatedly promised not to use force against Southern Rhodesian whites". Much to the dismay of his critics, the British Prime Minister failed even to "retain the option as a bluff to deter Southern Rhodesian action". 77/ From the outset, the British Government lacked the political will to exercise its power of enforcement.

Tirivafi gai, the Chief Representative of the Zimbabwe African National Union (ZANU) to the United Nations, the United States and the Caribbean from 1977 to 1980, recently claimed that the United Kingdom could have brought down the Smith régime had it imposed a total blockade and seriously enforced economic sanctions. Had the United Kingdom taken such a position, Kangai maintained, the armed struggle, and the horrific bloodshed that it entailed, could have been avoided. 78/

"I that those sanctions were doomed from the start", charged John Deary, an active opponent of Ian Smith during UDI. "They were doomed from the moment the British allowed the oil [supply] to continue. The Government was totally aware of the fact that it was going on, and they were totally aware of how it was arriving here", Mr. Deary claimed. As head of Southern Rhodesia's Catholic Commission for Justice and Peace, Mr. Deary made several visits to the British Foreign Office during the sanctions period. According to him, he and other members of the Commission:

> "had to go to the Foreign Office and on our knees beg them to cut off the supply of oil. The hypocrisy of their denial that they were capable of doing so is something that will forever stick in my gut." 79/

The United Kingdom, however, was not the only guilty party. According to Betty Jo Dorsey, an American living in Southern Rhodesia during UDI, "You could tell which countries were breaking sanctions ... by the cars that were in the country - German, Japanese and French. Peugeots, Mercedeses, Volkswagens, all the Japanese lines were there". 80/ As early as 1967, the Financial Mail reported that "United Nations members have paid lip service to United Nations resolutions on the subject [of sanctions] and allowed their nationals to go about their Southern Rhodesian business quietly and profitably". That the firms of numerous countries were actively breaking sanctions was "obvious to anyone doing a spot of window shopping". 81/ The Financial Mail predicted that if such sanctions busting activities continued, "Southern Rhodesia could soon be out of the dog box economically and therefore, in the end, politically". 82/

The home Governments of the companies violating sanctions were, for the most part, aware of the illegal activities. According to a prominent businessman employed by the Associated Chambers of Commerce of Southern Rhodesia during the 1970s:

> "They had to have a pretty good idea of what was going on. They had to know. They had to know that a country of this size, with the sort of economy which we had in 1965 could not survive with all the taps shut. So they knew that we were getting things out. And it is quite probable that politically that was acceptable - in the sense that if they knew that in the long term [the Southern Rhodesian set-up] would not last, then it was also in their political interest to have something which was worthwhile at the end of it." 83/

Eddie Cross, an economist for the Agricultural Marketing Authority of the Southern Rhodesian Government from 1969 to 1980, maintained that "We were exporting commodities to countries which were essentially in violation of the United Nations sanctions". Consequently,

> "Those of us who were responsible for sanctions breaking in the agricultural sector ... followed a policy, meticulously, of ensuring that the buyer, no matter who he was, was aware of the fact that the product came from this country." 84/

Such a policy was necessary to ensure the consistent co-operation of the buyer, and ultimately, that Southern Rhodesia was going to be paid, he concluded.

As a result of massive sanctions busting by foreign corporations, with the collusion of many Governments, the illegal Southern Rhodesian régime continued to survive. In the light of the active connivance of the British Foreign Office in the sanctions-busting operation, Prime Minister Harold Wilson's prediction that sanctions would bring Southern Rhodesia down in "weeks, not months" was the epitome of cynicism. 85/

E. Long-term effects of sanctions

By 1975 most of the consumer goods that could be made within the constraints of the Southern Rhodesian economy were being produced. The limited domestic market and obstacles imposed by sanctions on external trade meant that Southern Rhodesian industries frequently did not produce enough to achieve economies of scale. Thus their manufactures were often costly, of inferior quality, and uncompetitive internationally. 86/

In September 1966, P. C. Aldridge, director of the Association of Southern Rhodesian Industries, expressed concern at the mushrooming of backyard industries. The reputation of established local products would be damaged, he maintained, "if supplies of shoddy or inferior goods should be finding their way to the market". The Financial Mail found that the public was "restive about the quality of some Southern Rhodesian-made goods" and unhappy about paying the higher prices. The correspondent queried whether it might not be more economical to import the finished product than to import so many of the components and to produce the article under less than optimal economic conditions. 87/

By the mid-1970s there was little room for further expansion in either the domestic or foreign markets. The sanctions-induced decline in export earnings meant that the country was desperately short of foreign exchange, which it needed either to produce capital goods or to import them. Hence, there was a serious structural limit to the growth of the manufacturing sector under sanctions. 88/

Ten years after the imposition of sanctions the Southern Rhodesian economy had reached a plateau. Machinery was wearing out. Spare parts could not be obtained. The country was "running down its capital goods stock right across the board", claimed Ruth Weiss, who covered Southern Rhodesia for the Financial Mail during the early sanctions period. Far from ensuring economic growth, sanctions had "made a massive holding operation necessary". 89/ A prominent businessman in the commercial sector concluded that "If you're not moving forward in economic terms, then you are actually going backwards". 90/ Southern Rhodesia, claimed a colleague, had finally "come to the crunch line". 91/

Sanctions severely limited Southern Rhodesia's access to foreign loans and direct investment. According to the Rhodesian Herald of 5 April 1973, "unless access to external sources of capital is eased soon, the rate of development necessary to sustain the population cannot be achieved". An entrepreneur involved in under-the-counter tobacco sales maintained that:

"The long, drawn-out effects of sanctions did harm us. There was no more capital investment from overseas. Exploration for new minerals, irrigation schemes, and new industries need overseas capital. This was frozen by sanctions. Sanctions restricted the growth of the country, of employment opportunities, of development." 92/

Southern Rhodesia's foregone growth potential was enormous. Eddie Cross estimated that over the course of the sanctions period, the value of lost exports approximated $R 3.6 billion. That is, the value of exports would have been 62 per cent higher than their actual value of $R 5.8 billion had sanctions not been imposed. 93/

F. Sanctions in conjunction with other factors

In the mid-1970s, a number of factors converged to intensify the damage done by sanctions. Firstly, petroleum prices increased dramatically, trebling the cost of Southern Rhodesian oil imports between 1973 and 1976. 94/ Although oil prices increased around the world, Southern Rhodesia was particularly affected in that it paid the sanctions premium in addition to the OPEC price increase. The oil price rise sparked a world economic recession, which caused a rapid deterioration in Southern Rhodesia's terms of trade. The prices offered for Southern Rhodesia's primary commodity exports fell sharply, while import prices skyrocketed. Southern Rhodesia was actually earning less foreign currency for its exports at a time when it needed that currency more than ever. By 1979 Southern Rhodesia's terms of trade were 40 per cent worse than they were when sanctions were imposed. 95/

In order to finance vital oil requirements, the Smith régime drastically cut non-petroleum import allocations from the mid-1970s onwards. Its supply of capital goods, spare parts and certain essential inputs practically ceased and the Southern Rhodesian manufacturing sector embarked upon a downward spiral.

It was during this period of increased economic hardship that Zambia and Mozambique began to intensify pressure on Southern Rhodesia. Interdependent as their economies were, the two countries were committed to applying sanctions to the greatest extent possible. In January 1973, in response to stepped-up guerrilla activities from the Zambian territory, Southern Rhodesia closed the border with its western neighbor. In retaliation, Zambia declared that it would keep the border closed permanently, regardless of a Southern Rhodesian decision to reopen it. Henceforth Zambia would reroute its copper exports through the United Republic of Tanzania, at tremendous loss to the Southern Rhodesian railways. 96/

The Zambian border closure eliminated a major source of foreign exchange earnings for Southern Rhodesia. Until sanctions were imposed in 1965, Zambia had been Southern Rhodesia's largest export market, accounting for approximately 65 per cent of total foreign sales. By 1967 the value of Southern Rhodesian manufactured goods consumed in Zambia was only one third the pre-sanctions value. Although the market for Southern Rhodesian consumer goods had shrunk considerably by 1973, revenues from transit freight to and from Zambia were still worth several million pounds sterling per year. The loss of these earnings caused a trebling of Southern Rhodesia's deficit in services in 1973. 97/

Until Portugal was forced to concede independence to Mozambique in June 1975, the colonial Power had been an important source of support for the Southern Rhodesian régime. The new Government, however, was openly antagonistic to Southern Rhodesia and allowed Zimbabwean liberation forces to use Mozambique as a rear base. Southern Rhodesia now had hostile territory on three sides. Matters came to a head in March 1976, when the Mozambique Government closed its border with Southern Rhodesia, forcing the Smith régime to reroute over 1.5 million tons of export goods per year through South Africa - at much greater expense. Southern Rhodesia, from that period, became almost totally reliant on South Africa to supply it with imports, to take its exports, and to allow passage of goods through its territory to and from the sea.

Until the Mozambique border closure, about half of all Southern Rhodesian exports were shipped through the Mozambican ports of Beira and Lourenço Marques. While Beira was 360 miles from the Southern Rhodesian capital, the South African port of Durban was 1,260 miles away. Thus, transport through Mozambique was faster and cheaper than transport through South Africa. Moreover, according to John Graylin, "Beira was a tremendously well run port at that time. It was handling more goods per person employed than almost any port in the world". 98/ Ports in South Africa, by contrast, were extremely congested. Trade was hampered by serious delays in loading and unloading and greatly increased shipping and freight costs, due to the much longer distances that goods were transported. 99/

The border closures by Mozambique and Zambia meant the loss of potential markets for new Southern Rhodesian manufactures. Failure to find new outlets for Southern Rhodesian goods meant stagnant or even diminished foreign exchange earnings, earnings that were crucial for further development of the economy. The inability of Southern Rhodesia to make inroads into the regional market stunted its nascent import substitution industries. Domestic demand was limited, primarily due to the low incomes of the African majority. Without expansion into the region, economies of scale could not be achieved. Thus, the application of sanctions by Mozambique and Zambia, exacerbated by the oil price increase and the world economic recession, was a serious blow to the Southern Rhodesian economy.

From 1974 onward, Southern Rhodesia was faced with "inadequate capital investment, as a result of the balance of payments constraint", according to a businessman who at that time worked for the Association of Southern Rhodesian Industries. Deterioration was evident "right the way across - through industry, agriculture, mining and inadequate capital replacement". Because of the shortage in foreign exchange, the country could not afford new machinery and equipment. Moreover, the businessman recalled, "We were fighting a war, so quite a lot of our import capacity had to be diverted to military hardware". 100/

It was during this period of economic decline that the liberation war began to escalate. By 1979, the war was consuming more than one third of the national budget, costing the régime approximately $R 1 million a day. Between 1975/76 and 1979/80 the budget deficit increased five-fold, primarily as a result of the war and oil import costs. 101/

The war also took its toll in other ways. "The relentless [military] call-up of all white men under 50 ... had a devastating impact on morale", according to Tony Hawkins, an economist who taught at the University of Southern Rhodesia during UDI. 102/ Eddie Cross recalled that he personally spent six months a year in the army, and that out of a white male population of about 110,000, approximately 60,000 were in the armed forces at any point in time. "People got fed up with having to go into the army for longish periods very frequently", often six weeks at a time, four to five times a year, John Graylin claimed. 103/

In the long run, the efficiency and productivity of the economy suffered from the frequent and prolonged absence of skilled [white] personnel. 104/ The fact that employers were required to pay men who were doing their military service ultimately became such an intolerable financial burden that the Government was forced to subsidize the operation. 105/ "We were running out of domestic revenue and foreign currency", one businessman summarized, "in addition to which the permanent call-up was wrecking what was left of the economy. The cost of the war was too high domestically". 106/ In 1976, for the first time since the post-UDI panic a decade earlier, more white people emigrated from Southern Rhodesia than immigrated to it. More than 7,000 whites left Southern Rhodesia that year, further draining the country of vital professional, technical and military manpower. 107/

The war was "the final nail in the coffin", concluded one businessman. "But there were a lot of other nails. ... The state of war, the state of economic sanctions, could not go on forever without a total collapse". 108/ The inability of the country to finance both the war and the economy "was in part attributable to sanctions", maintained a colleague formerly involved in the covert exportation of minerals. "If we had been able to continue our economic strength", he concluded, "the political side of the thing would have continued the war longer". 109/ Thus in the long run sanctions lessened the bloodshed by reducing the régime's ability to carry on the war, thereby shortening its duration.

G. South Africa imposes sanctions

The effectiveness of sanctions was dramatically enhanced when South Africa began to apply them. By all accounts, South Africa was the most notorious sanctions buster; without the massive support of its southern neighbor, Southern Rhodesia could not have withstood the onslaught of economic sanctions for as long as it did. However, the relationship between the two countries was not an altogether happy one. "The South Africans were totally mercenary about the sanctions against Southern Rhodesia", charged Eddie Cross, now general manager of the Cold Storage Commission, a Zimbabwe parastatal company. "They exploited the situation right from the word go. They exploited their monopolistic control over our transport routes. They exploited their favourable position as a supplier of spares and critical things that we could not buy internationally because of sanctions. We owe the South Africans nothing for 14 years of sanctions busting", he concluded. "They were making a good business out of it. For many South African businessmen sanctions against Southern Rhodesia were a boom, a tremendous thing". 110/

By the mid-1970s, South African Prime Minister John Vorster had come to consider the Smith régime a thorn in the side. He viewed it as a destabilizing factor in the region and determined that the fires of African nationalism had to be contained before they spread further south. Moreover, South Africa itself was beginning to feel the heat of external pressures. The United States Secretary of State Henry Kissinger warned Vorster that South Africa was the next candidate for international sanctions, if it failed to sever its ties with the illegal Southern Rhodesian régime. 111/

Hoping to force Smith to give way to a moderate, easily manipulable black Government, South Africa began to pressure the Southern Rhodesian régime. "Unexplained" snarl-ups in the South African transport system left Southern Rhodesian imports stranded south of the border. Oil and other vital supplies were cut off. The arms flow dwindled. Southern Rhodesian exports piled up on South African ports. South African loans, crucial for financing the war and large infrastructure projects, came to a halt. 112/ "If the border with Mozambique had been open, the South African situation could have been weathered", claimed a former employee of the Association of Southern Rhodesian Industries. 113/ However that option had been closed. Once South Africa began applying sanctions, Southern Rhodesia was doomed. A political settlement loomed not far in the future.

H. Will blacks suffer most

One of the most common arguments made by opponents of sanctions against South Africa is that blacks, rather than whites, will suffer most. Therefore, sanctions should not be imposed. Again, it is instructive to reflect upon the Southern Rhodesian case. Speaking to the United Nations-sponsored World Conference on Sanctions against Racist South Africa held in June 1986, the Zimbabwean Minister of Foreign Affairs, Witness Mangwende, claimed that sanctions were effective in Southern Rhodesia, but to a lesser degree than they would have been had they not been violated by major Western countries. He added that while Africans bore the brunt of United Nations sanctions against Southern Rhodesia; "at no stage did the blacks in Zimbabwe or the suffering neighbouring States ever ask for the lifting of those sanctions". On the contrary, Mr. Mangwende maintained, they called for a more rigorous enforcement of sanctions by the West. The Foreign Minister concluded that there was no reason to believe that blacks in South Africa would react differently. 114/

In a similar vein, while conducting an investigation in Southern Rhodesia in 1972, the British Government's Pearce Commission found that Africans strongly supported the retention of sanctions, in spite of the burden they imposed on the African population. The Commission reported that Africans were willing to make such sacrifices in order to achieve their objective of majority rule. 115/

The following year, Eddison Zvobgo, then Director of the External Commission of the African National Council (ANC) of Zimbabwe, pursued a different tack. Testifying at a United States Congressional hearing in February 1973, Mr. Zvobgo claimed:

"It is not us who need sheets to sleep on or cars to come into the city, or spare parts to run the industries. We do not own the economy. Those comforts which have been siphoned off by sanctions are totally irrelevant to the African people.

"Over 90 per cent of the African people live on the land. ... They are fed by the very soil. So that to suggest that sanctions hurt the Africans and therefore in the interest of the African we ought to drop sanctions, is nonsense." 116/

Recalling his work as Zimbabwe African National Union (ZANU) representative to the United Nations, the United States and the Caribbean during the sanctions period, Tirivafi Kangai maintained that the liberation movement consistently emphasized a two-pronged strategy consisting of sanctions and the armed struggle. So seriously did ZANU consider sanctions that it took the United States Government to court over the enactment of the Byrd Amendment, charging that the United States was violating international law through its abrogation of mandatory United Nations sanctions. Although the liberation movement did not win its case against the United States, it was successful in bringing the issue to the attention of the American people. Mr. Kangai asserted that while the war was the determining factor in the transition to majority rule, sanctions were critical in that they enlisted the support of other countries, isolating the régime politically and economically, ultimately contributing to its downfall. 117/

The Zimbabwean Minister of Information, Nathan Shamuyarira, reiterated the importance of sanctions as a political weapon. He said that as such they assist in mobilizing forces against the target State. The most critical aspect of sanctions against Southern Rhodesia, Mr. Shamuyarira maintained, was that they successfully mobilized the world opinion against the Smith régime.

Moreover, sanctions gave new leverage to black Zimbabweans inside the country. Confident that their actions were backed by the United Nations and the international community, they began to attack the Smith régime more openly, in public and in the court of law. However, Mr. Shamuyarira cautioned, it is important to remember that sanctions were one factor among many. Sanctions alone did not bring down the Smith régime. In the final analysis, it was sanctions in conjunction with other factors such as diplomatic and political pressure, and most importantly the armed struggle, that forced the country to accept the premise of majority rule. "This", concluded the Minister of Information, "should be the goal of economic sanctions against the apartheid régime". 118/

Judith Acton concurred that the liberation movement considered sanctions as an important component of the struggle against the Smith régime. "Sanctions had a very profound psychological effect within this country", she maintained.

"Sanctions helped to make the whites feel isolated. Some people would argue that when a group is isolated, it fights back more fiercely, but I do not think that was proved in our case ... Whatever they are saying, all the time they were trying to be acceptable and trying to get back into a normal relationship with the world." 119/

Mr. Kangai agreed that whites in Southern Rhodesia were extremely bitter toward the West, particularly the United Kingdom. Perceiving themselves to be part of the Western world, defending Christianity and civilization, they could not understand why the West spurned them, supporting instead the African "terrorists". 120/

I. Comparative reflections on South Africa

Addressing a meeting of the Zimbabwe-Mozambique Friendship Association in June 1986, Lieutenant Colonel Clemence Gaza, Director of Public Relations of the Zimbabwe National Army, declared:

"We know from our own experience in the struggle that sanctions can be a powerful economic and psychological weapon, that, linked to the armed struggle, helped to bring the Southern Rhodesian régime to its knees." 121/

If the imposition of economic sanctions played such a major role in the liberation of Zimbabwe, what role can they be expected to play in the future of South Africa?

"Sanctions have the capacity to really damage the South African economy", according to Eddie Cross. South Africa is even "more vulnerable" to economic sanctions than was Southern Rhodesia, he continued, "because they are so much more sophisticated, so much more dependent on access to technology, so much more dependent upon exports of sophisticated products". 122/

Like Southern Rhodesia 20 years ago, South Africa today is extremely reliant upon international trade and investment for its economic well-being and growth. In November 1985 the Standard Bank Review noted that:

"As a small, relatively open economy, the country's prosperity is based to a great extent on its ability to freely sell materials and products abroad. In turn, South Africa depends on the outside world for many essential inputs."

Foreign trade constitutes approximately 55 per cent of South Africa's gross domestic product, compared to 17 per cent for the United States. Capital goods, such as advanced technology, transport equipment and power generators comprise 40 per cent of all South African imports. 123/ Petroleum products and military goods constitute another one third of the total import bill. 124/ Agricultural machinery and certain essential fertilizers and pesticides are imported too. Computer systems and vital components such as aircraft, railway engines and rolling stock are, for the most part, purchased abroad. South Africa does not have the capability to produce most advanced machinery, components and spare parts, either on the scale needed, or at all. 125/

South Africa's massive foreign debt, equivalent to more than one third of its gross domestic product, makes it one of the world's top debtor nations. International lending has helped Pretoria to finance huge infrastructure and industrial projects and to cope with massive military expenditures, which have more than trebled since 1976. 126/ The high import requirements of these projects have given rise to severe balance of payments difficulties and a rapidly increasing inflation rate. 127/

Ironically, South Africa's dependence on Western finance has proved to be its undoing. Without explicitly labelling their actions as "sanctions", international banks have shown their ability to break the South African economy. With business confidence at an all-time low after the declaration of the state of emergency in July 1985, United States banks began cutting off new funds to South Africa. The actions of the United States banks caused a chain reaction: other banks followed suit, refusing to renew short-term credits and calling in long-term loans. Describing the scenario, one United States banker exclaimed: "It was like a 1929 run on a bank; everyone was trying to get out". 128/

As banks began demanding repayment of their dollar-based loans, a scramble for dollars ensued. The shortage of dollars and over-supply of rand caused the value of the rand to decrease sharply. It plummeted more than 20 per cent between late July and mid-August 1985, hitting bottom at $US 0.35, less than half its 1984 value. 129/ To keep the rand from falling further, the Government closed the Johannesburg Stock Exchange and suspended all trading on the currency market for a period of five days. On 1 September 1985, the Government announced a four-month moratorium on the repayment of South Africa's $US 14 billion foreign debt which was due at the end of the year. With the dramatic deterioration in the value of the rand, South African reserves were far too limited to repay the massive foreign debt. 130/

Simultaneous with the first initiatives of the United States banks, France imposed limited sanctions, prohibiting new investment in South Africa. The fear of more extensive sanctions, particularly against South African exports considered crucial to the country's economic recovery, caused a panic on the Johannesburg Stock Exchange. In only one week in late July 1985, more than R 11 billion were slashed off the value of the shares. A wave of selling followed, primarily among United States, British and French shareholders. Brokers described the situation as a "bloodbath". 131/ If such turmoil followed in the wake of relatively minor sanctions, the impact of comprehensive sanctions would in all probability be devastating.

Shaky business confidence has caused a steady outflow of private capital from South Africa since 1982. Between June and September 1985, foreign investors withdrew R 365 million from South Africa through the sale of shares

on the stock exchange. In September 1985, the press reported the largest
flight of capital since the aftermath of the Sharpeville massacre in
1960. 132/ During the 11-month period between May 1985 and March 1986,
capital flight from South Africa amounted to approximately $US 1 billion.
Since the onset of the 1985 debt crisis, foreign exchange volumes have fallen
by 50 per cent. 133/

Over the course of the past five years, United States direct investment in
South Africa has declined by one half, with virtually no new investments being
made during this period. During 1985 and 1986, more than 70 United States
companies pulled out of South Africa or announced their intention to do
so. 134/ An economic report prepared by the American Consulate in
Johannesburg in July 1986 described South Africa as a serious trade and
investment risk for American businesses. According to the consulate's
economic officers, South Africa is:

"a chronic debtor, import-starved, ridden with ethnic diversity, a
repressive régime unable to manage its own domestic constituency in any
positive way, whose only leverage is its ability to mani ulate foreign
Governments and attract international attention for better or for
worse." 135/

Until the last quarter of 1986, most of the foreign companies closing
operations in South Africa were relatively small firms. Then, in September
1986 Coca Cola announced its plans for departure. General Motors followed suit
on 20 October. The next day, IBM made known its intention to leave.
Honeywell and Warner Communications followed the day after that. In November,
Eastman Kodak announced that it was selling out. The largest single
divestiture came from Barclays, South Africa's largest commercial bank and the
first British company to divest itself of its South African holdings. 136/
All of these companies claimed that they were leaving South Africa for
political as well as economic reasons. The internal unrest was too serious,
the business climate too volatile, and the anti-apartheid pressure on the home
front too costly for them to continue. One investment broker predicted a
"stampede" by foreign firms, "prompted by both political pressure and lower
profits". 137/

The loss of foreign investment has serious implications for the South
African economy. According to Jan Steyn, director of South Africa's Urban
Foundation, the country is "desperately short of development capital". It is
"still a developing country ... with a very great need for investment". As
the deterioration of the economy causes a decline in domestic savings, "the
need for investment from abroad becomes yet more acute". 138/ Moreover,
direct investment through the subsidiaries of foreign corporations provides
not only capital, but the most advanced technology and skilled manpower, the
lack of which is among the most severe constraints upon South African economic
growth. 139/

Other forms of sanctions have long been eroding the health of the South
African economy. To circumvent the 1973 OPEC oil embargo, South Africa has
been paying US$ 2 per barrel over the regular price for oil, or a total of $US
300 million a year. This extra expense for purchasing on the spot market,
plus the costs of middlemen, rerouting, and other forms of camouflage, amount
to an extra $US 2.3 billion per year. 140/ With technical and financial
assistance from foreign corporations, South Africa has built

coal-to-oil conversion plants. However, the synthetically produced oil accounts for only 38 per cent of South Africa's requirements and it is extremely expensive, costing approximately $US 1.3 billion a year. 141/

Similarly, South Africa spends about $US 2.1 billion per year to circumvent the United Nations mandatory arms embargo. Although South Africa manufactures many of its own arms, it has failed to produce the most sophisticated weapons systems and must still import most of its aircraft, tanks, and other armoured vehicles at exorbitant prices. Moreover, 80 per cent of the components of the arms produced in South Africa are foreign made. Thus, rather than increasing South Africa's strategic self-sufficiency, the apartheid arms build-up has been increasing its dependence upon foreign collaboration. 142/

Unlike Southern Rhodesia in 1965, South Africa has long since passed the shallow phase of import substitution, such as the manufacture of consumer goods. Hence, sanctions will not serve to stimulate a period of growth in the manufacturing sector as they did in Southern Rhodesia. Even before the imposition of sanctions, the South African economy has reached the plateau that Southern Rhodesia reached some years after sanctions were imposed.

The deepening crisis in the South African economy is another factor that will work to the country's detriment if sanctions are imposed. The vigorous Southern Rhodesian economy in 1965 helped to soften the sanctions blow. South Africa, in contrast, is in the depths of its worst economic recession in 50 years. Since 1980, the rand has lost two thirds of its value. Inflation reached a 66-year high in January 1986, running at more than 20 per cent. 143/ Record black unemployment levels - surpassing the 6 million mark, mean that one out of two black workers may be jobless. The critical employment crisis is exacerbating already profound urban tensions. 144/ Hundreds of millions of rand have left South Africa. Scores of transnational corporations have shut down their South African subsidiaries, while foreign banks have refused to roll over their loans.

South Africa in 1986 bears a far closer resemblance to Southern Rhodesia in the mid-1970s than to that country when sanctions were imposed. In conjunction with its rapidly deteriorating economic situation, South Africa is confronted by mounting political pressures: escalating trade union and community action, intensified activity by the armed wing of the African National Congress of South Africa, and the general ungovernability of the black townships.

Already reeling from these internal strains, Pretoria is extremely vulnerable to external pressures. Like the Southern Rhodesian minerals exporter who attributed his country's political collapse to its loss of economic strength, South African newspaper editor Willem de Klerk has said that "the West has the power to do us considerable damage and if our economy is affected we will become increasingly politically defenceless". In such a context, for South Africa today as for Southern Rhodesia in the past, comprehensive mandatory economic sanctions would be a decisive blow that would hasten the downfall of apartheid.

Notes

1/   Robin Renwick, Economic sanctions, Harvard Studies in International Affairs, No. 45 (Cambridge, Massachusetts, Harvard University Center for International Affairs, 1981), pp. 2, 91 and 92; Deon Geldenhuys, "The political prospects for sanctions; interaction of international pressures and domestic developments", in South Africa and sanctions: genesis and prospects, a symposium (Johannesburg, South African Institute of Race Relations and South African Institute of International Affairs, 24 February 1979), p. 30.

2/   Geldenhuys, op. cit., p. 41; Margaret Doxey, Economic sanctions and international enforcement, 2nd ed. (New York, Oxford University Press, 1980), p. 84.

3/   General Assembly resolution 2145 (XXI) of 21 October 1966.

4/   Security Council resolutions 276 (1970) of 30 January 1970 and 284 (1970) of 29 July 1970.

5/   Doxey, op. cit., p. 63.

6/   Southern African Research and Documentation Centre, South Africa imposes sanctions against neighbours, Published for the Eighth Summit of the Non-Aligned Movement (Harare, Southern African Research and Documentation Centre, September 1986), p. 5.

7/   Chris Child, "Apartheid, economic collaboration and the case for the United Nations comprehensive mandatory sanctions against South Africa", Notes and Documents 6/84 (New York, United Nations Centre against Apartheid, July 1984), p. 51.

8/   Catholic Institute for International Relations, "Sanctions against South Africa", Comment, November 1985, p.3.

9/   General Assembly resolution 1761 (XVII) of 6 November 1962, as noted in Doxey, op. cit., p.61.

10/   Quoted in Geldenhuys, op. cit., p. 38.

11/   Charter of the United Nations, Article 27; see also: Doxey, op. cit., pp. 3 and 4.

12/   Security Council resolution 181 (1963) of 7 August 1963.

13/   Doxey, op. cit., pp. 61 and 62.

14/   Security Council resolution 182 (1963) of 4 December 1963.

15/   Security Council resolution 282 (1970) of 23 July 1970.

16/   Security Council resolution 418 (1977) of 4 November 1977.

17/   Security Council resolution 569 (1985) of 26 July 1985, as reported in the Financial Times (London), 27 July 1985.

18/ "US, Britain Veto Resolution to Condemn SA Raids", Herald (Zimbabwe), 26 May 1986.

19/ Doxey, op. cit., p. 62.

20/ B. Akporode Clark, "The case for a mandatory oil embargo against South Africa", Objective: Justice, vol. 13, No. 1 (May 1981), p. 3.

21/ Unless otherwise indicated, all quotations are taken from interviews conducted by the author in Zimbabwe between November 1985 and June 1986.

22/ Anonymous interview, Harare, Zimbabwe, 14 May 1986.

23/ Anonymous interview, Harare, Zimbabwe, 13 May 1986.

24/ Renwick, op. cit., p. 9.

25/ Harry R. Strack, Sanctions: the case of Rhodesia (Syracuse, Syracuse University Press, 1978), p. 22; William Minter, King Solomon's mines revisited: Western interests and the burdened history of southern Africa (New York, Basic Books, 1986), p. 209.

26/ Minter, op. cit., p. 203.

27/ Ibid., pp. 203 and 207-209.

28/ Strack, op. cit., p. 17; Donald L. Losman, International economic sanctions: the cases of Cuba, Israel and Rhodesia (Albuquerque, University of New Mexico Press, 1979), p. 94; Robert McKinnell, "Sanctions and the Rhodesian economy", The Journal of Modern African Studies, vol. 7, No. 4 (1969), p. 561.

29/ Losman, op. cit., pp. 95 and 105; Elaine Windrich, Britain and the politics of Rhodesian independence (London, Croom Helm Ltd., 1978), p. 63; Mervyn Frost, "Collective sanctions in international relations: an historical overview of the theory and practice", in South Africa and sanctions: genesis and prospects, a symposium (Johannesburg: South African Institute of Race Relations and South African Institute of International Affairs, 24 February 1979), p. 20.

30/ Security Council resolution 217 (1965) of 20 November 1965.

31/ Windrich, op. cit., pp. 64 and 65.

32/ Strack, op. cit., p. 17; McKinnell, op. cit., p. 561; Windrich, op. cit., p. 69; Renwick, op. cit., p. 27; Losman, op. cit., p. 89; Doxey, op. cit., p. 67.

33/ Strack, op. cit., p. 17; Frost, op. cit., p. 20; Losman, op. cit., p. 105; Doxey, op. cit., p. 68.

34/ Doxey, op. cit., p. 67; Windrich, op. cit., pp. 78 and 79; Renwick, op. cit., p. 27.

35/ Security Council resolution 232 (1966) of 16 December 1966.

36/   Losman, op. cit., p. 95.

37/   Security Council resolution 253 (1968) of 29 May 1968.

38/   Strack, op. cit., p. 16; E.G. Cross, "Economic sanctions as a tool of policy against Rhodesia", The World Economy, vol. 4, No. 1 (March 1981), p. 70; Donald L. Losman, "Rhodesia: a decade under sanctions", Il Politico (June 1978), p. 323.

39/   Losman, "Rhodesia ...", op. cit., p. 323.

40/   Robert McKinnell, "Assessing the economic impact of sanctions against Rhodesia, a note on T. R. C. Curtin's Article", African Affairs, vol. 67, No. 228 (1968), p. 231.

41/   E. G. Cross, op. cit., p. 73; Renwick, op. cit., p. 40.

42/   Strack, op. cit., p. 88.

43/   Cross, op. cit., p. 73; Losman, International ..., op. cit., p. 103; Financial Mail (Johannesburg), vol. 23, No. 1 (6 January 1967); Interview with John Graylin, Harare, Zimbabwe, 5 May 1986. Mr. Graylin was chairman of the Tobacco Export Promotion Council from 1965 to 1968. He subsequently chaired the National Export Council, and finally was named chief executive of the Association of Rhodesian Industries.

44/   Renwick, op. cit., p. 77; Strack, op. cit., p. 87.

45/   R. B. Sutcliffe, "Rhodesian trade since UDI", The World Today (October 1967), p. 420.

46/   Interview with E. G. Cross, Harare, Zimbabwe, 26 March 1986. Mr. Cross was an economist for the Rhodesian Government's Agricultural arketing Authority from 1969 to 1980.

47/   Interview with John Graylin.

48/   Renwick, op. cit., p. 32; interview with E. G. Cross.

49/   Ruth Weiss, "Rhodesia: truth or blind faith?", Financial Mail, vol. 27, No. 1 (5 January 1968), p. 31.

50/   Losman, International ..., op. cit., p. 107; Financial Mail, vol. 24, No. 12 (23 June 1967), pp. 989 and 992.

51/   Financial Mail, vol. 19, No. 6 (11 February 1966), p. 332; ibid., vol. 20, No. 13 (24 June 1966), p. 868; ibid., vol. 23, No. 5 (3 February 1967), p. 313; ibid., vol. 24, No. 6 (12 May 1967), p. 453.

52/   Financial Mail, vol. 22, No. 2 (14 October 1966), p. 115; ibid., vol. 22, No. 12 (23 December 1966), p. 951; Sutcliffe, op. cit., p. 421.

53/   Financial Mail, vol. 19, No. 12 (25 March 1966), p. 715; ibid., vol. 21, No. 10 (2 September 1966), p. 660.

54/   Financial Mail, vol. 22. No. 11 (10 June 1966), p. 693.

55/ _Financial Mail_, vol. 22, No. 2 (14 October 1966), p. 115; _ibid._, vol. 23, No. 7 (17 February 1967), pp. 447 and 449; _ibid._, vol. 23, No. 10 (10 March 1967), p. 652; _ibid._, vol. 24, No. 6 (12 May 1967), p. 453.

56/ _Financial Mail_, vol. 22, No. 4 (28 October 1966), p. 271; _ibid._, vol. 22, No. 7 (18 November 1966), p. 538; _ibid._, vol. 26, No. 7 (17 November 1967), p. 624.

57/ Minter, _op. cit._, p. 203; Garfield Todd, "Address regarding Rhodesian sanctions to the economic symposium, held at the University of Zimbabwe", Salisbury, 8-10 September 1980, p. 8; Martin Bailey, _Oilgate, the sanctions scandal_ (London, Hodder and Stoughton, 1979), p. 8.

58/ Security Council resolution 221 (1966) of 9 April 1966.

59/ Minter, _op. cit._, p. 210; Doxey, _op. cit._, p. 71. The British Government removed the blockade in 1976 when the newly independent Government in Mozambique announced that it would enforce sanctions.

60/ Windrich, _op. cit._, p. 204; Anthony Lake, _The "tar baby" option, American policy toward Southern Rhodesia_ (New York, Columbia University Press, 1976), p. 39; interview with Tirivafi J. Kangai, Harare, Zimbabwe, 11 June 1986. Mr. Kangai was Chief Representative of the Zimbabwe African National Union (ZANU) to the United Nations, the United States and the Caribbean from 1977 to 1980.

61/ B   y, _op. cit._, pp. 140, 173 and 241; Bernard Rivers, "Sanctions breaker - selling oil to Rhodesia", _Southern Africa_, vol. 10, No. 7 (September 1977), pp. 9-11; Center for Social Action of the United Church of Christ, _Oil conspiracy: an investigation into how multinational oil companies provide Rhodesia's oil needs_ (New York, Center for Social Action, 21 June 1976), p. 26. As early as December 1965, Shell, a British-Dutch firm that played a leading part in Shell/BP marketing arrangements in southern Africa, told the British Government that the only way to keep oil from getting to Southern Rhodesia was to cut off all oil supplies to South Africa. According to Robin Renwick, Head of the Rhodesia Department of the British Foreign Office during the Lancaster House negotiations, the British Government was unwilling to sever South African oil supplies, and the matter was dropped (see Renwick, _op. cit._, p. 29).

62/ Windrich, _op. cit._, p. 106; Renwick, _op. cit._, p. 35; Doxey, _op. cit._, pp. 3 and 4.

63/ Lake, _op. cit._, pp. 39 and 44; Windrich, _op. cit._, p. 218; T. Curtin, "Rhodesian economic development under sanctions and the 'the long haul'", _African Affairs_, vol. 67, No. 227 (1968), p. 102.

64/ Martin Bailey, _op. cit._, pp. 21 and 114; Bernard Rivers, _op. cit._, p. 10.

65/ For further details see: Bailey, Rivers and the Center for Social Action of the United Church of Christ, _op. cit._

66/ Unless otherwise indicated, all quotations are taken from an interview with Sir Garfield Todd, Harare, Zimbabwe, 13 May 1986.

67/ Bailey, op. cit., pp. 21 and 22; Rivers, op. cit., p. 11.

68/ Strack, op. cit., pp. 146 and 147; Edgar Lockwood, "An inside look at the sanctions campaign", Issue, vol. 4, No. 3 (Fall 1974), p. 73. When the Byrd Amendment was enacted, 60 per cent of United States chrome ore imports originated in the Soviet Union. During the five-year tenure of the amendment, the Soviet Union continued to be the leading supplier for the United States of the high grade chrome ore, supplying 52 per cent by volume compared to Southern Rhodesia's 11 per cent (Renwick, op. cit., p. 44; Strack, op. cit., p. 148).

69/ Strack, op. cit., p. 148; Gale W. McGee (Chair, Senate Sub-committee on Africa), "The United States Congress and the Rhodesian chrome issue", Issue, vol. 2, No. 2 (Summer 1972), p. 3.

70/ Strack, op. cit., p. 148; Renwick, op. cit., p. 44.

71/ Interview in U.S. News and World Report, 29 November 1971, quoted in Strack, op. cit., p. 162.

72/ Rhodesian Herald (Salisbury), 25 September 1971; 6 November 1971; 27 January 1972, quoted in Strack, op. cit., pp. 163 and 164.

73/ Interview with Judith Todd Acton, Harare, Zimbabwe, 13 May 1986.

74/ All quotations are taken from an interview conducted in Harare, Zimbabwe, on 20 May 1986, with a businessman who wished to remain anonymous.

75/ Losman, op. cit., p. 151.

76/ Interview with Nathan Shamuyarira, Minister of Information, Posts and Telecommunications, Harare, Zimbabwe, 4 June 1986.

77/ Minter, op. cit., p. 207. Also see Lake, op. cit., p. 42.

78/ Interview with Tirivafi J. Kangai.

79/ Interview with John Deary, Harare, Zimbabwe, 15 April 1986.

80/ Interview with Betty Jo Dorsey, Harare, Zimbabwe, 12 May 1986.

81/ Financial Mail, 29 September 1967, p. 1049.

82/ Financial Mail, vol. 24, No. 5, 5 May 1967, p. 368.

83/ Anonymous interview, Harare, Zimbabwe, 13 May 1986.

84/ Interview with Eddie Cross, Harare, Zimbabwe, 26 March 1986.

85/ Minter, op. cit., p. 210. On 10 September 1978, News of the World quoted the British Liberal Party leader, David Steel, as saying: "Those who shipped in the oil were not hostile Powers. They were British companies, backed by the British Foreign Office, with the connivance of British Cabinet Ministers and the knowledge of the Prime Minister ... The sanctions-busters were our own leaders!" (Quoted in Bailey, op. cit., p. 15)

86/ *Financial Mail*, vol. 24,   . 4 (28 April 1967), p. 281; *ibid.*, vol. 25, No. 8 (25 August 1967), p. 627; T. Curtin, "Total sanctions and economic development in Rhodesia", *Journal of Commonwealth Political Studies*, vol. 7, No. 2 (July 1969), p. 131.

87/ *Financial Mail*, vol. 21, No. 10 (2 September 1966), p. 660.

88/ Strack, *op. cit.*, p. 96; interview with Simon Gray, currently an economist for the Confederation of Zimbabwe Industries, Harare, Zimbabwe, 7 May 1986. Corroborated by a businessman formerly employed by the Association of Rhodesian Industries, Harare, Zimbabwe, 14 May 1986.

89/ Interview with Ruth Weiss, Harare, Zimbabwe, November 1985. Weiss wrote the "Rhodesia round-up" column for the *Financial Mail* from September 1965 until she was deported from Southern Rhodesia in early 1968. Also, *Financial Mail*, vol. 23, No. 4 (27 January 1967); *ibid.*, vol. 23, No. 13 (31 March 1967), p. 857; David Wield, "Manufacturing industry", in Colin Stoneman, ed., *Zimbabwe's inheritance* (London, The College Press and MacMillan Press, 1981), p. 160.

90/ Anonymous interview, Harare, Zimbabwe, 13 May 1986.

91/ Anonymous interview, Harare, Zimbabwe, 20 May 1986.

92/ Anonymous interview, Harare, Zimbabwe, 21 May 1986.

93/ Cross, *op. cit.*, p. 73.

94/ Strack, *op. cit.*, p. 88

95/ Renwick, *op. cit.*, p. 48.

96/ Renwick, *op. cit.*, p. 46; Windrich, *op. cit.*, p. 216.

97/ Windrich, *op. cit.*, p. 216; Losman, *International ...*, *op. cit.*, p. 103; *Financial Mail*, vol. 22, No. 6 (11 November 1966), p. 419; Richard Hall, *The high price of principles: Kaunda and the white South* (London, Hodder and Stoughton, 1969), pp. 165 and 166.

98/ Renwick, *op. cit.*, p. 46; Interview with John Graylin.

99/ Renwick, *op. cit.*, pp. 46 and 47; Losman, *International ...*, *op. cit.*, p. 101; interview with John Graylin; Carol Thompson, "Southern Africa: who is the 'dependent' one?", *ACAS Newsletter*, No. 19 (Fall 1986), p. 23.

100/ Anonymous interview, Harare, Zimbabwe, 14 May 1986.

101/ Renwick, *op. cit.*, pp. 51 and 54; *Zimbabwe Conference on Reconstruction and Development*, Salisbury, 23-27 March 1981, Conference Documentation, p. 9.

102/ Tony Hawkins, "The rise and fall of Smith's Rhodesia", *Financial Times* (London), 1 August 1986; interview with Tony Hawkins, Harare, Zimbabwe, 19 May 1986.

103/ Interviews with E. G. Cross and John Graylin.

104/ Interview with Tony Hawkins; Tony Hawkins, "The rise ...", op. cit.;
Tony Hawkins, "Rhodesian economy under siege", Bulletin of the Africa
Institute of South Africa, vol. 13, No. 1 (1975), p. 23.

105/ Anonymous interview, Harare, Zimbabwe, 14 May 1986.

106/ Anonymous interview, Harare, Zimbabwe, 20 May 1986.

107/ Losman, op. cit., pp. 121, 135 and 136; Strack, op. cit., p. 89;
Renwick, op. cit., p. 50.

108/ Anonymous interview, Harare, Zimbabwe, 13 May 1986.

109/ Anonymous interview, Harare, Zimbabwe, 20 May 1986.

110/ Interview with E. G. Cross.

111/ Strack, op. cit., pp. 68, 69 and 243; Renwick, op. cit., pp. 52-54.

112/ Renwick, op. cit., p. 53; Interview with E. G. Cross.

113/ Anonymous interview, Harare, Zimbabwe, 14 May 1986.

114/ Quoted in: Tommy Sithole, "West is accused of hypocrisy over
sanctions on SA", Herald (Harare), 18 June 1986.

115/ Lake, op. cit., p. 45; Renwick, op. cit., pp. 44 and 89.

116/ Hearings before the Sub-committee on Africa and the Sub-committee on
International Organizations and Movements of the House Foreign Affairs
Committee, 21 and 22 February and 15 March 1973, p. 52, quoted in Lake,
op. cit., p. 46. Eddison Zvobgo is currently the Minister of Justice, Legal
and Parliamentary Affairs in the Government of Zimbabwe.

117/ Interview with Tirivafi J. Kangai.

118/ Interview with Nathan Shamuyarira. Also see: "Shamuyarira raps US,
UK stand on Pretoria", Herald (Harare), 4 July 1986.

119/ Interview with Judith Todd Acton.

120/ Interview with Tirivafi J. Kangai.

121/ Speech by Lieutenant Colonel Clemence Gaza to the
Zimbabwe-Mozambique Friendship Association (ZIMOFA), Harare, Zimbabwe, 1 June
1986.

122/ Interview with E. G. Cross.

123/ Standard Bank Review, November 1985; C. W. Davids, "The impact of
economic sanctions against South Africa on the SADCC States", Harare (Harare),
17 February 1986, p. 28; "SA frantic steps to block sanctions", Herald
(Harare), 8 August 1986; Also see: John S. Saul and Stephen Gelb, The crisis
in South Africa, 2nd ed. (New York, Monthly Review Press, 1986), p. 75.

124/ Neva Makgetla, "Why we call for sanctions", Sechaba (September
1985), p. 10.

125/ Saul and Gelb, op. cit., p. 75; Child, op. cit., p. 28;
J. H. Cooper, "Economic sanctions and the South African economy",
International Affairs Bulletin, vol. 7, part II (1983), p. 37.

126/ Makgetla, op. cit., p. 12; Davids, op. cit., p. 32; "Many
ingredients have contributed to South Africa's economic crisis", Financial
Gazette (Harare), 19 July 1985.

127/ Saul and Gelb, op. cit., p. 75.

128/ Mark Nicholson, "The bankers' dilemma", African Business, November
1985, p. 10.

129/ "South Africa: running with the rand", West Africa, 2 September
1985; Financial Times (London), 17 August 1985; "Fragile recovery for RSA",
Financial Gazette (Harare), 17 January 1986; "South Africa: is there life
after sanctions?", Economist, 26 July 1986.

130/ "$US 10 billion bank deal bails out apartheid", Herald (Harare),
6 March 1986.

131/ "SA economy: recovery stalls", Financial Mail, 2 August 1985; Sunday
Star (Johannesburg), 28 July 1985.

132/ "South Africa: running with the rand", op. cit.; Herald (Harare),
3 September 1985; Vella Pillay, "Rising cost of apartheid: the economic
crisis", in Phyllis Johnson and David Martin, eds., Destructive engagement,
southern Africa at War (Harare, Zimbabwe Publishing House, 1986), p. 228.

133/ "Apartheid is finished and must be replaced - Shultz", Sunday Mail
(Harare), 27 July 1986; "SA frantic steps to block sanctions", Herald
(Harare), 8 August 1986.

134/ Phillip Van Niekerk, "US withdrew $500 million in '85", Weekly Mail
(Johannesburg), 25 April - 1 May 1986; Keith H. Hammonds, "Out of Africa?
Well, not really", The New York Times, 17 August 1986; Richard W. Stevenson,
"Kodak sets Pretoria pullout", The New York Times, 20 November 1986.

135/ Alan Cowell, "Consulate's economic report angers Pretoria", The New
York Times, 24 October 1986.

136/ "SA frantic steps to block sanctions", Herald (Harare), 8 August
1986; Steve Lohr, "Barclays pullout: business reasons", The New York Times,
25 November 1986; National Public Radio, 24 November 1986; BBC, 24 November
1986.

137/ Tamar Lewin, "Pullouts may spur South Africa flight", The New York
Times, 22 October 1986.

138/ "Urban Foundation head urges foreign investment", Business Day
(Johannesburg), 14 March 1986.

139/ Richard Moorsom, The scope for sanctions (London, Catholic Institute
for International Relations, 1986), p. 59.

140/ "Many ingredients ...", op. cit., Financial Gazette, 19 July 1985; Brian Bolton, "How sanctions would hurt", South, September 1985, p. 34; Shipping Research Bureau, South Africa's lifeline - violations of the oil embargo (Amsterdam, Shipping Research Bureau, 1986) quoted in Financial Times (London), 17 September 1986.

141/ Child, op. cit., p. 30; Denis Herbstein, "The oil option", West Africa, 19 August 1985; "How relaxed can Botha be?", Economist, 9 August 1986, p. 24; Shipping Research Bureau, op. cit.

142/ Child, op. cit., p. 30; Glenn Frankel, "U.N. arms ban proves costly to South Africans", Washington Post, 24 February 1985.

143/ "$US 10 billion bank deal bails out apartheid", Herald (Harare), 6 March 1986; "Urban Foundation head urges foreign investment", Business Day, 14 March 1986; Harry Anderson et al, "The squeeze on Pretoria gets tighter, sanctions as a fact of life", Newsweek, 30 June 1986; "South Africa: is there life after sanctions?", Economist, 26 July 1986; Alexander Camarque, "Save now and subsidise the borrowers", Weekly Mail, 9-16 October 1986; "SA polls signal white shift to support blacks", Herald, 26 June 1986.

144/ Anderson, op. cit.; "SA unemployment budget headache", Herald (Harare), 19 March 1986; Phillip Van Niekerk, "Every second black worker may be jobless", Weekly Mail, 12-18 September 1986.

III. SOUTH AFRICA IMPOSES SANCTIONS AGAINST ITS NEIGHBOURS

by

Phyllis Johnson and David Martin

[Ms. Johnson and Mr. Martin are directors of the Southern African Research and Documentation Centre (SARDC), an independent institution based in Harare, Zimbabwe, and editors of a recently published book entitled <u>Destructive engagement: Southern Africa at war</u>.]

SOUTH AFRICA IMPOSES SANCTIONS AGAINST ITS NEIGHBOURS

While the international community debates whether or not to impose sanctions against South Africa in an attempt to end that country's apartheid system and halt the spiral of violence, South Africa itself is imposing sanctions against other States in the region.

It is conservatively estimated that these sanctions have cost South Africa's independent black-ruled neighbours well in excess of $US 20 billion. Yet Pretoria claims to oppose the use of sanctions.

Sanctions are defined as "economic or military action to coerce a State to conform". The objective of sanctions is to restrict or prevent access and increase costs. There is ample evidence to prove that South Africa has adopted both economic and military means to coerce its neighbours, restricting their access to trade routes and vastly increasing their transportation costs.

To achieve this, Pretoria has relied largely on surrogate forces. Captured documents, prisoners and ballistics tests in at least three countries -- Mozambique, Zimbabwe and Angola -- have identified South Africa as the source of training, weapons and strategy. Those three countries, as well as Zambia, Lesotho and Botswana have also been subjected to direct attacks by the South African Defence Force (SADF).

This undeclared war against its neighbours is part of South Africa's "total strategy" policy defined by Pretoria as the mobilization of all forces -- political, economic, diplomatic and military -- in defence of apartheid.

Readers may be aware that officials in Pretoria have threatened retaliatory sanctions against neighbouring States in the event that sanctions are imposed against South Africa. While this debate continues in public, other actions have been quietly implemented. Pretoria is already imposing selective economic sanctions against the other States in southern Africa.

We intend to deal with this specific point of South Africa's relations in the region. But before we do, it is necessary to specify the context and the terminology. South Africa's activities in the region are most often referred to as destabilization, that is, the overspill of apartheid's war with its own people into the contiguous States of the region. The independent black-ruled States, especially Mozambique, Angola, Zimbabwe, Botswana and, up to a point, Lesotho, have been suffering the casualties and the destructive effects of war through direct or surrogate action.

This waging of war on its neighbours proves beyond doubt that South Africa is a threat to international peace and security. This is a very serious point and we will come back to it. But it is part of an overall strategy. It is not South Africa's objective simply militarily to destabilize those States which have the geographical misfortune to share its borders.

South Africa's policy of "total strategy" first emerged in the early 1970s in defence strategy drawn up by the then Minister of Defence, P. W. Botha. Although there may be some disagreements over tactics to employ in specific situations, "total strategy" is accepted by all institutions of the South African Government.

This policy uses destructive methods or "disincentives" and it also uses "incentives" toward more "formative" action, or what some people call "sticks" and "carrots". These may be military, economic, political or diplomatic. The objective is the creation of a network of regional relationships to be used to persuade neighbouring States that their interests lie with Pretoria. Central to understanding why South Africa is imposing sanctions against its neighbours is an insight into Pretoria's perception of its role, militarily and economically, as the region's "super-Power".

P. W. Botha has reorganized the structures of State power, and by this we do not mean the tricameral "parliament" but the main policy planning bodies, including four all-white cabinet committees, and in particular the State Security Council. This reorganization has given the military more direct involvement in the decision-making process, and this is often credited with a more "hawkish" approach to military intervention outside South Africa's borders. But military destabilization is only one aspect. The combination of tactics used against neighbouring countries has varied from State to State depending on its military, economic and political vulnerabilities. But the primary targets are invariably economic.

The regional objective is to maintain a dependence that will be economically lucrative and politically submissive, and act as a bulwark against the imposition of international sanctions against apartheid. Key to this is the destruction of alternative transportation routes.

Of the regional railway links running east, west and south, it is more than coincidence that the only one not to be sabotaged since 1980 is that which runs straight south from Zambia through Zimbabwe to the South African ports of Durban, Port Elizabeth, East London and Cape Town. That is certainly a route in which Pretoria has a vested interest and which provides South Africa with considerable foreign currency earnings.

The other main regional outlets to the sea are west through Angola and east through Mozambique. Running west from Zambia to Lobito on the Atlantic coast is the Benguela railway which has been used to transport copper from Zambia, accounting for 90 per cent of its exports. It has also served Zaire's Shaba province. This route has not functioned fully for more than a decade due to sabotage in Angola.

Since 1980, when Zimbabwe's independence brought an end to sanctions against Southern Rhodesia and Mozambique reopened its border, the railway routes east through Mozambique have been systematically sabotaged. This has destroyed any opportunity for land-locked countries in central Africa to use trade routes to the Indian Ocean ports of Nacala, Beira and Maputo, and has deprived Mozambique of one third of its potential foreign currency earnings.

An early policy determination of the Mugabe Government in Zimbabwe was to
return to these routes and three years after independence more than half of
Zimbabwe's trade transitted Mozambique. This reduced dependence on South
Africa at the expense of the southern railway network and port facilities.
For Zambia and Zaire, the alternative through Mozambique was cheaper and
shorter than the southern route. Malawi sought to return to its traditional
route through Mozambique, and there was also the option for Botswana to divert
its trade.

But Pretoria had other plans. P. W. Botha had proposed a "constellation
of southern African States". This would have maintained and increased the
economic dependence of neighbouring States, provided a security buffer, and
given de facto recognition to the bantustans by their inclusion in this scheme.

Pretoria's hopes for implementation of this plan were shattered by two
related events in the space of 27 days in early 1980.

The first event was the announcement on 4 March 1980 of the results of the
Zimbabwe's independence election in which Robert Mugabe's party won an
outright majority. Zimbabwe, commanding access to the regional hinterland,
was key to the "constellation" scenario. But it needed a maleable government
and the South African-backed candidate, Bishop Abel Muzorewa, lost the
election.

The second event occurred on 1 April 1980, when leaders from nine
countries in the region formed the Southern African Development Co-ordination
Conference (SADCC) with the stated aim of reducing the region's dependence on
the apartheid régime.

Central to the creation of SADCC was the development of the regional
transportation system away from South African routes. However, the SADCC
analysis that the focal point for reducing dependence on South Africa lay in
the communications system was equally apparent to Pretoria's policy planners
and it was this new option for the contiguous States that Pretoria set out to
destroy.

Today the only lines functioning on Mozambique's four main railway systems
are those which South Africa has an interest in keeping open or those which
are defended at massive military cost. The Beira route containing Zimbabwe's
oil pipeline, as well as its shortest road and railway to the sea, is kept
open by the Zimbabwean army.

The portion of Zimbabwe's trade transitting Mozambique, which was 53.9 per
cent in 1983, is now at about 5 per cent. The cheapest route for Zimbabwe's
bulk exports such as sugar and steel is the railway to Maputo, but that route
has been closed since it was sabotaged on 20 August 1983 and this trade now
passes through South African ports. In the case of steel, this amounts to
almost three times the freight cost.

Having ensured dependence on the southern route, South African authorities
can divert or delay this traffic at will. Their insistence that Zimbabwe use
ports other than Durban added $500 per ton to the transportation cost of

tobacco exports.   There are hundreds of other examples of selective sanctions dating back to 1981.

A British junior minister said in Harare recently that sanctions could not be imposed against South Africa because there were no alternative routes for other States in the region.   For South Africa, this simply confirms its policy that destruction of regional routes is protection against sanctions.

Angola's case is sometimes seen as different because that country has been fighting an undeclared war since South African troops invaded - before there were any Cuban combat troops - in August 1975.   But similar economic considerations apply, and its Benguela railway, lifeline for copper exports from Zambia and Zaire, has been blocked for over a decade.

South Africa has a direct national interest at stake in Angola in that the capture and control of the Cabinda oilfields would give Pretoria fuel security in the event of effective imposition of the international oil embargo.   And sophisticated United States military equipment given to the National Union for the Total Independence of Angola (UNITA) rebels may soon find its way into the arsenal that South Africa uses against the other front-line States.

Mozambique used to be an exporter of cement with its Maputo factory drawing materials from a quarry at Salamanga, south of the capital.   However, the railway line linking the quarry and the factory has been continuously sabotaged since October 1984.   The result is that Mozambique no longer exports cement but spends 90,000 rand per month importing clinker from South Africa. Consequently, the local price of cement has risen by 50 per cent.

South Africa has also restricted Mozambique's foreign currency income by cutting its usage of Maputo port to only 16.1 per cent of the 1974 level and reducing the Mozambican migrant labour force in South Africa in the same period by about two thirds.

The incredible social cost cannot be quantified either now or in its implications for the future.   This is starkly illustrated in Mozambique, where 40 per cent of primary schools have been destroyed and 25 per cent of primary school children are without places in educational institutions.   The national cattle herd has been slaughtered and the network of rural stores and health clinics has been destroyed.   Mozambique's exports in 1985 were not enough to cover the oil import bill, yet it has a coal "mountain" at Moatize that it cannot get to the sea and a tea "hill" nearby.

The estimated costs to the region do not take into account the number of people displaced as refugees, often within their own countries, a figure running into several million.   In addition, more than 100,000 people have died as a result of famine in Mozambique and in southern Angola, famine resulting, for the most part, from war.

Nor do the estimates fully take into account the lost manufacturing output, development arrested or deterred, lost investment and tourism, monies diverted to defence, and so on.

We have spent the past three years doing a study of this "destabilization" and the evidence that South Africa is imposing sanctions against neighbouring countries is overwhelming and irrefutable.

Before returning to the details of this fundamental point, it is necessary to draw attention to the historical perspective.

Just over a quarter of a century ago, Harold Macmillan spoke in Cape Town about the "wind of change" gusting through the African continent. That was in January 1960, and only eight African nations were independent. By the end of 1961, a further 18 had become independent. This was the era in which the late John Kennedy spoke of "new frontiers", and when hopes ran high among African nationalists.

Until the mid-1960s, South Africa sought the direct incorporation of the High Commission territories of Botswana, Lesotho and Swaziland, then administered by the United Kingdom of Great Britain and Northern Ireland. This course of action held several advantages for the apartheid administration, not the least of which was the legitimacy it would have given to the policy of bantustan "independence". Once it became clear that the United Kingdom would not agree to this, the Verwoerd régime proposed the establishment of a common market or a commonwealth in southern Africa. The first step would have been a free trade zone to strengthen economic links in the region, laying the basis for a regional political institution.

This failed to materialize in its totality but, as the independence of the High Commission territories approached, Pretoria took steps, with varying degrees of success, to try to ensure that sympathetic administrations came to power. Botswana, Lesotho and Swaziland were incorporated into a South African-dominated customs union and into the rand monetary area. These formal economic links gave Pretoria enormous leverage over the affairs of these States, which it continues to use to great effect.

Until the mid-1970s, Pretoria's regional policy concerned itself with attempts to thwart activities by liberation movements which were growing in strength in neighbouring States as well as at home. It was shielded in this by a ring of "buffer" States that included the Portuguese colonies of Mozambique and Angola, the British rebel colony of Southern Rhodesia, and by the illegally occupied Namibia. Regional policy was directed toward reinforcing this barrier of States through various alliances, including economic and military.

With its regional base apparently secure, the Vorster régime launched its "outward-looking" policy of dialogue in the late 1960s, seeking allies within the newly-formed Organization of African Unity (OAU). There were a few initial successes. The most spectacular of these was the establishment of diplomatic relations with Malawi and an exchange of State visits. Although this "dialogue" initiative was finally condemned and blocked by OAU in 1971, Malawi has remained one of apartheid's most consistent allies.

After the Caetano Government fell in Portugal in 1974, the face of southern Africa changed almost overnight, with the independence of Mozambique and Angola the following year, and then, in 1980, of Zimbabwe. This was not achieved without considerable bloodshed. It is of great importance in the context of this discussion that during these liberation wars, the Portuguese and the Southern Rhodesians created or co-opted groups to use as surrogates against the nationalist parties.

In the case of Angola, there were three of these groups of which only one remains relevant today. That is UNITA led by Jonas Savimbi. We have copies of the documents which reveal that when UNITA was supposedly fighting against Portuguese colonialism, it was in reality an adjunct of the Portuguese armed forces. These documents have been dismissed by Savimbi as forgeries. However, during the course of our study we visited Portugal on three occasions to interview the commanders of the Portuguese army who were in Angola in the early 1970s.

Among those we interviewed was Marshall Costa Gomes, who was Portugal's commander in Angola from 1970 to 1972, and later president after the coup d'état. We also talked to, among others, General Bettencourt Rodrigues, the commander in eastern Angola at that time, and Brigadier Passos Ramos, the head of Portuguese military intelligence in Angola. None of them can be described as a radical seeking to belittle UNITA. On the contrary, they are gentlemen who harbour a nostalgic warmth for Savimbi and the role he played in support of the war they were fighting. But all three of them, and many others who served in the Portuguese army in that period, confirmed that the documents were authentic.

Furthermore, they said that they had a "gentlemen's agreement" with UNITA under which they armed that movement to fight against the Popular Movement for the Liberation of Angola (MPLA), which today forms the Government of that country. One of the main tactics was the disruption of the Benguela railroad, a main artery not only for the Angolan interior but for trade from Zambia and Zaire.

On the other side of the continent is the Mozambique National Resistance (MNR) which is fighting against the Government of Mozambique and disrupting the other main trade routes to the sea for the land-locked African hinterland. MNR was created by the Southern Rhodesian Central Intelligence Organization (CIO), in Southern Rhodesia, in 1976. This has been admitted by Ken Flower, who was head of CIO, and confirmed by MNR itself. We have spent many hours interviewing Flower and the men who trained, armed, administered and paid MNR on behalf of Southern Rhodesia.

We have stressed the origins of MNR and UNITA for, after the fall of the Portuguese empire and then of Southern Rhodesia, they were inherited by South Africa. They are now used as proxies, not only in the destabilization of the region but in the sanctions that South Africa is imposing on its neighbours to retain their dependence on its trade and transportation.

The collapse of Portuguese colonialism gave rise to a hasty reformulation of South Africa's regional strategy. Military capacity was expanded, while

Vorster launched his diplomatic "détente" initiative, vaguely defined as a constellation of independent States presenting a united front against common enemies. This was coupled with minor internal changes and with removal of some forms of "petty apartheid". However, the détente initiative began to crumble with the invasion of Angola in 1975 and the eventual expulsion of South African forces by Angolan and Cuban troops in March 1976. Some impetus to maintain dialogue was dashed with the brutal repression of the Soweto uprising. African States could not be seen to be collaborating with a régime that slaughtered unarmed black schoolchildren in the streets.

By the end of 1976, South Africa's regional policy had collapsed and the régime faced a growing internal crisis. Top military strategists, including the Defence Minister, P. W. Botha, began to flesh out the "total strategy" which they had proposed as early as 1973, with its economic, political and military implications. This was laid out in the 1977 Defence White Paper which identified the need to "maintain a solid military balance relative to neighbouring States", while advocating economic and other "action in relation to transport services, distribution and telecommunications" with the purpose of promoting "political and economic collaboration" in the region.

Another, more recent historical development must just be mentioned before we return to the question of sanctions, and this is the assumption to power of P. W. Botha in 1978, with the subsequent reorganization of the state structures and the adoption of "total strategy" as the official state policy.

Shortly after taking office, Botha elaborated on the proposal for a constellation of southern African States (CONSAS), a regional grouping to be dominated by South Africa. As mentioned earlier, this plan was disrupted by the result of the Zimbabwean independence election in early 1980 and the formation, less than a month later, of SADCC, a regional grouping which excluded South Africa.

At the formative meeting of SADCC in Lusaka, the late President of Botswana, Sir Seretse Khama, sounded an ominous warning when he said: "The struggle for economic liberation will be as bitterly contested as has been the struggle for political liberation."

Sir Seretse stressed that the creation of SADCC was not a declaration of war on South Africa. But Pretoria saw it otherwise. Instead of CONSAS, which it could have dominated, there was SADCC, of which South Africa was not a member and which sought to reduce, rather than consolidate, the region's dependence on South Africa. That was unacceptable to Pretoria.

Central to the creation of SADCC and the lessening of dependence on South Africa was the regional system of transport and communications. While some geographical arguments could be made for regional economic relations involving South Africa, albeit without apartheid, this does not apply to transportation, other than for Botswana, Lesotho and Swaziland. For other States in the region there is no logical geographical reason for using transportation routes through South Africa. Other routes are shorter and cheaper; therefore, South Africa has ensured that they do not function.

Zimbabwe's independence and the reopening of routes through Mozambique to the Indian Ocean ports of Beira and Maputo offered the opportunity for the landlocked hinterland immediately to reduce its dependence on the South African transportation system.

At the time of Zimbabwe's independence in 1980, Mozambique's border with Southern Rhodesia had been closed for four years in compliance with United Nations sanctions against the rebel British colony. Thus, the trade from which Mozambique had derived a third of its foreign exchange earnings through rail tariffs and port charges was non-existent.

An early determination of the Mugabe Government was to resume maximum usage of those routes, for economic as well as political reasons, since they represented the shortest and cheapest trade routes to the sea. By the end of 1983, just over half of Zimbabwe's trade was transitting Mozambique, a level of dependence reduction clearly unacceptable to South Africa. In 1984, the figure was down to a third, and by the end of 1985, the total of Zimbabwe's trade passing through Mozambique was about 5 per cent.

The cause of this forms part of the basis of our thesis that South Africa is already imposing sanctions against its neighbours.

From 1980, South Africa set out to destroy the Mozambique economy directly and through its inherited surrogates, MNR. Particular targets included transportation routes, SADCC projects, development schemes and foreign aid workers, communal villages, schools and medical facilities.

Zimbabwe and Zambia are dependent for their trade routes upon two railway systems through Mozambique. The most important, and by far the cheapest, with the largest port handling capacity, is the route through Chicualacuala to Maputo. As a result of sabotage, that route has been totally closed to Zimbabwe since 20 August 1983.

The second route is through Mutare to the port of Beira. This route, which also carries the oil pipeline, is Zimbabwe's shortest access route to the sea. However, the gradients on the Beira line and the limited handling capacity of Beira port impose restrictions on the amount of traffic which can transit this route.

Sabotage of the Beira line began in earnest in June 1982. When one of the pumping stations along the oil pipeline was damaged later in the year, Zimbabwe committed some 2,000 troops to guard its lifeline. Had Zimbabwe not pursued this course of action, it is almost certain that this route would also have been closed to traffic.

To illustrate the implications for Zimbabwe of the destruction of its eastern routes, attached in annex I is a list of comparative freight tariff charges on the four alternative routes for four bulk items. These figures relate to 1984 and they reveal that Zimbabwe's export bills for freight on items such as steel have, as a minimum, doubled as a result of the destruction of these routes.

We mentioned earlier that more than half of Zimbabwe's trade was transitting Mozambique in 1983, and that by 1984 this had been reduced to one-third. There is a further point about the 1984 figure that requires emphasis. The total tonnage through Mozambique that year was just over half a million, and of this more than half had to transit South Africa to reach the port of Maputo. The first two columns of annex I, containing the comparative freight rate charges, illustrate the financial implications.

In addition to the cost to Zimbabwe, there is the cost to Mozambique. As mentioned, Mozambique lost one third of its foreign exchange earnings when it closed its frontiers and imposed sanctions against Southern Rhodesia. Today, given the sabotage of the lines to Beira and Maputo, Mozambique is suffering a similar loss.

Another chart, contained in annex II, illustrates the selective destruction of the Mozambican railway systems.

Mozambique has four railway systems -- south, central, north and Zambezia. There is no need to deal with the Zambezia system as it is purely internal. The other three all provide trade routes for neighbouring countries.

The southern system has four separate railways. Today, because of sabotage, trains in Mozambique operate only in the daylight hours, so the percentages shown reflect the amount of time the railways were able to operate, during approximately a 12-hour day, during the period in question, which is the beginning of January to mid-November 1985.

The first of the tower blocks on the extreme left is the route to South Africa through Ressano Garcia. This is a major outlet for exports from the northern Transvaal, and thus South Africa has a considerable interest in keeping it open. The result is that it has been comparatively unscathed by sabotage by MNR, who are given target instructions by SADF, as will be shown later.

The next line, shown as Limpopo, is the one referred to earlier as Zimbabwe's main route through Chicualacuala to the port of Maputo. Usage in the first ten and a half months of 1985 was less than one per cent, and even this represents usage of part of the line rather than the whole.

While it could be said that South Africa has a positive interest in the Ressano Garcia line, it definitely has a negative interest in the Limpopo line. While South Africa would wish to keep the former open, it certainly wants to keep the latter closed.

South Africa also has a positive interest in the next line, to Goba, which serves Swaziland, with whom it has the warmest relations of all of the contiguous States. Positive interest in this line is reinforced as it continues through Swaziland into South Africa.

The fourth line on the southern system, to Salamanga, definitely fails into the negative interest category. Salamanga is located south of Maputo and the only function of this line is to service the Maputo cement factory from the quarry at Salamanga.

That quarry used to supply the cement factory more than adequately, and Mozambique earned valuable foreign currency from exporting cement. But, as a result of sabotage, the Salamanga line has been closed since October 1984. The irony now is that the Maputo factory has to import clinker from South Africa to produce cement at a cost of some 90,000 rand a month, to be paid in foreign currency. The effect of this on the local market is that a ton of cement which used to cost $US 42.50 now costs $US 62.50, an increase of almost 50 per cent.

Pretoria's interest in all of the lines on the central and northern systems is negative, as none passes through South Africa and they therefore pose the danger of the land-locked hinterland using them to reduce their dependence.

The Machipanda route to Beira is the one referred to earlier as Zimbabwe's shortest outlet to the sea. The high usage rate on this route is due to the presence of soldiers of the Zimbabwe National Army, who have been guarding the line since October 1982. We cannot quantify the cost to Zimbabwe of this commitment since that date. But, since additional Zimbabwean troops went into Mozambique in a combat role in July 1985, an additional amount equivalent to $US 24 million has been approved in military subventions.

The next line shown as Sena, where there was zero usage in 1985, is a particularly interesting case. This line heads north-west from Beira, dividing at a small town called Nhamalabue. From there, one line goes north to Malawi and the second goes west to the provincial capital of the Tete province and the coal mines at Moatize.

This route previously carried 60 per cent of Malawi's trade through the port of Beira. Today, as a result of sabotage, it carries nothing. In 1985, Malawi had to fly out its tea and coffee crops, and its freight bills are now roughly five times what they used to be.

The Moatize mine has coal worth $US 12 million to US$ 14 million, which it cannot get to the coast, and it has virtually closed down production. The contribution to the Mozambique economy from Moatize coal could be $US 40 million to US$ 50 million. Today it is nothing.

The next link, shown as Dondo-Muanza, links the Beira cement factory to a quarry to the north-west. Traffic on this route has been irregular since 1980 and non-existent since 1983. As a result, the Beira factory has stopped production. In 1978, Mozambique earned $US 5.6 million from the export of cement. Today it does not earn anything from cement exports and the decline in cement production resulting from South African aggression has a ripple effect that is halting production in other industries such as asbestos-cement sheeting.

The northern route, although shown as two lines, is in fact a single line from the Indian Ocean port of Nacala which has an enormous potential. This route runs through the provincial capital of Nampula and on to the Malawi border in the west. A very heavy Mozambican military presence has meant a reasonably high operational rate on the sector from Nampula to the sea. But the remainder of the line, which used to carry 30 per cent of Malawi's trade, today carries none at all.

To achieve this destruction in Mozambique, Pretoria has relied largely on a surrogate force, the MNR. Some examples of directives to MNR from SADF to sabotage economic targets in Mozambique are contained in two sets of captured documents.

The first set of documents was found on 5 December 1981, when the Mozambican army overran a large MNR base at Garagua in the eastern Manica province. One of these documents from Garagua contained the minutes of a meeting held at an MNR training camp in South Africa, at Zoabostad, on 25 October 1980. The MNR delegation was led by Alonso Dhlakama, who had been appointed by the Southern Rhodesians to head MNR after the death of his predecessor. The South African delegation was led by Colonel Charles van Niekerk, a military intelligence officer who had been the liaison to the Southern Rhodesians when MNR was still under their control.

This document emphasized the need to open new fronts. It also ordered "the closure to traffic of the railway Beira-Umtali and the traffic by road on the Inchope-Vila Franco do Save section". Regarding the increasing of the struggle, the South Africans suggested: "Interrupt the railway traffic Malvernia-Gwelo (Zimbabwe), establish a base near the South African border, open the Maputo province front, arrange for urban incidents in Maputo and Beira. These should be done as from now until December 1981."

Another document containing the minutes of another meeting held at Zoabostad, on 5 November 1980, stated: "Attack cities with mortar bombs in order to create a higher impact in national and international levels. Destroy the Cahora Bassa power lines to South Africa to cover the idea of South African support to MNR as the importance of these power lines to South Africa is only 7 per cent."

In August 1985, Mozambican/Zimbabwean military action resulted in the capture of the main MNR base at Gorongosa, about 150 kilometres north of Beira. More than 200 kilograms of documents were recovered, including the daily diaries kept by Dhlakama's secretary.

One of the entries referred to a meeting which began in Pretoria on 23 February 1984, about a month before Mozambique and South Africa signed the Nkomati Agreement. The objective of the meeting, according to the diary, was interesting; it read "Planning the war in the face of the situation taken up by the South African Republic".

Equally fascinating was the record of participants. The MNR delegation was again led by Dhlakama. The South African team was extremely high-powered. It included the head of the Directorate of Military Intelligence, General Pieter van der Westhuizen, who has since been promoted as secretary to the powerful State Security Council. It also included the commander of the SADF Special Forces, General André Liebenberg, as well as a Brigadier from military intelligence, whom we believe is called van Tonder, and inevitably, Colonel van Niekerk.

The diary for that day, Thursday, 23 February 1984, recorded the following points of significance:

"We [that is, the South African] soldiers will continue to give support without the consent of our politicians in massive numbers so as to win the war... Machel can only fall immediately through a cut in the economy and communications routes".

That meeting continued for a further two days, during which economic targets were defined as: "Railways, Cahora Bassa, co-operantes and other targets of an economic nature such as the ones belonging to SADCC."

"Co-operantes" means foreign aid workers. From 1981 until March 1986, at least 34 foreign aid workers were murdered, 66 kidnapped and 5 wounded by MNR. They came from countries as diverse as Brazil, Portugal, the Union of Soviet Socialist Republics, Sweden and the United Kingdom of Great Britain and Northern Ireland. The result of the action against them was of course that foreigners were withdrawn from the rural areas, bringing many development projects to a standstill.

It should be clear from the above that, by various means, South Africa deliberately and systematically set out from, at the latest, October 1980 to undermine the Mozambican economy and sabotage communications routes which would have enabled the neighbouring land-locked countries to reduce their dependence on South Africa.

We would like to stay with the question of communications routes a little longer for these are fundamental to the attempts of the SADCC countries to reduce their dependence upon South Africa.

Running west from Zambia to Lobito on the Atlantic coast is the Benguela railway. It used to handle Zambia's copper exports as well as exports from Zaire's Shaba province. This route has hardly functioned for more than a decade due to sabotage in Angola.

From Zimbabwe, running south, there are two railway systems. The one that goes to South Africa through Botswana was attacked on a number of occasions from 1981, within Zimbabwe, by people whom our recent book proves beyond any doubt are being trained, armed and supported by South Africa.

The other main route to the south is direct, through Beitbridge to the South African ports of Durban, East London, Port Elizabeth and Cape Town. Of all of the railway systems running to the east, west and south, this is the only one which has not been sabotaged in the past six years. That, certainly, is more than coincidence.

For almost six years, South Africa has been applying economic sanctions in one form or another against the States of the region. No two cases are exactly alike, and certainly Angola's is quite different because that country has been at war with South Africa and its surrogates for 11 years. Moreover, it is now confronted again with direct United States intervention.

But there are many more subtle tactics which South Africa employs and which stem from its regional economic stronghold, which SADCC is trying to break. These have now reached the stage where they amount to economic sanctions.

Having destroyed transportation routes to the east and the west, ensuring Zimbabwe's dependence on the southern route, South Africa then insisted that Zimbabwe must use ports other than Durban. As shown in annex I, containing comparative tariff rates, this added another $500 per ton to the transportaion cost of tobacco exports.

There are many examples of selective economic sanctions, dating back to 1981. Zimbabwe was then still in the process of buying its own locomotives and was exporting a bumper maize crop when the South African Transport Services withdrew leased locomotives, causing chaos in the transport system.

South Africa is at present applying further sanctions against Zimbabwe. The normal wagon turnaround time to South African ports is 13 days, but this has been increased to 18 days as a means of delaying Zimbabwe's trade. That this is again occurring at a time when Zimbabwe has a bumper maize crop is no coincidence.

In late 1982, the oil pipeline and the oil storage tanks at Beira were sabotaged in a direct South African (not surrogate) operation. This caused a major fuel crisis for Zimbabwe, with queues several kilometres long at all gasoline stations. Zimbabwe became entirely dependent upon South Africa for the delivery of fuel and South Africa imposed limitations on fuel deliveries, demanding a meeting at ministerial level, which the Prime Minister Robert Mugabe refused. At one point, the country had only one day's supply of gasoline and diesel.

Mozambique has suffered similarly, through lost foreign exchange from rail and port charges, as shown. Add to that the termination of the preferential gold agreement under which a portion of the salaries of migrant workers was remitted in gold at a fixed rate; the reduction in the number of migrant workers from Mozambique by some 60 per cent since independence; the reduction of South African traffic through Maputo port to only 16 per cent of its 1973 level; and the sabotage of domestic routes which prevent Mozambique from getting out its own exports. That overview gives an idea of the scale of sanctions against Mozambique. Its exports in 1985, amounting to $US 80 million to US$ 90 million, will not even cover its 1986 bill for oil imports.

In considering the price that the front-line States have been and are paying as a result of South Africa's "total onslaught", attention is normally focused on the economic price while ignoring the social cost. It is not possible to quantify fully the social cost in relation, for example, to what it will mean in the years to come to a nation whose children have been deprived of education. No area more starkly illustrates the social cost than primary education in Mozambique. By the end of 1985 about 25 per cent of primary school-age children were out of school, some 40 per cent of primary schools had been destroyed and almost 5,000 teachers were out of work. According to figures provided by the Ministry of Education, the situation had deteriorated markedly since the signing of the Nkomati Agreement with South Africa.

In November 1983, four months before Nkomati, 840 of a total of 4,727 primary schools were closed, destroyed by South Africa's surrogates. By April 1985, the number had risen to 1,863, an increase of over 1,000. During the same period, the number of pupils out of school, "displaced" as they are described in Mozambique, rose from 152,688 to 313,766. The number of teachers "displaced" rose from 2,396 to 4,992.

Education is precious in Mozambique. If one remembers that the legacy of 500 years of Portuguese colonialism when Mozambique became independent in 1975 was an illiteracy rate of 97 per cent, it is possible to grasp the enormity of this problem in relation to the country's future development.

For people in the rural areas, the health posts, clinics and hospitals are another fundamental requirement. These have been destroyed since 1980 at the rate of about 100 per year and by 1986, 10 per cent of the total had been closed. Yet another vital need is the rural store network. The Portuguese settler exodus of 1974-1975, the population growth and the bandit activity meant that to restore the population-per-store ratio to its 1971 level, Mozambique would require another 12,723 stores. However, even if the stores were built, the impact of sabotage of the country's economic infrastructure, and therefore the revenues generated by exports, was such that there would be little to put in them. The mining sector, as an example, which could earn between $US 120 million and US$ 150 million a year, earned only about $US 2 million in 1985.

One of the most vital facets of rural life is livestock. In 1980, Mozambique's national cattle herd numbered 1.5 million, about half of these owned by the peasants. By the end of 1985, it numbered only 900,000 and even then few were what the Mozambique Government described as "under control". In the southern Maputo province, for example, only 36,000 of the estimated 200,000 cattle were "under control". The remainder were running wild in the forests and bush.

Although we have chosen to discuss a particular situation in some detail, examples abound throughout the region, as seen from turning briefly to Botswana, Lesotho and Swaziland, the "captive States". Nothing in recent times more dramatically illustrates their vulnerability than the case of Lesotho. On 1 January 1986, South Africa imposed an economic blockade on Lesotho, restricting and delaying the movements of people and supplies. Three weeks later, the Government of Chief Jonathan fell in a military coup d'état, the first one in southern Africa. It is not our purpose here to deal with the internal contradictions which existed; rather it is to re-emphasize the point about vulnerability.

Lesotho is a tiny, impoverished and completely dependent nation of 1.5 million people, completely surrounded by South Africa. More than half of the adult population works at mines, farms and industries across the border; and most rural households rely for income on the remittances of these migrant workers. All imports and exports pass through South Africa. Almost all shops and businesses are branches of the South African system and so is the railway. Almost all of its tourists, its investment and its electricity comes from South Africa.

Lesotho and Swaziland are both part of the rand monetary zone and subject to the fluctuations of the South African currency. Botswana is no longer part of the rand zone and, as one of the world's three largest exporters of diamonds, has a sound economic base with more than a year's supply of foreign exchange. Though not as vulnerable in some ways, Botswana has similar dependencies on transportation routes, investment and business relations, as well as on jobs for migrant workers.

These "captive States" derived considerable income from the Southern African Customs Union, though leading economists argue that they could derive more from other customs and exise arrangements. Payments from the customs union amount to almost 40 per cent of Botswana's revenue, about 60 per cent of Swaziland's, and more than 70 per cent of Lesotho's. South Africa, who is also a member of the customs union, controls these payments and has withheld them for up to two years as a means of economic pressure. Another problem is the threat of renegotiation of the customs union agreement. P. W. Botha referred to these broader implications of the customs union when he said in a public speech: "We see this customs union not in isolation as a revenue-sharing arrangement, but as part of a comprehensive regional development strategy".

Another means of economic pressure, using a slightly different approach, is the setting up of projects and then threatening their withdrawal. One example is the Highlands Water Project, under which impoverished Lesotho is to sell one of its few natural resources to its thirsty neighbour, which Pretoria has threatened to cancel on more than one occasion. Another example is a threatened withdrawal of South African financing and market for a $300 million project to mine soda ash, potash and salt in the Sua Pan, a massive dry salt lake in northern Botswana.

Yet another South African pressure tool is the concept of "mutual defence" and the luring of regional States into "non-aggression pacts" or security agreements, such as the Nkomati Accord with Mozambique signed in March 1984, or the security agreement with Swaziland, signed two years earlier, and considerably more extensive.

In addition, there is the military pressure: through surrogate action, which we have already examined in some detail, and which in Zimbabwe defines white farmers as economic targets; direct South African sabotage of major economic installations, such as the oil storage tanks in Luanda and Beira, aircraft and ammunition dumps in Zimbabwe; direct commando strikes, such as the surprise attacks on Maseru and, more recently, on other Commonwealth capitals of Gaborone, Harare and Lusaka; and full-scale invasion, as in the case of southern Angola.

We have not mentioned Namibia at all, but briefly, the objective there is to create military and, especially, economic structures that will reinforce dependence on South Africa, even when it eventually gains an internationally acceptable independence; retention by South Africa of its only port facility at Walvis Bay; and the accumulation of a staggering debt-servicing bill.

Nor have we considered Zambia in detail, which suffered most from the imposition of sanctions against Southern Rhodesia, largely from the failure of the international community to make good on its promises of assistance, and which continues to suffer the effects of South African economic pressure, largely through the sabotage of the most direct routes to the sea for its copper exports and its imports.

An insight into the use of these "techniques of coercion", which in almost any other circumstances would be called sanctions, is offered by an academic paper produced in 1981 as part of a South African government consultancy. The paper, entitled "Some strategic implications of regional economic relationships for the Republic of South Africa" and written by Professor Deon Geldenhuys, a leading foreign policy adviser to Pretoria, was published before the extensive application of such tactics in practice. It recommended ways in which South Africa could use its economic links for strategic purposes; it remains a guide for regional policy.

Geldenhuys advocated limiting or prohibiting the use of South African railways and harbours for the trade of black-ruled neighbours, limiting or banning labour recruited from those States, creating delays at border posts, imposing import and export curbs, and curtailing or terminating the provision of technical expertise. These in fact amount to selective economic sanctions.

A number of the recommended measures have been applied or threatened, including:

(a) Limiting or prohibiting the use of South Africa's railway and harbour facilities for the export of goods from neighbouring States. There are, needless to say, numerous ways of limiting the use of these facilities, e.g. by manipulating the availability of railway trucks or berthing facilities in harbours, or by harsher measures such as imposition of surcharges on goods transported, or official announcement of restrictions on the amount of goods that may be exported via South Africa;

(b) Limiting or banning importation of labour from neighbouring States;

(c) Regulating the access to and movement through South Africa of nationals from neighbouring States. Without going to the extreme of prohibiting entry into South Africa, the authorities have various means open to them to make access more difficult, e.g. by deliberate delays at border posts;

(d) Placing curbs on the imports of goods from neighbouring States or regulating the export of goods to neighbouring States. The two most crucial items are undoubtedly food and oil, but machinery, spare parts and various other goods could also be added;

(e) Curtailing or terminating the provision of technical expertise to these States, e.g. in the operation of Maputo harbour.

An important point stressed by the author of that paper was that South Africa could not be seen to be openly applying economic coercion against its neighbours for that would leave it vulnerable to calls for sanctions against apartheid itself. Explanations, justifications and the use of surrogates were necessary, he said, to disguise the reality and to protect South Africa from the sanctions lobby.

Since then, South Africa has overseen the systematic destruction of the region's alternative communications infrastructure using military force to maintain economic dependence. In practice, some explanation has been proffered on each occasion that these techniques have been applied, such as port delays or congestion in the railway system, and so on.

Southern Africa today is at a highly dangerous crossroads. Inside South Africa, the violence escalates and so does the death toll. Apartheid's intransigence remains intact in the face of mounting international condemnation and calls for action. And in the international community, there remain pockets of opposition to serious action.

Meanwhile, South Africa has been implementing sanctions in various forms against the States of southern Africa. One needs only to look at the objective of sanctions, i.e. to restrict or prevent access or increase costs, or at the definition of sanctions as "a penalty for disobeying a law or reward for obeying it ... consideration helping to enforce obedience to any rule of conduct ... economic or military action to coerce a State to conform".

This has occurred while the international community has been deliberating, and while some members have been trying to deflect the debate by expressing fears as to what sanctions against South Africa would mean for the Africans of that country and for the contiguous States.

We would like to begin our concluding remarks with a quotation from the executive secretary of SADCC, Simba Makoni, who said in an interview with The Washington Post in November 1985: "Sanctions are a road not to a peaceful change but a less violent change. Yes, there is going to be suffering, but it's inevitable. South Africa's neighbours," he added, "were already suffering a lot. There can no longer be talk of a peaceful solution".

Opponents of mandatory sanctions have been using three main arguments as the basis of their opposition. These are:

(a) That sanctions did not work in the case of Southern Rhodesia;

(b) That sanctions would hurt blacks in South Africa;

(c) That sanctions would harm the front-line States.

The focus of this paper has been on the third of these points but in concluding we would like to deal briefly with the first two arguments.

Those who argue that sanctions do not work always point out the case of

Southern Rhodesia. We dispute the validity of that argument. Sanctions did work against Southern Rhodesia, despite the assistance of South Africa and others in sanctions-busting. Southern Rhodesia was forced to sell its goods at under world-market prices and to buy at a premium. That certainly helped to undermine the economy, and ultimately to shorten the war. So did the ban on Southern Rhodesian chrome. Furthermore, Southern Rhodesia was forced into greater self-sufficiency and import substitution. That created more jobs and, ironically, gave Zimbabwe a more broadly-based economic inheritance.

We must not forget the psychological impact on the Southern Rhodesian whites of being internationally condemned and shunned. Many white Southern Rhodesians who lived through the sanctions years have told us that this form of sanction had the most profound effect on them. They felt like international lepers, their passports were rejected in most countries, they were shunned in international sports arenas, films were withheld from their televisions and cinema screens.

The sports boycott on South Africa is having a similar effect. South Africa goes to extreme lengths to persuade rebel sportsmen and sportswomen to break the boycott, spending vast sums of money in foreign currency to bribe them. Now there is the threat of removing such "soap operas" as Dallas from their television screens. Psychologically, even if these measures are not fully effected, they hurt, and there is plentiful scope to bring the lesson home even more sharply to South Africa through other measures. An airline travel ban, or a ban on landing rights would have great psychological impact, for South Africans are considerable travellers.

It is true that in many ways the sanctions against the rebel British colony of Southern Rhodesia did not work. The cynical self-interest and racism of the United Kingdom and some other members of the international community ensured that they did not. But, in a number of important ways, sanctions against Southern Rhodesia did work.

The second argument used in opposition to sanctions is that they would hurt the black people of South Africa the most. This is the main contention of the apartheid régime. The Deputy Minister of Foreign Affairs, Louis Nel, reacting to the imposition of very limited economic sanctions by the United States in September 1985, said: "If the American Congress votes for sanctions against South Africa it could very well start a process leading to misery and suffering for millions of innocent blacks in the entire southern African region."

A few days later, Nel followed this up in a booklet, in which he said: "Let us be frank, our neighbouring States will suffer before we do." Nel reflected the stance adopted by his Prime Minister who had threatened to deport 1.5 million migrant workers from South Africa if the United Nations imposed economic sanctions.

Again, to use the case of Southern Rhodesia, it is simply not true that the front-line States and black South Africans would suffer most from sanctions. It is true that Zambia suffered considerably from the failure of the international community to make good on promises of assistance after the imposition of sanctions against Southern Rhodesia. But then, as now, the

Zambian Government believed that sanctions would shorten the period of suffering.

It is <u>apartheid</u> that is causing hardship for the people of southern Africa. For those living in the subsistence economy of South Africa, and in reality that includes most of the people in the townships as well as the rural areas, the banning of the importation of Camembert cheese from France, computers from the United States, Mercedes cars from the Federal Republic of Germany and others from Japan will not make any difference.

Furthermore, the people of South Africa themselves are loudly and clearly calling for sanctions to help them to end <u>apartheid</u>. If it means extra suffering, they are saying, they will endure that as a means of shortening the suffering they already endure under <u>apartheid</u>.

Bishop Desmond Tutu expressed this plea for action most eloquently in an interview in January 1986 with <u>The New York Times</u>.

"For goodness sake," he said, "let people not use us as an alibi for not doing the things they know they ought to do. We are suffering now, and this kind of suffering seems to be going to go on and on and on. If additional suffering is going to put a terminus to our suffering then we will accept it".

That plea leads us directly to the third argument used by the opponents of sanctions, that the front-line States would be the principal sufferers if sanctions were imposed against South Africa.

Those who make this argument are wilfully ignorant of two realities: the solidarity felt by the people of the front-line States for their brothers and sisters in their struggle to overthrow <u>apartheid</u>; and the extent to which the front-line States are already suffering.

For the front-line States, the harsh reality is that while the international community argues about sanctions, South Africa is already imposing selective economic sanctions against independent majority-ruled States in the region.

Annex I

TARRIF CHARGES: COST PER TONE

(in Zimbabwean dollars)

Commodity	Maputo vía Chicualacuala	Maputo vía Komatipoort	Durban vía Beitbridge	Port Elizabeth Plumtree
Steel	30.80	64.70	86.44	85.12
Sugar ex Chiredzi	29.32	44.01	–	–
Tobacco ex Harare (box rate)	806.00	1 196.40	1 366.80	1 876.40
Jet A1 (Fuel)	99.15	125.94	151.74	173.47

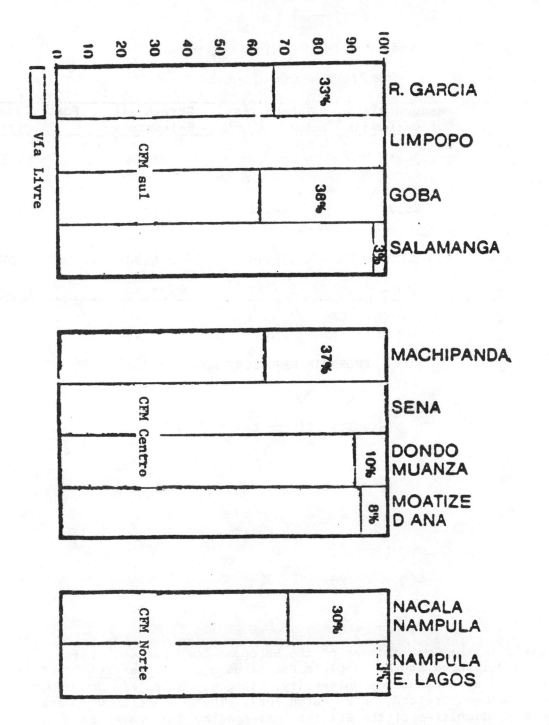

PPARALYSIS OF THE RAILWAY SYSTEM IN 1985

Annex II

IV. PEOPLE'S SANCTIONS NOW

by

Stanley Clinton Davis

[Mr. Davis is the Commissioner of the European Communities. This
statement was delivered at the People's Sanctions against Apartheid Conference
which took place at Strathclyde University, Glasgow, United Kingdom of Great
Britain and Northern Ireland, on 21 March 1987. The Conference was organized
by the Scottish Committee of the British Anti-Apartheid Movement in
co-operation with the Special Committee against Apartheid.]

Today's rallies against apartheid - optimistic rallies, full of hope for a free South Africa - are taking place right across the country. Despite the suppression of news, the shootings, the intimidation and the harassment, the voices of the oppressed, the voices of the evicted in Langa, the cries of those mourning their dead, are being heard inside and outside South Africa.

The voices protest against the so-called "reforms", designed not to dismantle but simply to modernize apartheid, aware that each one merely highlights to the deprived the enormity of their political disabilities. And the voices are reaching such a crescendo of defiance and indignation that the South African Government is left confused, its reaction indecisive and inconsistent. Day in and day out, one by one, the props of the régime are being pulled out. The industrialists and the bankers are leaving one after the other, the process is inexorable, for business is becoming desperate to divorce itself from apartheid, and time is running out. And even some Afrikaners are turning against apartheid as they are beginning to feel the pinch. That then is the background against which I find myself here today.

I do not know how many times in the past the Anti-Apartheid Movement in Scotland has received greetings from the European Commission. If it has never received any, then I am delighted to make that good today.

There is an important point here. As the clamour for full-scale economic sanctions has increased in recent months and as the apartheid State has become more vicious in the defence of white supremacy, so it is right that all Governments and all international institutions are asked to account for their contribution to the defeat of apartheid and the illegal occupation of Namibia.

There can be no innocent bystanders, no casual observers, no neutrals in the sanctions debate. And the European Commission, the organization in which I serve, must be prepared to have its record scrutinized, just like everybody else.

Nobody could say that the performance of the European Community has been anything other than mixed. But we have in recent months made some important breakthroughs - breakthroughs which have been achieved with the crucial support of comrades in the British Labour Group and in the Socialist Group of the European Parliament. I would like to tell you about these briefly.

For instance, this year the European Economic Community (EEC) will spend about £14 million on a special programme for victims of apartheid inside South Africa. This fund, managed by the Commission, is used to provide direct support for the South African Council of Churches, the Southern African Catholic Bishops' Conference and trade unions like the Congress of South African Trade Unions (COSATU) and the Council of Unions of South Africa (CUSA). The money is used to provide legal assistance, training and education and humanitarian relief to those victimized in the anti-apartheid struggle. A small amount of money is also finding its way into Namibia via the Namibian Council of Churches.

For me, the emphasis on support for the trade unions is a vital one. Perhaps you will be aware that the Commercial, Catering and Allied Workers Union, an affiliate of COSATU, recently won a three-month-long strike over pay and conditions against OK Bazaars, South Africa's largest supermarket chain. The strike was won in the face of mass dismissals and fierce assaults on trade union activism. Thousands of workers became involved in the stoppage and they won. This is the kind of victory we must advertise, nourish, extend.

Now, of course, the ultimate conquest of apartheid, or the success of black trade unionism, will not turn upon relatively small transfers of cash to apartheid's victims from EEC. But the decision to send this money has a longer-term significance for the anti-apartheid campaign: it represents the acceptance on the part of community institutions that they are, in part, responsible for defraying the human costs of apartheid's excesses. You will not be surprised to learn that even this modest step has drawn criticism from both Chief Buthelezi and a number of Conservative MP's, who had predictable ideas about how the available money should be spent. Their efforts, I am pleased to say, did no more than impel the Commission to state quite unequivocably that no cash would be channelled through the Pretoria régime or the homeland administrations.

Secondly, I am also pleased to report that the Commission has hardened its outright condemnation of apartheid and taken a position on the question of sanctions that would have been unimaginable only a short time ago. Some months back, in the context of an official statement deploring the state of emergency in South Africa, the Commission said the following:

> "The Commission calls upon South Africa to change its attitude as quickly as possible; otherwise economic sanctions will, it believes, become inevitable. The Community must, in the Commission's view, prepare itself for this eventuality."

Now, that does not sound like much in itself. Indeed, to those who have craved effective action against Pretoria for so long it will seem positively feeble. But for an institution which had long been mute on the question of South Africa, which had no profile on the issue, but which - and here is the key point - is the manager of the European trading bloc this was indeed a breakthrough. And despite the objections of certain Governments - perhaps I do not need to invite you to speculate on their identity - the Commission has been developing this position ever since.

Last May, the Commission joined publicly in the condemnation of the attacks made by the South African forces on targets in Botswana, Zambia and Zimbabwe, three countries which are signatories to the Lomé Convention. In the same statement, the Commission associated itself with the call for the release of Nelson Mandela. Some time later, the Commission also condemned the arrest of Father Mkhkatshwa, General Secretary of the South African Catholic Bishops' Conference. It is all too rare for the Commission to make statements about human rights cases anywhere, but it was felt that the situation inside South Africa had deteriorated to such an extent that silence on our part would be impossible to comprehend. As indeed it would be.

Now, these initiatives, though small in themselves, have served to amplify the signal going out to Pretoria that the campaign against apartheid and the call for sanctions were achieving a new pitch of intensity, and that the Anti-<u>Apartheid</u> Movement was reaching into parts not reached before. The bankers and the business community needed the Movement to tell them where their long-term commercial interests lay, and that it was dangerous to ignore the political hazards, that <u>apartheid</u> was unworkable and that it was necessary to disengage from a dangerous commitment.

But of course we have not yet managed to get a full-scale sanctions programme off the ground. Too many national Governments have dragged their feet. They are always looking for "glimmers of hope" for they have to find a reason - any reason - for doing nothing. So Pretoria has a special department to supply glimmers. Of course, the trade measures actually agreed within EEC are very weak indeed. Some progress has been made on new investments, iron and steel imports, gold coins and crude oil, but these measures lack real punch and do not compare, for example, with the Nordic Programme of Action. Both Norway and Sweden, for example, are moving rapidly towards a total trade ban. Inside EEC, some individual countries have, to their lasting credit, added new measures to the consensus package agreed by the Council of Ministers. France is stopping its coal business with South Africa; Ireland is banning agricultural imports; Denmark has imposed a total trade ban.

But the record is patchy. And the Botha régime is desperate for the sanctions campaign to peter out. That is why the sanctions campaign must constantly renew itself, revitalize itself. Pretoria is just waiting for us to catch our breath in order to make up lost ground. The pro-<u>apartheid</u> effort in Europe is still intense. Let me give you some examples of this. Just recently, I was asked if the South African Ambassador to EEC - yes, unfortunately, we have one - could pay me a courtesy call. When he was told that representatives of racist Governments could expect no courtesy from me, he wrote back, his innocence injured, to say this:

> "I do regret that you are unwilling to discuss matters of mutual interest. I view my position as one representing a changing South Africa, I have a personal commitment to working for a just and open society...", etc., etc.

He followed this with another letter enclosing a briefing on sanctions, a briefing designed to convince me that "roughly 75 per cent of the present black population in urban areas oppose economic sanctions" and that "South Africans themselves do not believe that the imposition of sanctions will contribute to the abolition of <u>apartheid</u>". Just before I received this, I had received another unsolicited letter from the South African Mission telling me that "sanctions are ill-conceived and misguided actions which solicit approval among radicals and revolutionaries only".

Of course, it is all a gigantic confidence trick - genuinely bogus. But the <u>apartheid</u> propaganda effort in Europe is very sophisticated. Its proponents can absorb a great deal of abuse; they are skilled at exploiting any space, any chance at dialogue to try to lower the anti-<u>apartheid</u> temperature. They contact everybody; they wait for South Africa to leave the headlines of our newspapers; they chase every opportunity to be respectable. And if we, in turn, let the pressure slacken, become the slightest bit less strident in our demand for sanctions, they will advance.

But of course from behind the smooth public relations machine, the sheer ugliness of the apartheid State frequently breaks through. I am the Commissioner responsible for transport policy, and a short time ago officials in my department were approached by the South African Embassy in Paris; they wanted to arrange meetings for officials from the South African National Institute for Transport and Road Research and the National Road Safety Council. The supportive material they sent seemed innocent enough, all about the keeping of traffic registers, driving licences, insurance, etc. But the last paragraph of the briefing declared that they wanted "to investigate the latest developments to record, compute and reproduce images such as photographs and fingerprints by computer". In other words, what they were really after was police technology, assistance in creating a police car terminal system which could check fingerprints - black fingerprints - on the spot. Needless to say, they got short shrift, but the persistence of the servants of apartheid and their many apologists is remarkable and we must be continuously on our guard.

Comrades, the apartheid State knows that it is crucial to its very survival to win the argument about sanctions. Its people lobby intensively to prove that sanctions will hurt only blacks, only the front-line States, only the economies of those countries which impose them; to prove that they will not work, even that they will lengthen the life of apartheid; or to prove that they will harden attitudes and push Afrikaners irretrievably to the right, forcing them "to retreat back into the laager". And the more they lobby, the more they shout, the more they reveal that sanctions are indeed what they fear above all, because they know that real sanctions will bleed apartheid dry. And this is beginning to happen. John Vorster - giving the lie to those who assert, so misguidedly, that increased involvement will miraculously assist apartheid to cure itself - said in 1972 that "each trade agreement, each bank loan, each new investment is another brick in the wall of our continued existence".

Of course, the converse must be true: every trade agreement broken, every bank loan refused, every act of disinvestment represents another nail in the coffin of apartheid.

I very much support the concept of the peoples' sanctions campaign, the concept which underpins your conference today. It is vital for the message to go out that all of us as consumers, as church-goers, as local councillors, as students, can take our own sanctions against South Africa. We can, individually and collectively, be the bringers of economic disruption to the apartheid régime; we can all impose on apartheid the death of a thousand cuts. Moreover, it is vital for the sanctions campaign to continue to strengthen its presence in every area of policy; I myself have, for instance, made a close study of European air links with South Africa and have pushed for a rupture of those links. Though, as yet, it remains true that outside the Nordic countries there has been very little activity in Europe on this issue, we must keep up the pressure. South African exporters rely on air transport to move high-value or perishable exports such as diamonds, gold, fruit and flowers. It is high time that this export route was choked off. And it is high time, too, that as a counterpart to this we begin to build up an alternative infrastructure of rail and air routes in neighbouring black States to limit the dangerous dependence on South Africa.

Comrades, we have been making some small progress out in Europe. At least the debate there is now only about sanctions: how deep they should cut, which sectors should be covered, etc. We have, thankfully, left behind the sterile argument about codes of conduct, a device which was central to the now long-discredited policy of constructive engagement. It must be our collective objective now to build up the peoples' sanctions campaign to the point where it reaches critical mass, where it becomes such a programme of destructive disengagement that even the <u>apartheid</u> State cannot withstand its effects. And I am convinced that the rulers are losing confidence in their palsied theories and the ruled are beginning to think they can win. And so sanctions are needed, and needed now, as Malcolm Fraser said, "not to bring South Africa to its knees but to its senses".

I was delighted to be invited to join you today and I wish the Scottish Committee of the Anti-<u>Apartheid</u> Movement every success in its campaign for peoples' sanctions.

V.   SANCTIONS AGAINST SOUTH AFRICA:

A selective bibliography, 1981-1986

[This bibliography was prepared by the Dag Hammarskjöld Library of the United Nations Secretariat.]

INTRODUCTORY NOTE

In pursuance of resolutions 34/93 C of 12 December 1979 and 35/206 I of 16 December 1980, the General Assembly decided to organize, in collaboration with the Organization of African Unity, the International Conference on Sanctions against South Africa, which was held in UNESCO House, Paris, from 20 to 27 May 1981. At the request of the Centre against Apartheid, the Dag Hammarskjöld Library prepared a bibliography for the Conference. 1/

In resolution 40/64 C of 10 December 1985, the General Assembly decided to organize, in co-operation with the Organization of African Unity and the Movement of Non-Aligned Countries, a World Conference on Sanctions against Racist South Africa. This conference was held in UNESCO House, Paris, from 16 to 20 June 1986.

At the request of the Centre against Apartheid, the bibliography prepared for the 1981 Conference was updated for the World Conference. 2/ In response to the need for more recent information, that bibliography is now being updated to cover the period 1981-1986. As the prior bibliographies, it shall be divided into two parts, the first listing references to periodical articles and monographs, and the second containing references to reports, studies, resolutions and other selected documents and publications of the United Nations.

It is hoped that this bibliography will prove helpful to all who are engaged in the study of this international problem.

1/ ST/LIB/SER.B/32 (United Nations publication, Sales No. E/F.81.I.13).

2/ A/CONF.137/Ref.1.

I. PERIODICAL ARTICLES AND MONOGRAPHS

Abernethy, David B.
   The major foreign policy positions of the Reagan Administration :
   implications for United States-South African relations / David B. Abernethy.
   - International affairs bulletin. - 5(2) 1981 : 18-44.

Adelman, Kenneth L.
   Alternative futures in Southern Africa / by Kenneth L. Adelman, John Seiler.
   - Arlington, Va. : SRI International, Strategic Studies Center, 1979.
      xi, 107 p.
      "SRI Project 8299". - Prepared for: Office of the Assistant Secretary of
      Defense for International Security Affairs, Contract MDA903-79-C-0256.
      Doc. No.: SSC-TN-8299-1

Africa in the United States.
   Africa report. - 30(3) May/June 1985 : 4-32, 49-80.
      Special issue.

Africa South of the Sahara.
   Current history. - 84(501) Apr. 1985 : 145-187.
      Special issue.

The American people and South Africa : publics, elites and policymaking
processes / edited by Alfred O. Hero, Jr., John Barratt.
   Lexington, Mass. : Lexington Books, 1981.
      ix, 229 p.
      Sequel to: Conflict and compromise in South Africa. - "Result of a joint
      program initiated by the South African Institute of International Affairs
      of Johannesburg and the World Peace Foundation of Boston". - Includes
      bibliographical references and index.
      ISBN: 0-669-04320-6

Archer, Robert.
   The South African game sport and racism / Robert Archer and Antoine
   Bouillon. - London : Zed Press, 1982.
      viii, 352 p.
      Bibliography: pp. 337-345. - Includes index.
      ISBN: 0-86232-066-6

Austin, Dennis.
   A South African policy : six precepts in search of a diplomacy? / Dennis
   Austin. - International affairs. - 62(3) Summer 1986 : 391-405.
      Concerns the United Kingdom and South Africa. - Includes bibliographical
      references.

Automating apartheid : U.S. computer exports to South Africa and the arms
embargo.
   Philadelphia, Pa. : NARMIC/American Friends Service Committee, 1982.
      ix, 107 p. : ill.
      Includes bibliographical references.
      ISBN: 0-910082-00-6

Aynor, H.S.
   Israel versus apartheid at the United Nations / H.S. Aynor. -
   Jerusalem journal of international relations. - 8(1) Mar. 1986 : 34-41.

Barber, James.
   The EEC Code for South Africa : capitalism as a foreign policy instrument /
   James Barber. - World today. - 36(3) Mar. 1980 : 79-87.

Barber, James.
   Sanctions against South Africa : options for the West / James Barber and
   Michael Spicer. - International affairs. - 55(3) July 1979 : 385-401.

Barber, James.
   Supping with the devil, Zimbabwe-South Africa relations / James Barber. -
   International affairs bulletin. - 6(1) 1982 : 4-16.

Barber, James.
   The uneasy relationship : Britain and South Africa / James Barber, with an
   appendix by Christopher R. Hill. - London : Heinemann for the Royal
   Institute of International Affairs, 1983.
      142 p.
      Appendix: p. 98-129 entitled "French and West German relations with South
      Africa. - Includes bibliographical references and index.
      ISBN: 0-435-83042-2

Barber, James.
   The West and South Africa / James Barber, Jesmond Blumenfeld and Christopher
   R. Hill. - London ; Boston [Mass.] : Routledge and Kegan Paul, 1982.
      vi, 106 p. - (Chatham House papers ; 14).
      Issued jointly with the Royal Institute of International Affairs. -
      Includes bibliographical references.
      ISBN: 0-7100-9232-6

Beit-Hallahmi, Benjamin.
    Israel and South Africa, 1977-1982 : business as usual and more / Benjamin
    Beit-Hallahmi. - New outlook. - 26(2) Mar./Apr. 1983 : 31-35.

Benenson, Robert.
    South Africa's total strategy / by Robert Benenson. - Editorial research
    reports. - 2(9) 9 Sept. 1983 : 655-676.
        Includes bibliographical references.

Berridge, Geoff.
    Apartheid and the West / by Geoff Berridge. - Year book of world affairs. -
    Vol. 35 1981 : 152-164.
        Concerns mainly the United States and the United Kingdom.

Bissell, Richard E.
    South Africa and the United States : the erosion of an influence
    relationship / Richard E. Bissell. - New York : Praeger, 1982.
        xx, 147 p. - (Studies of influence in international relations).
        "Praeger special studies". - "Praeger scientific". - Bibliography: pp.
        140-142. - Includes index.
        ISBN: 0-03-047026-9

Black America and U.S. Africa policy.
    Africa report. - 29(3) May/June 1984 : 4-15, 48-54.
        Series of articles.

Blumenfeld, Jesmond.
    South Africa : economic responses to international pressures / Jesmond
    Blumenfeld. - World today. - 41(12) Dec. 1985 : 218-221.
        Includes bibliographical references.

Botha, Pieter Willem.
    South Africa : some perspectives for the future / Pieter Willem Botha. -
    Aussenpolitik : German foreign affairs review. - 35(3) 1984 : 272-280.
        Journal also available in German: X A932.

Bouillon, Antoine.
    Le sport et l'apartheid / Antoine Bouillon, Robert Archer. - Paris :
    Editions Albatros, 1981.
        319 p. - (Collection Sports ; v. 3).
        Bibliography: pp. 305-314. - Includes index.

Bourgi, Albert.
   Afrique noire-Israël : une relance problématique / Albert Bourgi. - Revue
   d'études palestiniennes. - No 11 printemps 1984 : 47-60.

Brooks, Pierre E.J.
   Security Council decisions and private contracts in conflict of law
   situations / Pierre E.J. Brooks. - South African yearbook of international
   law. - Vol. 3 1977 : 33-48.
      Concerns calls for sanctions against South Africa and Southern Rhodesia.

Buheiri, Marwan.
   L'alliance Israël-Afrique du Sud et le Tiers-Monde / Marwan Buheiri. - Revue
   d'études palestiniennes. - No 13 automne 1984 : 59-70.
      Includes bibliographical references.

Bunzel, Jeffrey H.
   The myth of the "Laager" : using U.S. business to pressure South Africa /
   Jeffrey H. Bunzel. - Fletcher forum. - 5(1) Winter 1981 : 133-139.

Bush, Ray.
   Steel : the South African connection / Ray Bush, Lionel Cliffe and Peter
   Sketchley. - Capital and class. - No. 20 Summer 1983 : 65-87.

Business in the shadow of apartheid : U.S. firms in South Africa / edited by
Jonathan Leape, Bo Baskin, Stefan Underhill.
   Lexington, Mass. : Lexington Books, 1985.
      xxxvii, 242 p.
      Includes bibliographical references and indexes.
      ISBN: 0-669-08404-2

Campbell, Kurt M.
   The Soviet-South African connection / by Kurt M. Campbell. - Africa
   report. - 31(2) Mar./Apr. 1986 : 72-75.

Chandhoke, Neera.
   South Africa and Zimbabwe, links and interlinks / Neera Chandhoke. - Africa
   quarterly. - 21(2/4) 1982 : 69-80.

Charney, Craig.
   Thinking of revolution : the new South African intelligentsia / by Craig
   Charney. - Monthly review : an independent socialist magazine. - 38(7)
   Dec. 1986 : 10-19.
      Includes bibliographical references.

Chazan, Naomi.
   The fallacies of pragmatism : Israeli foreign policy towards South Africa /
   Naomi Chazan. - African affairs. - 82(327) Apr. 1983 : 169-199.

Chettle, John H.
   The law and policy of divestment of South African stock / John H. Chettle. -
   Law and policy in international business. - 15(2) 1983 : 445-528.
      Concerns corporate investments in South Africa.

Chettle, John H.
   The United States and South Africa : barriers to communication / by John
   Chettle. - Orbis. - 25(1) Spring 1981 : 145-163.

Christian Concern for Southern Africa (London).
   Arms for apartheid : British military collaboration with South Africa / Pat
   Fitzsimons and Jonathan Bloch. - London : Christian Concern for Southern
   Africa, 1981.
      i, 60 p.
      "The conclusion and recommendations are those of CCSA". - Bibliography:
      pp. 57-58.

Clarke, Simon.
   Changing patterns of international investment in South Africa and the
   disinvestment campaign / Simon Clarke. - London : Anti-Apartheid Movement,
   1978.
      32 p. - (Foreign investment in South Africa : a discussion series /
      Anti-Apartheid Movement ; 3).
      ISBN: 0-900065-03-6

Clough, Michael.
   Beyond constructive engagement / by Michael Clough. - Foreign policy. - No.
   61 Winter 1985/86 : 3-24.
      Concerns the United States and South Africa.

Coker, Christopher.
   Collective bargaining as an internal sanction : the role of U.S.
   corporations in South Africa / by Christopher Coker. - Journal of modern
   African studies. - 19(4) Dec. 1981 : 647-665.

Coker, Christopher.
   Constructive engagement : reflections on American policy under the Nixon and
   Reagan administrations / Christopher Coker. - Journal of contemporary
   African studies. - 2(1) Oct. 1982 : 1-30.
      Concerns United States policy towards South Africa.

Coker, Christopher.
    East Germany and Southern Africa / by Christopher Coker. - Journal of social
    and political studies. - 5(3) Fall 1980 : 231-244.

Coker, Christopher.
    South Africa's strategic importance : a re-assessment / by Christopher
    Coker. - R.U.S.I. : journal of the Royal United Services Institute for
    Defence Studies. - 124(4) Dec. 1979 : 22-26.

Coker, Christopher.
    The United States and South Africa : can constructive engagement succeed? /
    Christopher Coker. - Millennium. - 11(3) Autumn 1982 : 223-241.

Conrad, Thomas.
    South Africa circumvents embargo / by Thomas Conrad. - Bulletin of the
    atomic scientists. - 42(3) Mar. 1986 : 8-13.
        Includes bibliographical references.

Coons, Christopher A.
    The response of colleges and universities to calls for divestment /
    Christopher A. Coons. -
    Washington, D.C. : Investor Responsibility Research Center, 1986.
        iii, 148 p. : map
        Includes bibliographical references.
        ISBN: 0-931035-08-2

Cooper, J.H.
    Economic sanctions and the South African economy / J.H. Cooper. -
    International affairs bulletin. - 7(2) 1983 : 25-47.

Cooper, J.H.
    Southern Africa and the threat of economic sanctions / J.H. Cooper. - South
    African journal of economics. - 52(3) Sept. 1984 : 266-281.

Corporate responsibility and the institutional investor / Christian Concern for
Southern Africa.
    London : CCSA, 1974.
        22 p.
        "Report of a seminar held at the London Graduate School of Business
        Studies, 1st November 1973".

Crocker, Chester A.
    The U.S. and South Africa : a framework for progress / by Chester A.
    Crocker. - Department of State bulletin. - 85(2103) Oct. 1985 : 4-7.

Crocker, Chester A.
   A U.S. policy for the '80s / by Chester A. Crocker with Mario Greznes and
   Robert Henderson. - Africa report. - 26(1) Jan./Feb. 1981 : 7-14.
      Concerns Southern Africa.

Crocker, Chester A.
   U.S. response to apartheid in South Africa / by Chester A. Crocker. -
   Department of State bulletin. - 85(2099) June 1985 : 38-40.

Dam, Kenneth W.
   South Africa : the case against sanctions / by Kenneth W. Dam. - Department
   of State bulletin. - 85(2099) June 1985 : 36-38.
      Concerns the United States.

Danaher, Kevin.
   In whose interest? a guide to U.S.-South Africa relations / Kevin Danaher. -
   Washington, D.C. : Institute for Policy Studies, 1984.
      xi, 279 p. : maps.
      Bibliography: pp. 191-256. - Includes index.
      ISBN: 0-89758-038-9

David, Charles.
   Le Conseil national de sécurité et la politique sud-africaine des Etats-Unis
   de 1969 à 1976 / Charles David. - Etudes internationales. - 12(4) déc. 1981
   : 657-690.
      Summary in English.

Davis, Jennifer.
   Economic disengagement and South Africa : the effectiveness and feasibility
   of implementing sanctions and divestment / Jennifer Davis, James Cason, Gail
   Hovey. - Law and policy in international business. - 15(2) 1983 : 529-563.
      Concerns economic relations between the United States and South Africa.

Dugard, John.
   Silence is not golden / by John Dugard. - Foreign policy. - No. 46 Spring
   1982 : 37-48.
      Concerns foreign relations between the United States and South Africa.

Economic sanctions against South Africa.
   Geneva : International University Exchange Fund, 1980.
      Vol. 1-11, 13-14 : ill.
      Includes bibliographical references.
      Vol. 12 not to be issued.

Eickhoff, Ekkehard.
   Aspects of German-South African relations / Ekkehard Eickhoff. -
   International affairs bulletin. - 7(1) 1983 : 25-34.

Eidelberg, P.G.
   South Africa between East and West : Pretoria-Moscow détente? / P.G.
   Eidelberg. - Africa insight. - 10(2) 1980 : 59-65.

European business and South Africa : an appraisal of the EC-Code of Conduct /
Anne Akeroyd...[et al.].
   München [Federal Republic of Germany] : Kaiser, 1981.
      257 p. - (Reihe Entwicklung und Frieden : Materialien / Wissenschaftliche
      Kommission des Katholischen Arbeitskreises Entwicklung und Frieden ; 13).
      Bibliography: pp. 251-254.
      ISBN: 3-459-01319-2

Faltas, Sami.
   Philips, electronics and the arms trade / Sami Faltas. - Current research on
   peace and violence. - 4(3) 1981 : 195-217.
      Includes bibliographical references.

Fierce, Milfred C.
   Black and white American opinions towards South Africa / by Milfred C.
   Fierce. - Journal of modern African studies. - 20(4) Dec. 1982 : 669-687.

Fisher, Scott.
   Coping with change : United States policy toward South Africa / by Scott
   Fisher. - Washington, D.C. : National Defense University Press, 1982.
      ix, 83 p. : map. - (National security affairs monograph series / National
      Defense University, Research Directorate / National Defense University,
      Research Directorate ; 82-7).
      Includes bibliographical references.

Foreign investment in South Africa and Namibia : a directory of U.S., Canadian
and British corporations operating in South Africa and Namibia... / by Anne
Newman and Cathy Bowers.
   Washington, D.C. : Investor Responsibility Research Center, 1984.
      ii, 279 p.
      "With a survey of the 100 largest U.S. bank holding companies and their
      practices and policies on lending toSouth Africa". - Bibliography: p.
      4. - Includes index.
      ISBN: 0-931035-00-7

Franck, Thomas M.
   An investment boycott by the developing countries against South Africa : a
   rationale and preliminary assessment of feasibility / Thomas M. Franck [et
   al]. - Human rights quarterly. - 4(3) Aug. 1982 : 309-332.

Franko, Lawrence G.
   The European stake in South Africa / Lawrence G. Franko. - Washington
   quarterly. - 2(2) Spring 1979 : 85-95.

Fraser, Malcolm.
   What to do about South Africa / Malcolm Fraser, Olusegun Obasanjo. -
   Foreign affairs. - 65(1) Fall 1986 : 154-162.

Freer, P.A.
   South Africa, business prospects re-assessed / by P.A. Freer and D. Samson.
   - London : Economist Intelligence Unit, 1982.
      107 p. : map. - (EIU special report ; no. 126).
      Includes bibliographical references.

Geldenhuys, Deon.
   The diplomacy of isolation : South African foreign policy making / Deon
   Geldenhuys. - Johannesburg [South Africa] : Macmillan South Africa for the
   South African Institute of International Affairs, 1984.
      iii, 295 p.
      Includes bibliographical references and indexes.
      ISBN: 0-86954-188-9

Geldenhuys, Deon.
   Instability and conflict in Southern Africa : South Africa's role in
   regional security / Deon Geldenhuys, William Gutteridge. - Conflict studies.
   - No. 148 1983 : 27 p.

Geldenhuys, Deon.
   Some foreign policy implications of South Africa's "Total national
   strategy", with particular reference to the "12-point plan" / Deon
   Geldenhuys. - Braamfontein, South Africa : South African Institute for
   International Affairs, 1981.
      63 p. - (Special study = Spesiale studie / South African Institute of
      International Affairs).
      Includes bibliographical references.
      ISBN: 0-909239-80-0

Geldenhuys, Deon.
   The United States and South Africa : a dialogue of the deaf? / Deon
   Geldenhuys. - International affairs bulletin. - 4(1) 1980 : 21-27.

Gosiger, Mary C.
   Strategies for divestment from United States companies and financial
   institutions doing business with or in South Africa / Mary C. Gosiger. -
   Human rights quarterly. - 8(3) Aug. 1986 : 517-539.
      Includes bibliographical references.

Guillerez, Bernard.
   ONU-Afrique du Sud : la croisade des clercs / par Bernard Guillerez. -
   Défense nationale. - Vol. 42 juin 1986 : 131-136.

Gupta, Anirudha.
   The struggle against Pax Pretoriana : strategic retreat or pragmatic
   accommodation? / by Anirudha Gupta. - Non-aligned world. - 2(2) Apr./June
   1984 : 304-316.

Gutteridge, William.
   South Africa, strategy for survival? / William Gutteridge. - Conflict
   studies. - No. 131 June 1981 : 32 p.
      Special issue.

Harshé, Rajen.
   France, francophone African states and South Africa : the complex triangle
   and apartheid / Rajen Harshe. - Alternatives. - 9(1) Summer 1983 : 51-72.

Hauck, David.
   Two decades of debate : the controversy over U.S. companies in South Africa
   / David Hauck, Meg Voorhes, Glenn Goldberg. - Washington, D.C. : Investor
   Responsibility Research Center, 1983.
      ii, 163 p.

Heath, Edward.
   The changing world around South Africa / Edward Heath. - International
   affairs bulletin. - 5(2) 1981 : 6-17.

Herbstein, Denis.
   Under Thatcher's coattails / by Denis Herbstein. - Africa report. -
   31(5) Sept./Oct. 1986 : 20-23.

Hill, Walter W.
   A rejoinder to the Hübner-Dick and Seidelmann South African sanctions model
   / Walter W. Hill, Jr. - Journal of peace research. - 17(1) 1980 : 77-83.
      Comment on article by Gisela Hübner-Dick and Reimund Seidelmann in:
      Journal of peace research. - 15(2) 1978.

Holland, Martin.
   The EEC code for South Africa : a reassessment / Martin Holland. - World
   today. - 41(1) Jan. 1985 : 12-14.

Holland, Martin.
   The European Community and South Africa : economic reality or political
   rhetoric? / Martin Holland. - Political studies. - 33(3) Sept. 1985 :
   399-417.

Howe, Herbert.
   United States policy in Southern Africa / by Herbert Howe. - Current
   history. - 85(511) May 1986 : 206-208, 232-234.
      Includes bibliographical references.

Hunt, Meg.
   South Africa's sanctions put region at risk / by Meg Hunt. - Journal
   of defense and diplomacy. - 4(9) Sept. 1986 : 6-7.

Hunter, Jane.
   Israel and the Bantustans / by Jane Hunter. - Journal of Palestine studies.
   - 15(3) Spring 1986 : 53-89.
      Includes bibliographical references.

Hunter, Jane.
   Israël, l'Afrique du Sud et les Bantoustans / Jane Hunter. - Revue
   d'études palestiniennes. - No 21 automne 1986 : 43-78.
      Includes bibliographical references.

Husain, Azim.
   The West, South Africa and Israel : a strategic triangle / Asim Husain. -
   Third World quarterly. - 4(1) Jan. 1982 : 44-73.

ICI (Imperial Chemical Industries Limited) in South Africa / prepared by Rodney
Stares.
   London : CCSA, 1977.
      37 p.

International Peace Research Association.
   Peace and the apartheid system : militarization and conflict formation in
   South Africa / The International Peace Research Association. - UNESCO
   yearbook on peace and conflict studies . - 1982 : 67-148.

Investment in _apartheid_ : list of companies with investment and interests in South Africa.
    Brussels : International Confederation of Free Trade Unions, 1981.
        40 p.

Investment in South Africa : the options / Christian Concern for Southern Africa.
    London : CCSA, 1976?.
        i, 59 p.
        "Report of a seminar held at the Methodist Missionary Society, London 24th Feb. 1976".
        Includes bibliographical references.

Iordanskii, Vladimir Borisovich.
    Apartheid on the skids / Vladimir B.Iordanskü. - New times. - No. 28 21 July 1986 : 28-30.
        Journal also available in French, Russian and Spanish.

Jaster, Robert S.
    Politics and the "Afrikaner bomb" / by Robert S. Jaster. - Orbis. - 27(4) Winter 1984 : 825-851.
        Concerns South African nuclear development.

Johnson, Shaun.
    Between the devil and the deep black sea? : black perception of British policy towards South Africa / Shaun Johnson. - International relations: the journal of the David Davies Institute of International Studies. - 8(5) May 1986 : 443-454.
        Includes bibliographical references.

Kaempfer, William H.
    A model of the political economy of international investment sanctions: the case of South Africa / William H. Kaempfer and Anton D. Lowenberg. - Kyklos. - 39(3) 1986 : 377-396.
        Summaries in French and German. - Bibliography: pp. 394-395.

Kane-Berman, John.
    A constructive approach to constructive engagement / John Kane-Berman. - Braamfontein, South Africa : South African Institute of International Affairs, 1983.
        11 p. - (Occasional paper = Geleentheidspublikasie / South African Institute of International Affairs).
        ISBN: 0-908371-16-0

Kannyo, Edward.
   The Latin balancing act / by Edward Kannyo. - Africa report. - 27(4)
   July/Aug. 1982 : 52-59.
      Concerns Latin American relations with Africa.

Karis, Thomas G.
   Revolutions in the making : black politics in South Africa / Thomas G.
   Karis. - Foreign affairs. - 62(2) Winter 1983/84 : 378-406.

Keenleyside, T.A.
   The impact of human rights violations on the conduct of Canadian bilateral
   relations : a contemporary dilemma / T.A. Keenleyside and Patricia Taylor. -
   Behind the headlines. - 42(2) 1984 : 27 p.

Kennedy, Edward M.
   The sanctions debate / by Edward M. Kennedy. - Africa report. - 31(5)
   Sept./Oct. 1986 : 37-39.
      Concerns United States policy toward South Africa.

Kibble, Steve.
   Reform of apartheid and continued destabilisation in Southern Africa / by
   Steve Kibble and Ray Bush. - Journal of modern African studies. - 24(2)
   June 1986 : 203-227.
      Includes bibliographical references.

Killick, John.
   The total onslaught : how does it look from Moscow? / John Killick. -
   Braamfontein, South Africa : South African Institute of International
   Affairs, 1983.
      10 p. - (Occasional paper = Geleentheidspublikasie / South African
      Institute of International Affairs).
      Includes bibliographical references.
      ISBN: 0-908371-12-8

Klare, Michael T.
   Evading the embargo : illicit U.S. arms transfers to South Africa / Michael
   T. Klare. - Journal of international affairs. - 35(1) Spring/Summer 1981 :
   15-28.

Kreindler, Joshua David.
   South Africa, Jewish Palestine and Israel : the growing relationship,
   1919-1974 / Joshua David Kreindler. - Africa quarterly. - 20(3/4) 1981 :
   48-87.
      Includes bibliographical references.

Kuzmanic-Svete, Nila.
    A delicate stage in handling the crisis in the African South / Nila
    Kuzmanic-Svete. - Review of international affairs. - 36(837) 20 Feb. 1985 :
    27-28.
        Concerns relations between the United States and South Africa.
        Journal also available in French, Russian and Spanish.

Laïdi, Zaki.
    Washington et l'Afrique australe : le volontarisme à l'épreuve / Zaki Laïdi.
    - Politique internationale. - No 30 hiver 1985/1986 : 95-104.
        Summaries in English and Spanish.

Lake, Anthony.
    Do the doable / by Anthony Lake. - Foreign policy. - No. 54 Spring 1984 :
    102-121.
        Concerns United States foreign policy in Africa.

Landgren, Signe.
    South Africa : arms embargo disimplemented / Signe Landgren. - Bulletin of
    peace proposals. - 17(3/4) 1986 : 455-459.

Legum, Colin.
    The Western crisis over Southern Africa : South Africa, Rhodesia, Namibia /
    Colin Legum. - New York : Africana Pub. Co., 1979.
        xi, 260 p. : ill., maps.
        Includes bibliographical references.
        ISBN: 0-8419-0492-8

Leistner, G.M.E.
    Regional cooperation as a cornerstone of South African external policy /
    G.M.E. Leistner. - Africa insight. - 13(1) 1983 : 4-7.

Leistner, G.M.E.
    South Africa's relations with USA and Germany : some observations / G.M.E.
    Leistner. - Africa insight. - 13(3) 1983 : 202-207.

Leonard, Richard.
    The crisis in South Africa : rising pressures on multinationals / by Richard
    Leonard. - Multinational business. - No. 3 1986 : 17-29.
        Includes bibliographical references.

Leonard, Richard.
   South Africa at war : white power and the crisis in Southern Africa /
   Richard Leonard. - Westport, Conn. : Lawrence Hill, 1983.
      x, 280 p.
      Includes bibliographical references and index.
      ISBN: 0-88208-108-X

Litwak, Lawrence.
   Divesting from South Africa : a prudent approach for pension funds / by
   Lawrence Litwak, Julia Estrella, and Kathleen McTique. - Oakland, Calif. :
   Community Economics, Inc., 1981.
      iv, 53 p. - (Studies in pension fund investments ; 10).
      Published jointly with Conference on Alternative State and Local
      Policies, Washington, D.C.
      Includes bibliographical references.
      ISBN: 0-89788-058-7

Lotta, Raymond.
   The political economy of apartheid and the strategic stakes of imperialism /
   Raymond Lotta. - Race and class. - 27(2) Autumn 1985 : 17-34.

Lugar, Richard G.
   Making foreign policy : the Congress and apartheid / by Richard G. Lugar.
   - Africa report. - 31(5) Sept./Oct. 1986 : 33-36.

Lundahl, Mats.
   Economic effects of a trade and investment boycott against South Africa /
   Mats Lundahl. - Scandinavian journal of economics. - 86(1) 1984 : 68-83.
      Includes bibliographical references.

Luttig, A.J.
   Economic coercion and South Africa / A.J. Luttig, A.C. Cilliers. - South
   African yearbook of international law. - Vol. 3 1977 : 119-135.

Maasdorp G.G.
   Economic and political aspects of regional cooperation in Southern Africa /
   G.G. Maasdorp. - South African journal of economics. - 54(2) June 1986 :
   151-171.
      Bibliography: pp. 169-171.

Maddrey, Wendell C.
   Economic sanctions against South Africa : problems and prospects for
   enforcement of human rights norms / Wendell C. Maddrey. - Virginia journal
   of international law. - 22(2) Winter 1982 : 345-380.

Magumbane, Bernard.
   Constructive engagement or disingeneous support for apartheid / Bernard
   Magumbane. - Issue : a journal of Africanist opinion. - 12(3/4) Fall/Winter
   1982 : 8-10.

Magyar, Karl P.
   The American disinvestment in South Africa debate : short-term morality vs
   long-term economic development / Karl P. Magyar. - International affairs
   bulletin. - 9(1) 1985 : 28-48.

Makgetla, Neva Seidman.
   Outposts of monopoly capitalism : Southern Africa in the changing global
   economy / by Neva Makgetla and Ann Seidman. - Westport, Conn. : L. Hill and
   Co., 1980.
      xiii, 370 p.
      Includes bibliographical references and indexes.
      ISBN: 0-88208-114-4

Makgetla, Neva Seidman.
   Transnational corporations from the FRG and South Africa's
   military-industrial complex : a case study of transnational corporate
   activity in Africa / Neva Seidman Makgetla. - Wissenschaftliche Beiträge. -
   15(2) 1980 : 28-41.
      Summaries in Russian and Spanish. - Includes bibliographical references.

Malinga, Phineas.
   Sanctions : imperialism looks after its own / by Phineas Malinga. - African
   communist. - No. 104 1986 : 50-58.
      Concerns South Africa.

Manning, Robert A.
   Constructive engagement, round two / by Robert A. Manning. - Africa report.
   - 30(1) Jan./Feb. 1985 : 79-82.
      Concerns United States relations with South Africa.

Marcum, John A.
   South Africa : changing American perceptions / John A. Marcum. -
   International affairs bulletin. - 4(3) 1980 : 3-9.

Maren, Michael.
   The Africa lobby : building a constituency against apartheid / by Michael
   Maren. - Africa report. - 29(3) May/June 1984 : 55-59.

Martin, Paul.
   South African sport : <u>apartheid</u>'s Achilles heel? / Paul Martin. - World
   today. - 40(6) June 1984 : 234-243.

Matthews, Robert O.
   Human rights and foreign policy : principals and Canadian practice / Robert
   Matthews and Cranford Pratt. - Human rights quarterly. - 7(2) May 1985 :
   159-188.

Maull, Hanns W.
   Les minéraux sud-africains : talon d'Achille de la sécurité économique
   occidentale? / Hanns W. Maull. - Politique étrangère. - 51(2) été 1986 :
   515-526.
      Summary in English. - Includes bibliographical references.

Maull, Hanns W.
   South Africa's minerals : the Achilles heel of Western economic security? /
   Hanns W. Maull. - International affairs. - 62(4) Autumn 1986 : 619-626.
      Includes bibliographical references.

McHenry, Donald F.
   The goals of the West / Donald F. McHenry. - International affairs bulletin.
   - 8(1) 1984 : 36-40.
      Concerns South Africa.

Meister, Ulrich.
   Notes from South Africa / Ulrich Meister. - Swiss review of world affairs. -
   31(10) Jan. 1982 : 8-12.

Metrowich, F.R.
   South Africa's new frontiers / F.R. Metrowich. - Sandton [South Africa] :
   Valiant, c1977.
      160 p. : ill.
      Includes index.
      ISBN: 0-86884-023-8

Millar, T.B.
   South African dilemmas / by T.B. Millar. - Canberra : Dept. of International
   Relations, the Australian National University, 1985.
      82 p. - (Canberra studies in world affairs / Department of International
      Relations, Australian National University ; no. 17).
      Includes bibliographical references.
      ISBN: 0-86784-607-0

Minter, William.
    South Africa : straight talk on sanctions / by William Minter. -
    Foreign policy. - No. 65 Winter 1986/87 : 43-63.
        Includes bibliographical references.

Misconceptions about U.S. policy toward South Africa. -
    Department of State bulletin. - 86(2114) Sept. 1986 : 12-17.

Monteiro, Anthony.
    Shield of Western interests / Anthony Monteiro. - Political affairs. - 61(5)
    May 1982 : 30-34.
        Concerns South Africa and the United States.

Moshi, H.P.B.
    Multinational corporations and sanctions in Southern Africa / H.P.B. Moshi.
    - Utafiti. - 4(2) 1979 : 183-194.

Mugomba, Agrippah T.
    The foreign policy of despair : Africa and the sale of arms to South Africa
    / Agrippah T. Mugomba. - Kampala : East African Literature Bureau, 1977.
        xiii, 255 p.
        Bibliography: pp. [347]-355.

Murray, Martin J.
    South African capitalism and black political opposition / by Martin J.
    Murray. - Cambridge, Mass. : Schenkman 1982.
        xiii, 773 p.
        Includes bibliographical references.
        ISBN: 0-870873-719-8

Namibia : the crisis in the United States policy toward Southern Africa /
produced by Africa Committee, National Council of Churches of Christ in the
U.S.A...[et al.].
    Washington, D.C. : Transafrica, 1983.
        vi, 49 p.
        Includes bibliographical references.

National Action/Research on the Military-Industrial Complex (Philadelphia,
Pa.).
    Automating apartheid : U.S. computer exports to South Africa and the arms
    embargo / NARMIC, American Friends Service Committee. - Philadelphia, Pa. :
    The Committee, 1982.
        ix, 107 p. : ill.
        Includes bibliographical references.
        ISBN: 0-910082-00-6

Ndaba, Benjamin Alan.
  Political change in South Africa : the contribution of foreign investment
  and Western countries / Benjamin Alan Ndaba
  Genève : Institut universitaire de hautes études internationales, 1986.
    iii, 168 p.
      "Mémoire présenté en vue de l'obtention du diplôme". -
    Bibliography: pp. 159-168

Nelson Mandela : the struggle is my life : his speeches and writings brought
together with historical documents and accounts of Mandela in prison by
fellow-prisoners.
  Rev. ed. - London : International Defence and Aid Fund for Southern Africa,
  1986.
    i, 249 p. : ill.
    Includes index.
    ISBN: 0-904759-69-5

Nicol, Davidson.
  United States foreign policy in Southern Africa : Third World perspectives /
  by Davidson Nicol. - Journal of modern African studies. - 21(4) Dec. 1983 :
  587-603.

Nolutshungu, Sam C.
  Skeptical notes on "constructive engagement" / Sam C. Nolutshungu. - Issue :
  a journal of Africanist opinion. - 12(3/4) Fall/Winter 1982 : 3-7.
    Concerns South Africa's apartheid policy.

Nyangoni, Wellington W.
  The OECD and Western mining multinational corporations in the Republic of
  South Africa / by Wellington W. Nyangoni. - Waltham, Mass. : African and
  Afro-American Studies Dept., Brandeis University, [1980?].
    168 p.
    Includes bibliographical references.

Oil and apartheid : churches' challenge to Shell and BP.
  London : Christian Concern for Southern Africa, 1982.
    78 p. : ill.
    Includes bibliographical references.

Olivier, Gerrit C.
  Co-operation or national security : choices and options for white and black
  Africa / Gerrit C. Olivier. - International affairs bulletin. - 4(3) 1980 :
  26-31.

Olivier, Gerrit C.
   South Africa's response to shifting nuances in United States' foreign policy
   / Gerrit C. Olivier. - Africa insight. - 12(2) 1982 : 85-88.

O'Mahony, Patrick J.
   Investment : a blessing or a curse? / by Patrick J. O'Mahony. - Great
   Wakering, Eng. : Mayhew-McCrimmon, 1979.
      248 p.
      ISBN: 0-85597-279-3

Osia, Kunirum.
   Israel, South Africa and Black Africa : a study of the primacy of the
   politics of expediency / Kunirum Osia. - Washington, D.C. : University Press
   of America, 1981.
      xi, 116 p.
      Bibliography: pp. 103-108. - Includes index.
      ISBN: 0-8191-1938-5

Parker, Frank J.
   South Africa : lost opportunities / Frank J. Parker. - Lexington, Mass. :
   Lexington Books, 1983.
      xii, 290 p.
      Includes bibliographical references and index.
      ISBN: 0-669-02750-2

Patel, C.N.
   The politics of state expulsion from the United Nations : South Africa a
   case in point / C.N. Patel. - Comparative and international law journal of
   Southern Africa. - 13(3) Nov. 1980 : 310-323.

Pienaar, Sara.
   South Africa and the League of Nations, 1929-1939 [microforms] / Sara
   Pienaar. - Johannesburg [South Africa] : University of Witwatersrand, 1982.
      vi, 427 p.
      Thesis (Ph.D.)-University of Witwatersrand, Johannesburg, 1982. -
      Bibliography: pp. 412-427.

Pieterse, Jan Nederveen.
   Israel's role in the Third World : exporting West Bank expertise / Jan
   Nederveen Pieterse. - Race and class. - 26(3) Winter 1985 : 9-30.

- 106 -

Pifer, Alan.
    South Africa in the American mind / Alan Pifer. - Johannesburg : South
African Institute of International Affairs, 1981.
    17 p. - (Occasional paper / South African Institute of International
    Affairs).
    ISBN: 0-909239-93-2

Porter, Richard C.
    International trade and investment sanctions : potential impact on the South
African economy / Richard C. Porter. - Journal of conflict resolution. -
23(4) Dec. 1979 : 579-612.

Reagan and the limits of leverage. - Africa report. - 31(5) Sept./Oct.
    1986 : 12-15.
        Concerns policy toward South Africa.

Redekop, Clarence G.
    The Mulroney government and South Africa : constructive disengagement /
Clarence G. Redekop. - Behind the headlines. - 44(2) Dec. 1986 : 16 p.
    Includes bibliographical references.

Relly, Gavin.
    The costs of disinvestment / by Gavin Relly. - Foreign policy. - No. 63
Summer 1986 : 131-146.

Rich, Paul.
    Insurgency, terrorism and the apartheid system in South Africa /
Paul Rich. - Political studies. - 32(1) Mar. 1984 : 68-85.

Roberts, Esther.
    South Africa and the international community / by Esther Roberts. -
Contemporary review. - 239(1391) Dec. 1981 : 281-286.

The role of multinational corporations in South Africa / edited by Deon
Geldenhuys.
    [Johannesburg] : South African Institute of International Affairs, 1979.
        i, 25 p. - (Study group series / South African Institute of International
        Affairs ; 2).
        ISBN: 0-909239-62-2

Ropp, Klaus von der.
    Southern Africa under the sign of the Pax Pretoriana / Klaus von der Ropp. -
Aussenpolitik : German foreign affairs review. - 35(4) 1984 : 415-429.
        Journal also available in German.

Rotberg, Robert I.
    South Africa and U.S. policy / Robert I. Rotberg. - Braamfontein, South
    Africa : South African Institute of International Affairs, 1985.
        10 p. - (Occasional paper = Geleentheidspublikasie / South African
        Institute of International Affairs).
        Includes bibliographical references.

Sanctions against South Africa / edited by Deon Geldenhuys.
    Braamfontein, Johannesburg: South African Institute of International
    Affairs, 1979.
        i, 27 p. - (Study group series / South African Institute of International
        Affairs ; 1).
        ISBN: 0-909239-61-4

Schmidt, Elizabeth.
    Decoding corporate camouflage : U.S. business support for apartheid /
    Elizabeth Schmidt ; foreword by Ron Dellums. - Washington, D.C. : Institute
    for Policy Studies, c1980.
        x, 127 p. : ill.
        Bibliography: pp. 116-117.
        ISBN: 0-89758-022-2

Schomer, Howard.
    South Africa: beyond fair employment / Howard Schomer. - Harvard business
    review. - 61(3) May/June 1983 : 145-156.

Shultz, George Pratt.
    Toward a new South Africa / by George P. Shultz. - Africa report. - 31(5)
    Sept./Oct. 1986 : 16-19.

Schumacher, Edward.
    The United States and Libya / Edward Schumacher. - Foreign affairs. - 65(2)
    Winter 1986/87 : 329-348.

Sole, Donald.
    The goals of the West in Southern Africa : a South African view / Donald
    Sole. - International affairs bulletin. - 8(1) 1984 : 26-35.

South Africa : an appraisal : the sovereign risk criteria.
    Johannesburg : Nedbank Group Economic Unit, c1977.
        vii, 293 p.
        Bibliography: p. 273-275.
        ISBN: 0-620-02614-6

South Africa : moving towards independent defence production. - Military technology. - No. 13 Dec. 1986 : 36-45.

South Africa : public policy perspectives / edited by Robert Schrire.
   Cape Town : Juta and Co., 1982.
      viii, 374 p.
      Bibliography: pp. 371-374.
      ISBN: 0-7021-1272-0

South Africa : the free world's treasure house : why you should invest in this country.
   Sandton, South Africa : Broadside, 1977.
      333 p. : ill.
      Sponsored by the South Africa Foundation and the Standard Merchant Bank.
      ISBN: 0-620-02238-8

South Africa : the vital link / edited by Robert L. Schuettinger.
   Washington, D.C. : Council on American Affairs, c1976.
      120 p. - (Council on American Affairs monographs).
      Includes bibliographical references.

South Africa and the United Nations : a select and annotated bibliography / compiled by Elna Schoeman.
   Bramfontein, South Africa : South African Institute of International Affairs, 1981.
      iii, 244 p. - (Bibliographical series = Bibliografiese reeks / South African Institute of International Affairs ; no. 8).
      Includes indexes.
      ISBN: 0-909239-88-6

South Africa and the United States : an annotated bibliography / Kevin Danaher.
   Washington, D.C. : Institute for Policy Studies, 1979.
      26 p. : ill., map.
      Includes index.

South Africa in Southern Africa : the intensifying vortex of violence / edited by Thomas M. Callaghy.
   New York : Praeger, 1983.
      viii, 420 p. : map.
      "Praeger special studies". - "Praeger scientific". - Bibliography: pp. 405-412. - Includes index.
      ISBN: 0-03-060306-4

The South African labour scene in the 1980s : discussions of the Study Group on Multinational Corporations / edited by Deon Geldenhuys.
   Braamfontein, Johannesburg: South African Institute of International Affairs, 1980.
      1, 61 p. - (Study group series / South African Institute of International Affairs ; 3).
      ISBN: 0-909239-76-2

South Africa's foreign relations, 1961-1979 : a select and partially annotated bibliography / compiled by Gail Lynda Rogaly.
   Braamfontein, South Africa : South African Institute of International Affairs, 1980.
      ix, 462 p. - (Bibliographical series = Bibliografiese reeks / South African Institute of International Affairs; no. 7).
      ISBN: 0-909239-69-X

South Africa's foreign relations, 1980-1984 : a select and annotated bibliography / Jacqueline A. Kalley.
   Braamfontein, South Africa: South African Institute of International Affairs, 1984.
      v, 283 p. - (Bibliographical series = Bibliografiese reeks / South African Institute of International Affairs ; no. 12).
      Includes indexes.
      ISBN: 0-908371-21-7

South Africa's international relations.
   South African review. - Vol. 2 1984 : 185-255.
      Series of articles.

Spandau, Arnt.
   Economic boycott against South Africa : normative and factual issues / Arnt Spandau. - Kenwyn [South Africa] : Juta & Co., 1979.
      xiv, 200 p.
      Includes bibliographical references and index.
      TNC mimeo ed. (316 p.).
      ISBN: 0-7021-0988-6

Spence, J.E.
   South Africa : between reform and retrenchment / J.E. Spence. - World today. - 40(11) Nov. 1984 : 471-480.

Spence, J.E.
   South Africa, reform versus reaction / J.E. Spence. - World today. - 37(12) Dec. 1981 : 461-468.

Spicer, Michael.
   Sanctions against South Africa : the changing context / Michael Spicer. -
   Braamfontein, South Africa : South African Institute of International
   Affairs, 1982.
      9 p. - (Occasional paper = Geleentheidspublikasie / The South African
      Institute of International Affairs).
      Includes bibliographical references.
      ISBN: 0-908371-039

Spiro, Peter J.
   State and local anti-South Africa action as an intrusion upon the federal
   power in foreign affairs / Peter J. Spiro. - Virginia law review. -
   72(4) May 1986 : 813-850.
      Concerns the United States. - Includes bibliographical references.

Spring, Martin C.
   Confrontation : the approaching crisis between the United States and South
   Africa / Martin C. Spring. - Sandton, South Africa : Valiant, 1977.
      181 p.
      ISBN: 0-86884-028-9 (pbk.)

Stares, Rodney.
   British banks and South Africa : a report / prepared by Rodney Stares based
   on original research and material provided by Martin Bailey. - London :
   Christian Concern for Southern Africa, [198-?].
      87 p.
      ISBN: 01-935-5260

Stop them insuring apartheid.
   Wellington : National Anti-Apartheid Council, 1979.
      24 p. : ill.
      Includes bibliographical references.

Study Commission on U.S. Policy toward Southern Africa.
   South Africa, time running out : the report of the Study Commission on U.S.
   Policy toward Southern Africa. - Berkeley, Calif. : University of California
   Press, c1981.
      xxvii, 517 p. : ill., maps.
      At foot of title: Foreign Policy Study Foundation. - Bibliography: pp.
      479-490. - Includes index.
      ISBN: 0-520-04547-5 (pbk.)

Stultz, Newell M.
   Foreign pressures on South Africa : the thumbscrew as conceptual framework /
   Newell M. Stultz. - International affairs bulletin. - 4(1) 1980 : 27-42.

Sullivan, Leon.
    Agents for change : the mobilization of multinational companies in South
    Africa / Leon Sullivan. - Law and policy in international business. - 15(2)
    1983 : 427-444.

Sullivan, Leon.
    The role of multinational corporations in South Africa / by Leon Sullivan. -
    Johannesburg [South Africa] : South African Institute of Race Relations,
    1980.
        25 p. - (The Alfred and Winifred Hoernlé memorial lecture / South African
        Institute of Race Relations ; 1980).
        "The 1980 Hoernlé memorial lecture, delivered in the Great Hall of the
        University of the Witwatersrand, Thursday, September 4, 1980".
        ISBN: 0-86982-191-1

Svetic, Filip.
    Sanctions : what kind and against whom? : the power and impotence of the
    international penalty mechanism / Filip Svetic. - Review of international
    affairs. - 37(881) 20 Dec. 1986 : 22-24.
        Journal also available in French, Russian and Spanish.

Taillefer, Bernard.
    Le dernier rempart : France-Afrique du Sud / Bernard Taillefer. - Paris : Le
    Sycomore, 1980.
        259 p. : ill., maps.
        "Contradictions". - Includes bibliographical references and index.
        ISBN: 2-86262-077-7

Tennyson, Brian Douglas.
    Canadian relations with South Africa : a diplomatic history / Brian Douglas
    Tennyson. - Washington, D.C. : University Press of America, 1982.
        xvi, 238 p.
        Bibliography: p. 213-232. - Includes index.
        ISBN: 0-8191-2633-0

Thompson, Richard.
    Rugby, apartheid and the Commonwealth Games / Richard Thompson. - New
    Zealand international review. - 9(1) Jan./Feb. 1984 : 16-19.
        Concerns New Zealand and South Africa.

Tjoneland, Elling Njal.
    Okonomiske sanksjonar som verkemiddel i internasjonal politikk / Elling
    Njal Tjonneland. - Internasjonal politikk. - No. 1 1986 : 49-67.
        Summary in English. - Includes bibliographical references.

Toler, Deborah.
   Constructive engagement : reactionary pragmatism at its best / Deborah
   Toler. - Issue : a journal of Africanist opinion. - 12(3/4) Fall/Winter 1982
   : 11-18.
      Concerns United States policy towards Southern Africa.

Tötemeyer, Gerhard.
   Détente or aggression : South Africa's Namibian policy / Gerhard Tötemeyer.
   - Braamfontein, South Africa : South African Institute of International
   Affairs, 1985.
      14 p. - (Occasional paper = Geleentheidspublikasie / South African
      Institute of International Affairs).
      ISBN: 0-908371-41-1

Turner, Terisa.
   Control of the oil market : OPEC initiatives to embargo South Africa : a
   case study of the exercise of national sovereignty / by Terisa Turner. -
   Development and socio-economic progress. - No. 4 Oct./Dec. 1981 : 38-63.

U.S. business in South Africa : the economic, political and moral issues /
Desaix Myers...[et al.].
   Bloomington, Ind. : Indiana University Press, c1980.
      xiv, 375 p.
      Includes bibliographical references.
      ISBN: 0-253-11486-1

Ungar, Sanford J.
   South Africa : why constructive engagement failed / Sanford J. Ungar, Peter
   Vale. - Foreign affairs. - 64(2) Winter 1985/86 : 234-258.

United States. Congress. House of Representatives. Committee on Foreign
Affairs. Subcommittee on Africa.
   Economic sanctions and their potential impact on U.S. corporate involvement
   in South Africa : hearing before the Subcommittee on Africa of the Committee
   on Foreign Affairs, House of Representatives, Ninety-ninth Congress, first
   session, January 31, 1985. - Washington, D.C. : U.S.G.P.O., 1985.
      iii, 105 p.

United States. Congress. House of Representatives. Committee on Foreign
Affairs. Subcommittee on International Economic Policy and Trade.
   U.S. corporate activities in South Africa : hearings and markup before the
   Subcommittees on International Economic Policy and Trade and on Africa of
   the Committee on Foreign Affairs, House of Representatives, ninety-seventh
   Congress on H.R. 3008, H.R. 3597, H.R. 6393, September 24, October 15 and
   22, 1981 ; May 18 and June 10, 1982. - Washington [D.C.] : U.S.G.P.O., 1983.
      iii, 327 p.

United States. Congress. House of Representatives. Committee on the District of
Columbia. Subcommittee on Fiscal Affairs and Health.
   South Africa divestment : hearing and markups before the Subcommittee on
   Fiscal Affairs and Health of the Committee on the District of Columbia,
   House of Representatives, Ninety-eighth Congress, second session on H. Con.
   Res. 216 and H. Res. 372...January 31 and February 7, 1984. - Washington,
   D.C. : U.S.G.P.O., 1984.
      iv, 520 p.

Uys, Stanley.
   Prospects for an oil boycott / by Stanley Uys. - Africa report. -
   25(5) Sept./Oct. 1980 : 15-18.

Vale, C.A.
   Quo vadis South Africa? / by C.A. Vale. - Contemporary review. - 246(1431)
   Apr. 1985 : 169-179.

Vale, Peter C.J.
   South African-Australian relations and the politics of perception : kissing
   cousins or a quarrel in the family? / Peter Vale. - Braamfontein, South
   Africa : South African Institute of International Affairs, 1983.
      8 p. - (Occasional paper = Geleentheidspublikasie / South African
      Institute of International Affairs).
      Includes bibliographical references.
      ISBN: 0-908371-13-6

Vale, Peter C.J.
   Through light glasses darkly : some thoughts on the formulation and nature
   of South African foreign policy / Peter C.J. Vale. - International affairs
   bulletin. - 6(2) 1982 : 27-34.

Venter, Denis.
   South Africa and Black Africa : some problem areas and prospects for
   rapproachement / Denis Venter. - Pretoria : Africa Institute of South
   Africa, 1980.
      40 p. - (Occasional papers of the African Institute ; 47).
      Bibliography: pp. 36-40.
      ISBN: 0-7983-0071

Vorster, M.P.
   Security Council Resolution 418 (1977) / M.P. Vorster and N.J. Botha. -
   South African yearbook of international law. - Vol. 1 1978 : 130-147.
      Concerns call by the UN for a mandatory arms embargo against South
      Africa.

Wassermann, Ursula.
   Apartheid and economic sanctions / Ursula Wassermann. - Journal of world
   trade law. - 15(4) July/Aug. 1981 : 366-369.

Watson, Rupert.
   Southern Africa at the crossroads / Rupert Watson. - New Zealand
   international review. - 8(4) July/Aug. 1983 : 6-8.

Weissman, Stephen.
   Dateline South Africa : the opposition speaks / by Stephen Weissman. -
   Foreign policy. - No. 58 Spring 1985 : 151-170.

Where is South Africa heading?.
   Africa report. - 26(5) Sept./Oct. 1981 : 4-57.
      Special issue on South Africa and U.S. foreign policy.

Whitehill, Robert.
   The sanctions that never were : Arab and Iranian oil sales to South Africa
   / Robert Whitehill. - Middle East review. - 19(1) Fall 1986 : 38-46.
      Includes bibliographical references.

Willers, David.
   The disinvestment debate / by David Willers. - Africa report. - 27(5)
   Sept./Oct. 1982 : 45-49.
      Concerns American foreign investments in South Africa.

Willers, David.
   South Africa and regional security / by David Willers. - R.U.S.I. :
   journal of the Royal United Services Institute for Defence Studies. -
   131(3) Sept. 1986 : 49-54.
      Includes bibliographical references.

Woolford, Guy.
   The United States disinvestment campaign : the emergent threat to South
   Africa / Guy Woolford. - International affairs bulletin. - 9(2) 1985 : 4-21.
      Includes bibliographical references.

Wörmann, Claudia.
    Osthandel als Problem der Atlantischen Allianz : Erfahrungen aus dem
Erdgas-Röhren-Geschäft mit der UdSSR / Claudia Wörmann. -
Bonn : Forschungsinstitut der Deutschen Gesellschaft für Auswärtige
Politik, 1986.
    243 p.
    (Arbeitspapiere zur internationalen Politik / Forschungsinstitut der
Deutschen Gesellschaft für Auswärtige Politik, ISSN 0344-9815 ; 38)
    Includes bibliographical references.
    ISBN: 3-7713-0272-2

Zagajac, Milivoje.
    Sanctions against South Africa / by Milivoje Zagajac. - Contemporary review.
    - 240(1396) May 1982 : 247-250.

II. DOCUMENTS AND PUBLICATIONS OF THE UNITED NATIONS

[ST/]DPI/682
   International Conference on Sanctions against South Africa, UNESCO House,
   Paris, 20-27 May 1981. - New York : UN, 1981.
      [6] p.
   Printed.

[ST/]DPI/696
   Objective : justice, Vol. 13, no. 2, November 1981. - New York : UN, 1981.
      40 p.
      Contains text of Panama Declaration and Programme of Action, 1981, on
      Namibia question and Paris Declaration, 1981, on sanctions against South
      Africa.
   Printed.
   Price: $US 1.50.

[ST/]DPI/706
   International Year of Mobilization for Sanctions against South Africa.
   Berlin Declaration and Appeal to the Mass Media adopted by the
   International Seminar on Publicity and the Role of Mass Media in the
   International Mobilization against Apartheid, held in Berlin in September
   1981. - New York : UN, 1982.
      [12] p.
      Contains text of the Berlin Declaration and Appeal to the Mass Media.
   Printed.

[ST/]DPI/707
   Objective : justice, v. 14, no. 1, Apr. 1982. - New York : UN, 1982.
      52 p.
      Special issue on International Year of Mobilization for Sanctions against
      South Africa.
   Printed.
   Price: $US 1.50.

[ST/]DPI/708
   Paris Declaration on Sanctions against South Africa adopted by the
   International Conference on Sanctions against South Africa, held in Paris in
   May 1981. - New York : UN, 1982.
      13 p.
   Printed.

[ST/]DPI/711

The case for sanctions against South Africa. - New York : UN, 1982.
    45 p.
Photo-offset.

[ST/]DPI/770

Main obstacles to the full eradication of racism, racial discrimination and
apartheid. - [New York] : UN Department of Public Information, 1983.
    6 p. - (Background paper / 2nd World Conference to Combat Racism and
    Racial Discrimination ; no. 7).
Printed.

[ST/]DPI/771

Assisting peoples and movements struggling against racism, denying support
to racist regimes and ensuring their isolation. - [New York] : UN Department
of Public Information, 1983.
    3 p. - (Background paper / 2nd World Conference to Combat Racism and
    Racial Discrimination ; no. 8).
Printed.

[ST/]DPI/773

Declaration and Programme of Action to Combat Racism and Racial
Discrimination adopted by the 1978 World Conference to Combat Racism and
Racial Discrimination. - New York : UN, 1983.
    19 p.
Printed.

[ST/]DPI/823

African Regional Symposium on South Africa's Illegal Occupation of Namibia :
the Threat to International Peace and Security, Arusha, United Republic of
Tanzania, 2-5 April 1984. - New York : UN, 1985.
    38 p. : graphs, tables.
    Includes bibliographical references.
Printed.

[ST/]DPI/824

Seminar on the Activities of Foreign Economic Interests in the Exploitation
of Namibia's Natural and Human Resources, Ljubljana, Yugoslavia, 16-20 April
1984. - New York : UN, 1985.
    57 p. : chart, tables.
Printed.

[ST/]DPI/826

Extraordinary plenary meetings of the United Nations Council for Namibia,
Bangkok, Thailand, 21-25 May 1984. - New York : UN, 1985.
    34 p. : ill.
Printed.

[ST/]DPI/891
  Political developments related to Namibia : report, dated 30 April 1986, of
  Standing Committee II of the UN Council for Namibia. - New York : UN, 1986.
     24 p.
     Includes bibliographical references.
  Printed.

[ST/]DPI/903
  Objective : justice, v. 18, no. 1/2, Dec. 1986. - [New York] : UN, Dept. of
  Public Information, Dec. 1986.
     43 p. : ill., map.
     "A United Nations review dedicated to the promotion of justice through
     the self-determination of peoples, the elimination of apartheid and
     racial discrimination, and the advancement of human rights".
  Printed.
  Price: $US 5.00.

Africa's call for sanctions against South Africa : a lecture delivered by
His Excellency Mr. James Victor Gbeho of the United Nations Special
Committee against Apartheid and Permanent Representative of Ghana to the
United Nations at a special meeting to launch the International Year of
Mobilization for Sanctions against South Africa on Wednesday, 13 January
1982, in London. - London : Africa Centre, 1982.
     14 p.
     Jointly published by: Africa Centre, London, United Nations Centre
     against Apartheid, New York and Anti-Apartheid Movement, London.
  Printed.

Africa's call for sanctions against South Africa / by His Excellency Mr.
James Victor Gbeho, Permanent Representative of Ghana to the United Nations.
- New York : UN, Feb. 1982.
     9 p. - (Notes and documents / United Nations Centre against Apartheid ;
     5/82).

Analytical compendium of actions by Governments with respect to sanctions on
South Africa / by Paul Conlon. - New York : UN, Sept. 1986.
     20 p. - (Notes and documents / United Nations Centre against Apartheid ;
     16/86).
  Photo-offset.

Apartheid, economic collaboration, and the case for the United Nations
comprehensive mandatory sanctions against South Africa / by Chris Child. -
[New York] : UN, July 1984.
     ii, 60 p. - (Notes and documents / United Nations Centre against
     Apartheid ; 6/84).
  Photo-offset.

Apartheid : the propaganda and the reality / by Donald Woods. - [New York] :
UN Centre against Apartheid ; London : Commonwealth Secretariat, 1986.
  vi, 35 p.
  "A study commissioned jointly by the UN Centre against Apartheid and the
  Commonwealth Secretariat".
Printed.

Appeal for an international boycott of South Africa / by the Reverend Dr.
Martin Luther King, Jr. - New York : UN Centre against Apartheid, 1982.
  13 p. : ill.
Printed.

The arms embargo, international law and the struggle against apartheid /
by Kader Asmal. - [New York] : UN, 1981.
  13 p. - (Notes and documents / United Nations Centre against Apartheid;
  23/81).
  Published at the request of the United Nations Special Committee against
  Apartheid.
Mimeographed.

Australia's changing policies toward apartheid / by Keith D. Sutter. - New
York : UN, Feb. 1985.
  i, 33 p. - (Notes and documents / United Nations Centre against
  Apartheid ; 3/85).
  "Published at the request of the Special Committee against Apartheid". -
  Includes bibliographical references.
Mimeographed.

Bishop Desmond Tutu calls upon the international community to apply punitive
sanctions against the apartheid regime. - New York : UN, Apr. 1986.
  6 p. - (Notes and documents / United Nations Centre against Apartheid ;
  7/86).
Photo-offset.

Call for sanctions against South Africa. - [New York] : UN, Jan. 1983.
  14, 16, 19 p. - (Notes and documents / United Nations Centre against
  Apartheid ; 3/83).
  Consists of three addresses by Alhaji Yusuff Maitama-Sule, Chairman of
  the Special Committee against Apartheid, Nov.-Dec. 1982.
Photo-offset.

Canadian governmental policy, banks, and corporate relations with South
Africa / by Sheila Kappler. - |New York] : UN, Aug. 1984.
   9 p. - (Notes and documents / United Nations Centre against Apartheid ;
   8/84).
   Includes recommendations of the Taskforce on the Churches and Corporate
   Responsibility Brief, May 1981.
Photo-offset.

Canadian policy on human rights in South Africa. - |New York] : UN, Aug.
1984.
   4 p. - (Notes and documents / United Nations Centre against Apartheid ;
   9/84).
   "Presented by the Canadian Government".
Photo-offset.

The care for the cultural boycott of apartheid South Africa / by Joseph N.
Garba, Chairman of the Special Committee against Apartheid. - New York : UN,
May 1985.
   3 p. - (Notes and documents / United Nations Centre against Apartheid ;
   5/85).
Mimeographed.

The case for South Africa's expulsion from international psychiatry / by
Rachel Jewkes. - |New York] : UN, May 1984.
   36 p. - (Notes and documents / United Nations Centre against Apartheid ;
   4/84).
   Includes bibliographical references.
Photo-offset.

Conference of West European Parliamentarians on an Oil Embargo against South
Africa, ACP House, Brussels, 30-31 January 1981. - |New York] : UN, Centre
against Apartheid, Dept. of Political and Security Council Affairs, April
1981.
   24 p. : ill.
Printed.

Consolidated list of sportsmen and sportswomen who participated in sports
events in South Africa from 1 September 1980 to 31 December 1985. - New York
: UN, Sept. 1986.
   54 p. - (Notes and documents / United Nations Centre against Apartheid ;
   22/86).
Photo-offset.

The cost of apartheid / by Judith Kim. - New York : UN, Sept. 1986.
   18 p. - (Notes and documents / United Nations Centre against Apartheid ;
   17/86).
Photo-offset.

Crisis in South Africa and need for greater international action against the
apartheid regime and its collaborators : conclusions and recommendations of
the annual report adopted by the United Nations Special Committee against
Apartheid on 17 October 1984. - New York : UN, 1984.
    18 p. - (|Notes and documents]/ United Nations Centre against Apartheid ;
    17/84).
Mimeographed.

Declaration of the International Seminar on the United Nations Arms Embargo
against South Africa. - New York : UN, Aug. 1986.
    8 p. - (Notes and documents / United Nations Centre against Apartheid ;
    11/86).
Photo-offset.

Declaration of the Seminar on Oil Embargo against South Africa. - New York :
UN, Aug. 1986.
    6 p. - (Notes and documents / United Nations Centre against Apartheid ;
    12/86).
Photo-offset.

Declaration of the World Conference on Sanctions against Racist South
Africa. - New York : UN, Aug. 1986.
    19 p. - (Notes and documents / United Nations Centre against Apartheid ;
    8/86).
Photo-offset.

Declarations of conferences and seminars organized or co-sponsored by the
United Nations Special Committee against Apartheid, 1981-1985. - New York :
UN, Mar. 1986.
    iii, 110 p. - (Notes and documents / United Nations Centre against
    Apartheid).
    "Special issue".
Photo-offset.

Divest from apartheid South Africa now : appeal issued on 17 April 1985 by
Joseph N. Garba, Chairman, United Nations Special Committee against
Apartheid. - New York : UN, April 1985.
    1 p. - (Notes and documents / United Nations Centre against Apartheid).
    "Special issue".
Mimeographed.

Divestment action by state and local authorities / by the American Committee on Africa. - New York : UN, Sept. 1986.
    16 p. : tables. - (Notes and documents / United Nations Centre against Apartheid ; 15/86).
Photo-offset.

Emblem for International Year of Mobilization for Sanctions against South Africa. - New York : UN, Mar. 1982.
    3 p.
Photo-offset.

European parliamentarians call for sanctions against South Africa. - [New York] : UN, Jan. 1983.
    10 p. - (Notes and documents / United Nations Centre against Apartheid ; 4/83).
    Includes the Declaration and resolution adopted by the Conference of West European Parliamentarians on Sanctions against South Africa, the Hague, 26-27 Nov. 1982.
Photo-offset.

The financing of South Africa's nuclear programme / by Reverend David Haslam. - New York : UN, Mar. 1981.
    [5] p. - (Notes and documents / United Nations Centre against Apartheid ; 17/81).
Photo-offset.

Implementation of United Nations resolutions on action against apartheid by Member States. - New York : UN, Sept. 1986.
    29 p. - (Notes and documents / United Nations Centre against Apartheid ; 14/86).
Photo-offset.

The implications of sanctions against South Africa for the mining and related industries in Britain / by Steven Bundred. - New York : UN, Apr. 1983.
    14 p. - (Notes and documents / United Nations Centre against Apartheid ; 7 Rev.1/83).
Photo-offset.

International boycott of apartheid sports. - [New York] : UN, June 1982.
    26 p. - (Notes and documents / United Nations Centre against Apartheid; 13/82).
    "Published at the request of the Special Committee against Apartheid".
Mimeographed.

International Conference on Sanctions against South Africa, Unesco House,
Paris, 20-27 May 1981. - New York : UN Centre against Apartheid, 1981.
   3 v. : ill.
   Contents: vol. 1. Main documents. - vol. 2. Observance of Africa
Liberation
   Day (25 May) : record of the special meeting of the International
   Conference on Sanctions against South Africa held at Unesco House, Paris,
   25 May 1981. - vol. 3. Statements.
Printed.

International Convention against Apartheid in Sports. - New York : UN, Feb.
1986.
   8 p. - (Notes and documents / United Nations Centre against Apartheid ;
   2/86).
Photo-offset.

International policy options / by Robert Hughes. - New York : UN, Mar. 1983.
   19 p. - (Notes and documents / United Nations Centre against Apartheid ;
   9/83).
   Includes bibliographical references.
Photo-offset.

International Year of Mobilization for Sanctions against South Africa, 1982
: programme of action. - New York : UN Centre against Apartheid, [1982].
   23 p.
   "Paris Declaration on Sanctions against South Africa": p. 11-20. -
   "Special Declaration on Namibia": pp. 21-23.
Printed.

The legacy of Dr. Martin Luther King, Jr., and the campaign for sanctions
against South Africa. - New York : UN, Feb. 1982.
   7 p. - (Notes and documents / United Nations Centre against Apartheid ;
   3/82).
Photo-offset.

Legal aspects of unilateral sanctions against South Africa : comments from
the Netherlands university lecturers in international law. - New York : UN,
1984.
   14 p. - Includes bibliographical references. - (Notes and documents /
   United Nations Centre against Apartheid ; 16/84).
Mimeographed.

The need for greatly expanded international action against apartheid :
proposals by the Special Committee against Apartheid. - New York : UN,
Sept. 1983.
21 p. - (Notes and documents / United Nations Centre against Apartheid).
Consists of the conclusions and recommendations of the Special Committee
against Apartheid in its report to the thirty-eighth session of the
General Assembly. - "Special issue".
Photo-offset.

The new France in the campaign against apartheid : report on the mission to
France (1-3 March 1982) by H.E. Alhaji Yusuff Maitama-Sule (Nigeria),
Chairman of the Special Committee against Apartheid. - [New York] : UN.
Centre against Apartheid, June 1982.
10 p.
Includes messages from President François Mitterand.
Printed.

News digest, No. 1 Jan. 1986-
New York : United Nations Centre against Apartheid, 1986.
Monthly.
Photo-offset.

News digest, special issue, Oct. 1986 / United Nations Centre against
Apartheid. - New York : UN, [1986].
20 p.
"For concerted international action against apartheid: summaries and
excerpts from statements made during the debate of the forty-first
session of the General Assembly".
Photo-offset.

News digest, special issue no. 2, Nov. 1986 / United Nations Centre against
Apartheid. - New York : UN, 1986.
19 p.
"Resolutions on apartheid adopted by the United Nations General Assembly
in Nov. 1986".
Photo-offset.

Non-aligned movement and the struggle against apartheid / by Hari Sharan
Chhabra. - New York : UN, 1984.
22 p. - (Notes and documents / United Nations Centre against Apartheid ;
18/84).
Includes bibliographical references.
Mimeographed.

The Organization of African Trade Union Unity : a decade of action against
apartheid and racism / by James Dennis Akumu, Secretary-General of OATUU. -
New York : UN, Apr. 1983.
    7 p. - (Notes and documents / United Nations Centre against Apartheid).
    "Special issue".
Photo-offset.

Plan of action for the promotion of the international campaign against
apartheid. - [New York] : United Nations Centre against Apartheid, 1986.
    17 p.
    "Concluding statement adopted by a strategy session organized by the
    United Nations Special Committee against Apartheid in New York on 25 and
    26 November 1985".
Printed.

Programme of Action against Apartheid adopted by the Special Committee
against Apartheid at its 530th meeting, New York, 25 October 1983. - [New
York] : United Nations Centre against Apartheid, 1984.
    24 p.
Printed.

Register of entertainers, actors and others who have performed in apartheid
South Africa. - New York : UN, Oct. 1983.
    18 p. - (Notes and documents / United Nations Centre against Apartheid ;
    20/83).
Photo-offset.

Register of entertainers, actors and others who performed in apartheid South
Africa. - New York : UN, 1984.
    16 p. - (Notes and documents / United Nations Centre against Apartheid;
    19/84).
    "Published at the request of the United Nations Special Committee
    against Apartheid".
Mimeographed.

Register of entertainers, actors and others who performed in apartheid South
Africa. - New York : UN, Apr. 1986.
    18 p. - (Notes and documents / United Nations Centre against Apartheid ;
    3/86).
Photo-offset.

Register of sports contacts with South Africa, 1 April-31 December 1981 :
report by the Special Committee against Apartheid. - New York : UN, Feb.
1982.
    62 p. - (Notes and documents / United Nations Centre against Apartheid ;
    7/82).
Photo-offset.

Register of sports contacts with South Africa, 1 January-30 June 1982. - New
York : UN, May 1983.
    xi, 25 p. - (Notes and documents / United Nations Centre against
    Apartheid ; 11/83).
    Photo-offset.

Register of sports contacts with South Africa, 1 July-31 December 1982. -
New York : UN, Aug. 1983.
    xi, 25 p. - (Notes and documents / United Nations Centre against
    Apartheid ; 16/83).
Photo-offset.

Register of sports contacts with South Africa, 1 January-30 June 1983. -
[New York] : UN, Jan. 1984.
    iv, 21, 1 p. - (Notes and documents / United Nations Centre against
    Apartheid ; 2/84).
Photo-offset.

Register of sports contacts with South Africa, 1 July-31 December 1983. -
[New York] : UN, Mar. 1984.
    34 p. - (Notes and documents / United Nations Centre against Apartheid ;
    3/84).
Photo-offset.

Register of sports contacts with South Africa, 1 January-30 June 1984. - New
York : UN, 1984.
    48 p. - (Notes and documents / United Nations Centre against Apartheid ;
    20/84).
Mimeographed.

Register of sports contact with South Africa, 1 July-31 December 1984. - New
York : UN, 1985.
    43 p. - (Notes and documents / United Nations Centre against Apartheid ;
    7/85).
Mimeographed.

Register of sports contacts with South Africa, 1 July-31 December 1985. -
New York : UN, Aug. 1986.
    30 p. - (Notes and documents / United Nations Centre against Apartheid ;
    9/86).
Photo-offset.

Register of sports contacts with South Africa, 1 January-30 June 1986. - New
York : UN, Dec. 1986.
   33 p. - (Notes and documents / United Nations Centre against Apartheid;
   24/86).
Photo-offset.

Relations between Canada and South Africa / by Joanne Naiman, Joan Bhabha
and Guy Wright. - [New York] : UN, Aug. 1984.
   11, 61 p. - (Notes and documents / United Nations Centre against
   Apartheid; 10/84).
Photo-offset.

Relations between the United States and South Africa / by George Houser. -
[New York] : UN, Aug. 1984.
   iii, 57 p. - (Notes and documents / United Nations Centre against
   Apartheid; 11/84).
Photo-offset.

Resolutions on apartheid adopted by the United Nations General Assembly in
1985. - New York : UN, Jan. 1986.
   37 p. - (Notes and documents / United Nations Centre against Apartheid;
   1/86).
Photo-offset.

Resolutions on apartheid adopted by the United Nations General Assembly in
1986. - New York : UN, Dec. 1986.
   26 p. - (Notes and documents / United Nations Centre against Apartheid;
   no. 25/86).
Photo-offset.

Role of banks in strengthening South Africa's military capability / by Terry
Shott. - [New York] : UN, 1981.
   15 p. : tables. - (Notes and documents /United Nations Centre against
   Apartheid, Department of Political and Security Council Affairs;
   no. 21-81).
   Includes bibliographical references. Published at the request of the
   Special Committee against Apartheid.
Mimeographed.

Sanctions against South Africa. - New York : United Nations Centre against
Apartheid, 1983.
   39 p. : ill.
   "Record of the special meeting of the General Assembly for the
   International Year of Mobilization for Sanctions against South Africa and
   presentation of awards for distinguished service in the struggle against
   apartheid, 5 November 1982".
Printed.

The Sasol coal liquefaction plants : economic implications and impact on South Africa's ability to withstand an oil cut-off / by Paul Conlon.
"Published at the request of the Special Committee against Apartheid ". - Includes bibliographical references.
Mimeographed.

Sheffield and Southern Africa. - London : Anti-Apartheid Movement on behalf of the Sheffield City Council and United Nations Centre against Apartheid, Mar. 1983.
22 p. : ill.
"An anti-apartheid movement publication".
Printed.

Solemn observance of the 25th anniversary of the Sharpeville massacre / by the Special Committee against Apartheid , 21 March 1985. - New York : UN, June 1985.
56 p. - (Notes and documents / United Nations Centre against Apartheid).
"Special issue".
Mimeographed.

South Africa : the case for mandatory economic sanctions. - New York : UN, Sept. 1986.
21 p. : table. - (Notes and documents / United Nations Centre against Apartheid ; 18/86).
Photo-offset.

South African propaganda : how the contagion of racism is spread / by John C. Laurence. - [New York] : UN, Aug. 1982.
26 p. - (Notes and documents / United Nations Centre against Apartheid ; 15/82).
Mimeographed.

South Africa's attempts to reduce dependence on imported oil / by Paul Conlon. - New York : UN, 1985.
24 p. - (Notes and documents / United Nations Centre against Apartheid ; 9/85).
"Published at the request of the Special Committee against Apartheid".
Mimeographed.

South Africa's offshore oil exploration / by Paul Conlon. - New York : UN, 1985.
24 p. - (Notes and documents / United Nations Centre against Apartheid ; 8/85).
"Published at the request of the Special Committee against Apartheid". - Mimeographed.

Sportsmen and sportswomen who participated in sports events in South Africa : consolidated list, 1 September 1980-31 December 1982. - New York : UN, Aug. 1983.
    28 p. - (Notes and documents / United Nations Centre against Apartheid ; 17/83).
Photo-offset.

The struggle in South Africa has united all races / by Mary Benson. - [New York] : UN, Aug. 1984.
    21 p. - (Notes and documents / United Nations Centre against Apartheid ; 7/84).
    Includes bibliographical references.
Photo-offset.

Time for sanctions against apartheid South Africa is now : statements, September 1981 to July 1982 / by H.E. Alhaji Yusuff Maitama-Sule. - [New York] : United Nations Centre against Apartheid, [1983].
    iv, 45 p.
Printed.

United Nations actions against apartheid. - New York : UN, Sept. 1986.
    12 p. - (Notes and documents / United Nations Centre against Apartheid ; 13/86).
Photo-offset.

United States bank policy and apartheid's financial crisis / by Diana Bratcher and Timothy Smith. - New York : UN, Apr. 1986.
    14 p. - (Notes and documents / United Nations Centre against Apartheid ; 6/86).
    "Issued at the request of the United Nations Special Committee against Apartheid".
Photo-offset.

United States student movement against apartheid : hearings at United Nations Headquarters, New York, 27 June 1986. - New York : UN, Sept. 1986.
    48 p. : ill., tables. - (Notes and documents / United Nations Centre against Apartheid ; 10/86).
Photo-offset.

Western Europe and the South African oil embargo / by Martin Bailey. - [New York] : UN, 1981.
    4 p. - (Notes and documents / United Nations Centre against Apartheid ; no. 9/81).
    "Published at the request of the United Nations Special Committee against Apartheid".
Mimeographed.

World against _apartheid_. - New York : UN, Mar. 1986.
  62 p.- (Notes and documents / United Nations Centre against _Apartheid_ ; 4/86)
  "Excerpts from statements made during the commemoration of the Fortieth Anniversary of the United Nations".
Photo-offset.

World Health Organization discontinues relations with World Medical Association. - New York : UN, Feb. 1982.
  8 p. - (Notes and documents / United Nations Centre against _Apartheid_ ; 4/82).
Photo-offset.

A/35/22/Add.1-3
  Special reports of the Special Committee against _Apartheid_. - New York : UN, 1981.
    iii, 104 p. : tables. - (GAOR, 35th sess., Suppl. no. 22A).
  Photo-offset.

A/35/802
S/14395
  Credentials of representatives to the thirty-fifth session of the General Assembly.
  - Letter dated 6 March 1981 from the Permanent Representative of South Africa to the United Nations addressed to the Secretary-General. - New York : UN, 9 Mar. 1981.
    [13] p., including annex.
  Mimeographed.

A/36/2
  Report of the Security Council, 16 June 1980-15 June 1981. - New York : UN, 1981.
    v, 58 p. - (GAOR, 36th sess., Suppl. no. 2).
  Photo-offset.

A/36/22
  Report of the Special Committee against _Apartheid_. - New York : UN, 1981.
    viii, 116 p., including annex : tables. - (GAOR, 36th sess., Suppl. no. 22).
  Photo-offset.

A/36/22/Add.1 and 2
  Special reports of the Special Committee against _Apartheid_. - New York : UN, 1982.
    iii, 17 p. - (GAOR, 36th sess., Suppl. no. 22A).
  Photo-offset.

A/36/23/Rev.1
   Report of the Special Committee on the Situation with regard to the
   Implementation of the Declaration on the Granting of Independence to
   Colonial Countries and Peoples. - New York : UN, 1982.
      viii, 171 p. - (GAOR, 36th sess., Suppl. no. 23).
   Photo-offset.

A/36/24
   Report of the United Nations Council for Namibia. - New York : UN, 1982.
      ix, 240 p. - (GAOR, 36th sess., Suppl. no. 24).
   Printed.

A/36/36
   Report of the Ad Hoc Committee on the Drafting of an International
   Convention against Apartheid in Sports. - New York : UN, 1981.
      iv, 8 p. - (GAOR, 36th sess., Suppl. no. 36).
   Photo-offset.

A/36/36/Corr.1
   Report of the Ad Hoc Committee on the Drafting of an International
   Convention against Apartheid in Sports: corrigendum. - New York : UN,
   20 Oct. 1981.
      1 p. - (GAOR, 36th sess., Suppl. no. 36, Corrigendum).
      Corrects text.
   Photo-offset.

A/36/190
S/14442
   Policies of apartheid of the Government of South Africa. - Letter dated
   10 April 1981 from the Chairman of the Special Committee against Apartheid
   to the Secretary-General. - New York : UN, 15 Apr. 1981.
      [5] p., including annex.
      Transmits Declaration of the International Seminar on the Implementation
      and Reinforcement of the Arms Embargo against South Africa, London, 1-3
      April 1981.
   Mimeographed.

A/36/201
S/14443
   Policies of apartheid of the Government of South Africa. - Letter dated
   10 April 1981 from the Chairman of the Special Committee against Apartheid
   to the Secretary-General. - New York : UN, 15 Apr. 1981.
      [8] p., including annex.
      Transmits Declaration of the International Seminar on Loans to South
      Africa, Zurich, 5-7 April 1981.
   Mimeographed.

- 132 -

A/36/290

    Policies of <u>apartheid</u> of the Government of South Africa. - Letter dated
    27 May 1981 from the Chargé d'affaires a.i. of the Permanent Mission of
    South Africa to the United Nations addressed to the Secretary-General. - New
    York : UN, 29 May 1981.
        [5] p., including annex.
        Transmits letter from Mr. R.F. Botha commenting on the International
        Conference on Sanctions against South Africa.
    Mimeographed.

A/36/319
S/14531

    Policies of <u>apartheid</u> of the Government of South Africa. - Letter dated
    11 June 1981 from the Chairman of the Special Committee against <u>Apartheid</u> to
    the Secretary-General. - New York : UN, 15 June 1981.
        [20] p., including annexes.
        Transmits Paris Declaration on Sanctions against South Africa adopted
        by the International Conference on Sanctions against South Africa,
        Paris, 20-27 May 1981.
    Mimeographed.

A/36/327
S/14546

    Question of Namibia. - Letter dated 12 June 1981 from the Acting President
    of the United Nations Council for Namibia to the Secretary-General. -
    New York : UN, 22 Jun. 1981.
        [13] p., including annex.
    Mimeographed.

A/36/430

    Implementation of the Declaration on the Denuclearization of Africa. -
    Report of the Secretary-General. - New York : UN, 3 Sep. 1981.
        1 p.
    Mimeographed.

A/36/496
S/14686

    Policies of <u>apartheid</u> of the Government of South Africa. - Letter dated
    10 September 1981 from the Acting Chairman of the Special Committee against
    <u>Apartheid</u> to the Secretary-General. - New York : UN, 14 Sep. 1981.
        [16] p., including annexes.
    Mimeographed.

A/36/665
S/14750
  Policies of <u>apartheid</u> of the Government of South Africa. - Letter dated
  9 November 1981 from the Permanent Representative of Kuwait to the United
  Nations addressed to the Secretary-General. - New York : UN, 12 Nov. 1981.
    [4] p., including annex.
    Transmits resolution of the Council of Ministers of the Arab Petroleum-
    Exporting Countries, 5 May 1981, on oil embargoes against South Africa
    and Israel.
  Mimeographed.

A/37/2
  Report of the Security Council, 16 June 1981-15 June 1982. - New York : UN,
  1982.
    [88] p. - (GAOR, 37th sess., Suppl. no. 2).
  Photo-offset.

A/37/22
  Report of the Special Committee against <u>Apartheid</u> [1982]. - New York : UN,
  1982.
    ix, 136 p. - (GAOR, 37th sess., Suppl. no. 22).
  Photo-offset.

A/37/22/Add.1 and 2
  Special reports of the Special Committee against <u>Apartheid</u>. - New York : UN,
  1985.
    iii, 20 p. - (GAOR, 37th sess., Suppl. no. 22A).
    1st special report includes bibliographical references.
    Contents: Document A/37/22/Add.1: special report : recent developments
    concerning relations between Israel and South Africa - Document
    A/37/22/Add.2: 2nd special report : trade union action against <u>apartheid</u>
    in South Africa.
  Photo-offset.

A/37/23/Rev.1
  Report of the Special Committee on the Situation with regard to the
  Implementation of the Declaration on the Granting of Independence to
  Colonial Countries and Peoples [1982]. - New York : UN, 1983
    ix, 206 p. - (GAOR, 37th sess., Suppl. no. 23).
  Photo-offset.

A/37/24
  Report of the United Nations Council for Namibia [1982]. - New York : UN,
  1983.
    x, 218 p. : tables. - (GAOR, 37th sess., Suppl. no. 24).
    Originally issued in mimeographed form as A/37/24(Part I) and
    A/37/24(Part II).
  Photo-offset.

A/37/36
    Report of the Ad Hoc Committee on the Drafting of an International
    Convention against Apartheid in Sports, 1982. - New York : UN, 1982.
        iv, 10 p. - (GAOR, 37th sess., Suppl. no. 36).
    Photo-offset.

A/37/230
S/15089
    Question of Namibia. - Letter dated 14 May 1982 from the President of the
    United Nations Council for Namibia to the Secretary-General. - New York :
    UN, 19 May 1982.
        [12] p., including annex.
        Contains Arusha Declaration and Programme of Action on Namibia,
        adopted 13 May 1982.
    Mimeographed.

A/37/265
S/15157
    Policies of apartheid of the Government of South Africa. - Letter dated
    26 May 1982 from the Chairman of the Special Committee against Apartheid
    to the Secretary-General. - New York : UN, 3 Jun. 1982.
        5 p.
        Transmits Manila Declaration for Action against Apartheid adopted by
        Asian Regional Conference for Action against Apartheid (1982).
    Mimeographed.

A/37/413
    Adverse consequences for the enjoyment of human rights of political,
    military, economic and other forms of assistance given to colonial and
    racist regimes in southern Africa. - Note by the Secretary-General. - New
    York : UN, 23 Sep. 1982.
        2 p.
        Transmits summary of resolutions and decisions adopted since 1980 by the
        General Assembly, the Economic and Social Council and the Commission
        on Human Rights and its Sub-Commission.
    Mimeographed.

A/37/474
    Comprehensive and mandatory sanctions against South Africa : report of the
    Secretary-General. - [New York] : UN, 4 Oct. 1982.
        2 p.
    Mimeographed.

A/37/474/Corr.1
   Comprehensive and mandatory sanctions against South Africa : report of the
   Secretary-General : corrigendum. - New York : UN, 29 Oct. 1982
      1 p.
      Corrects text.
   Mimeographed.

A/37/568
   Question of Namibia. - Implementation of the Declaration on the Granting of
   Independence to Colonial Countries and Peoples by the specialized agencies
   and the international institutions associated with the United Nations. -
   Letter dated 13 October 1982 from the President of the United Nations
   Council for Namibia to the Secretary-General. - New York : UN, 25 Oct. 1982.
      [71] p. : tables.
      Transmits report on IMF relations with South Africa.
   Mimeographed.

A/37/607
   Policies of apartheid of the Government of South Africa. - South Africa's
   application for credit from the International Monetary Fund : report of the
   Secretary-General. - New York : UN, 10 Nov. 1982.
      4 p.
   Mimeographed.

A/37/691
S/15508
   Policies of apartheid of the Government of South Africa. - Letter dated
   1 December 1982 from the Chairman of the Special Committee against Apartheid
   to the Secretary-General. - New York : UN, 3 Dec. 1982.
      8 p.
      Transmits text of Declaration of Conference of West European Parliamen-
      tarians on Sanctions against South Africa, The Hague, 1982.
   Mimeographed.

A/37/PV.56
   Provisional verbatim record of the 56th meeting of the thirty-seventh
   session of the General Assembly, held at United Nations Headquarters,
   New York, on Friday, 5 November 1982.
   New York : UN, 6 Nov. 1982
      [45] p.
      Special meeting devoted to the International Year of Mobilization for
      Sanctions against South Africa.
   Mimeographed.
   Distribution: Provisional (not for deposit).

A/38/2

    Report of the Security Council, 16 June 1982-15 June 1983. - New York : UN, 1984.
       vi, 70 p. - (GAOR, 38th sess., Suppl. no. 2).
    Photo-offset.

A/38/22

    Report of the Special Committee against Apartheid [1983]. - New York : UN, 1983.
       vii, 103 p. : tables. - (GAOR, 38th sess., Suppl. no. 22).
    Photo-offset.

A/38/22/Add.1

    Special report of the Special Committee against Apartheid. - New York : UN, 1985.
       10 p. - (GAOR, 38th sess., Suppl. no. 22A).
    Includes bibliographical references.
    Photo-offset.

A/38/23

    Report of the Special Committee on the Situation with regard to the Implementation of the Declaration on the Granting of Independence to Colonial Countries and Peoples. - New York : UN, 1984.
       ix, 198 p. - (GAOR, 38th sess., Suppl. no. 23).
    Originally issued in separate mimeographed parts (1983). - Includes bibliographical references.
    Photo-offset.

A/38/24

    Report of the United Nations Council for Namibia. - New York : UN, Nov. 1983.
       xi, 295 p.: tables, including annexes.- (GAOR, 38th sess., Suppl. no. 24).
    Photo-offset.

A/38/36.

    Report of the Ad Hoc Committee on the Drafting of an International Convention against Apartheid in Sports [1983]. - New York : UN, 1983.
       iv, 10 p. - (GAOR, 38th sess., Suppl. no. 36).
    Photo-offset.

A/38/36/Corr.1
Report of the Ad Hoc Committee on the Drafting of an International
Convention against Apartheid in Sports : corrigendum. - New York : UN,
11 Nov. 1983.
1 p.- (GAOR, 38th sess., Suppl. no. 36, Corrigendum).
Corrects text.
Photo-offset.

A/38/74
Policies of apartheid of the Government of South Africa. - Letter dated
14 January 1983 from the Permanent Representative of Jamaica to the United
Nations addressed to the Secretary-General. - New York : UN, 17 Jan. 1983.
5 p.
Transmits statement on tour of South Africa by a group of Jamaican and
other West Indian cricketers.
Mimeographed.

A/38/95
Policies of apartheid of the Government of South Africa. - Letter dated
15 February 1983 from the Permanent Representative of Trinidad and Tobago
to the United Nations addressed to the Secretary-General.-New York:
UN, 22 Feb. 1983.
3 p.
Transmits statement concerning visit of team of West Indian cricketers to
South Africa.
Mimeographed.

A/38/181
Policies of apartheid of the Government of South Africa. - Letter dated
6 May 1983 from the Permanent Representative of Venezuela to the United
Nations addressed to the Secretary-General. - New York : UN, 9 May 1983.
3 p.
Mimeographed.

A/38/189
S/15757
Question of Namibia. - Letter dated 9 May 1983 from the President of the
United Nations Council for Namibia to the Secretary-General. - New York :
UN, 17 May 1983.
17 p.
Transmits text of Paris Declaration on Namibia, 1983, and text of report
and Programme of Action on Namibia, 1983.
Mimeographed.

A/38/272
S/15832

Policies of <u>apartheid</u> of the Government of South Africa. - Letter dated 11 June 1983 from the Chairman of the Special Committee against <u>Apartheid</u>. - New York : UN, 16 June 1983.
   5 p.
   Transmits Declaration adopted by International Conference of Trade Unions on Sanctions and Other Actions against the <u>Apartheid</u> Regime in South Africa, Geneva, 1983.
Mimeographed.

A/38/289

Policies of <u>apartheid</u> of the Government of South Africa. - Note verbale dated 28 June 1983 from the Permanent Representative of the Bahamas to the United Nations addressed to the Secretary-General. - New York : UN, 1 July 1983.
   3 p.
   Transmits resolution on <u>apartheid</u> in sports adopted by House of Assembly of Bahamas.
Mimeographed.

A/38/310
S/15882

Policies of <u>apartheid</u> of the Government of South Africa. - Letter dated 15 July 1983 from the Acting Chairman of the Special Committee against <u>Apartheid</u> to the Secretary-General. - New York : UN, 25 July 1983.
   7 p.
   Transmits text of the Declaration adopted by the International Conference on Sanctions against <u>Apartheid</u> in Sports, London, 1983.
Mimeographed.

A/38/529

Letter dated 24 October 1983 from the Permanent Representative of the Sudan to the United Nations addressed to the Secretary-General. - New York: UN, 25 Oct. 1983.
   35 p.
   Transmits resolutions of 70th Inter-Parliamentary Conference, Seoul, 12 Oct. 1983.
Mimeographed.

A/38/539
S/16102

Policies of <u>apartheid</u> of the Government of South Africa. - Letter dated 26 October 1983 from the Acting Chairman of the Special Committee against <u>Apartheid</u> to the Secretary-General. - New York : UN, 8 Nov. 1983.
   26 p.
   Transmits Programme of Action against <u>Apartheid</u> adopted by the Special Committee against <u>Apartheid</u>, 25 Oct. 1983.
Mimeographed.

A/39/2
   Report of the Security Council, 16 June 1983-15 June 1984. - New York :
  UN, July 1985.
     vii, 70 mpl. - (GAOR, 39th sess., Suppl. no. 2).
  Photo-offset.

A/39/22
   Report of the Special Committee against <u>Apartheid</u>. - New York : UN, 1984.
     vii, 78 p. - (GAOR, 39th sess., Suppl. no. 22).
     Includes bibliographical references.
  Photo-offset.

A/39/22/Add.1
   Special report of the Special Committee against <u>Apartheid</u>. - New York : UN,
  Feb. 1985.
     12 p. - (GAOR, 39th sess., Suppl. no. 22A).
  Photo-offset.

A/39/23
   Report of the Special Committee on the Situation with regard to the
  Implementation of the Declaration on the Granting of Independence to
  Colonial Countries and Peoples. - New York : UN, 1984.
     ix, 221 p. - (GAOR, 39th sess., Suppl. no. 23).
  Photo-offset.

A/39/24
   Report of the United Nations Council for Namibia. - New York : UN, 1985.
     xi, 311 p. (GAOR, 39th sess., Suppl. no. 24).
  Photo-offset.

A/39/36
   Report of the <u>Ad Hoc</u> Committee on the Drafting of an International
  Convention against <u>Apartheid</u> in Sports. - New York : UN, 1984.
     iv, 13 p. (GAOR, 39th sess., Suppl. no. 36).
  Photo-offset.

A/39/133
S/16417
   Letter dated 15 March 1984 from the Chargé d'affaires a.i. of the Permanent
  Mission of Bangladesh to the United Nations addressed to the Secretary-
  General. - [New York] : UN, 19 Mar. 1984.
     290 p.
     Transmits resolutions of the 14th Islamic Conference of Foreign
    Ministers, Dhaka, 6-10 Dec. 1983.
    Mimeographed.

A/39/167/Add.2
E/1984/33/Add.2
    Implementation of the Programme of Action for the Second Decade to Combat
    Racism and Racial Discrimination. - Draft plan of activities for the period
    1985-1989 in accordance with General Assembly resolution 38/14 : report of
    the Secretary-General. - [New York] : UN, 4 Sept. 1984.
        7 p.
    Mimeographed.

A/39/370
S/16686
    Policies of apartheid of the Government of South Africa. - Letter dated
    25 July 1984 from the Chairman of the Special Committee against Apartheid
    to the Secretary-General. - [New York] : UN, 2 Aug. 1984.
        10 p.
        Transmits Declaration adopted by the North American Regional Conference
        for Action against Apartheid, New York, 18-21 June 1984.
    Mimeographed.

A/39/423
S/16709
    Policies of apartheid of the Government of South Africa. - Letter dated
    20 August 1984 from the Chairman of the Special Committee against Apartheid
    to the Secretary-General. - [New York] : UN, 27 Aug. 1984.
        14 p.
        Includes Declaration of the Seminar on the Legal Status of the Apartheid
        Régime and Other Legal Aspects of the Struggle against Apartheid, Lagos,
        13-16 Aug. 1984.
    Mimeographed.

A/39/466
    Implementation of the Declaration on the Denuclearization of Africa. Nuclear
    capability of South Africa. - Report of the Secretary-General. - [New York]
    : UN, 6 Sept. 1984.
        2 p.
        Includes operative paragraphs of General Assembly resolution 38/181 B.
    Mimeographed.

A/39/590
    Letter dated 16 October 1984 from the Permanent Representative of the
    Sudan to the United Nations addressed to the Secretary-General. -
    [New York] : UN, 19 Oct. 1984.
        14 p.
        Transmits resolutions adopted by the 72nd Inter-Parliamentary Conference
        held at Geneva on 29 Sept. 1984.
    Mimeographed.

A/40/2
  Report of the Security Council. - [New York] : UN, 18 Nov. 1985.
    148 p.
    Mimeographed version to be reissued as GAOR, 40th sess., Suppl. no. 2.
  Mimeographed.

A/40/22
  Report of the Special Committee against Apartheid. - New York : UN, 1986
    viii, 89 p. - (GAOR, 40th sess., Suppl. no. 22).
  Photo-offset.
  Price: $US 11.00.

A/40/22/Add.1-4
  Special reports of the Special Committee against Apartheid. - New York :
  UN, Jan. 1986.
    iii, 96 p. - (GAOR, 40th sess., Suppl. no. 22A).
  Photo-offset.
  Price: $US 11.00.

A/40/23
  Report of the Special Committee on the Situation with regard to the
  Implementation of the Declaration on the Granting of Independence to
  Colonial Countries and Peoples. - New York : UN, 1987.
    x, 250 p. - (GAOR, 40th sess., Suppl. no. 23).
    Originally issued in separate parts.
  Photo-offset.
  Price: $US 30.00.

A/40/24
  Report of the United Nations Council for Namibia. - New York : UN, 1986.
    xi, 315 p. - (GAOR, 40th sess., Suppl. no. 24).
    Originally issued in separate parts.
  Photo-offset.
  Price: $US 30.00.

A/40/36
  Report of the Ad Hoc Committee on the Drafting of an International
  Convention against Apartheid in Sports. - New York : UN, 1985.
    iv, 15 p. - (GAOR, 40th sess., Suppl. no. 36).
  Photo-offset.
  Price: $US 4.00.

A/40/307
S/17184

    Letter dated 8 May 1985 from the Permanent Representative of India to the United Nations addressed to the Secretary-General. - [New York] : UN, 14 May 1985.
      13 p.
    Includes Final Document of the Extraordinary Ministerial Meeting of the Co-ordinating Bureau of Non-Aligned Countries on the question of Namibia, held at New Delhi from 19 to 21 April 1985.
    Mimeographed.

A/40/343
S/17224

    Policies of _apartheid_ of the Government of South Africa. - Letter dated 23 May 1985 from the Acting Chairman of the Special Committee against _Apartheid_ addressed to the Secretary-General. - [New York] : UN, 29 May 1985.
      8 p.
    Transmits Declaration adopted by the Second International Conference on Sports Boycotts against South Africa.
    Mimeographed.

A/40/475
S/17336

    Policies of _apartheid_ of the Government of South Africa. - Letter dated 10 July 1985 from the Permanent Representative of Canada to the United Nations addressed to the Secretary-General. - [New York] : UN, 11 July 1985.
      7 p.
    Transmits statement on its relations with South Africa.
    Mimeographed.

A/40/514
S/17367

    Policies of _apartheid_ of the Government of South Africa. - Letter dated 27 July 1985 from the Permanent Representative of India to the United Nations addressed to the Secretary-General. - [New York] : UN, 29 July 1985.
      3 p.
    Transmits communiqué adopted by the Co-ordinating Bureau of the Movement of Non-aligned Countries on 27 July 1985 regarding the situation in South Africa.
    Mimeographed.

A/40/539
S/17391

    Policies of <u>apartheid</u> of the Government of South Africa. - Letter dated
9 August 1985 from the Chargé d'affaires a.i. of the Permanent Mission of
Indonesia to the United Nations addressed to the Secretary-General. - [New
York] : UN, 9 Aug. 1985.
      2 p.
    Transmits statement on recent development in South Africa.
Mimeographed.

A/40/553

    Concepts of security. - New York : UN, 1986.
      ix, 53 p. - (Disarmament study series ; 14).
    At head of title: Department for Disarmament Affairs; Report of the
Secretary-General. - Originally issued in mimeographed version as:
General and complete disarmament: study on concepts of security: report
of the Secretary-General, 26 Aug. 1985.
Photo-offset.
Sales No. E.86.IX.1.
Price: $US 8.50.

A/40/555
S/17402

    Policies of <u>apartheid</u> of the Government of South Africa. - Letter dated
15 August 1985 from the Chargé d'affaires a.i. of the Permanent Mission of
Brazil to the United Nations addressed to the Secretary-General. - [New
York] : UN, 15 Aug. 1985.
      4 p.
Mimeographed.

A/40/557
S/17405

    Policies of <u>apartheid</u> of the Government of South Africa. - Letter dated
16 August 1985 from the Permanent Representative of Senegal to the United
Nations addressed to the Secretary-General. - [New York] : UN, 16 Aug. 1985.
      3 p.
    Transmits statement by the President of Senegal and Chairman of the OAU
concerning the latest developments in South Africa.
Mimeographed.

A/40/565
S/17411

    Letter dated 20 August 1985 from the Acting Permanent Representative of Australia to the United Nations addressed to the Secretary-General. - [New York] : UN, 21 Aug. 1985.
       4 p.
    Includes statement by the Australian Foreign Minister, Mr. Bill Hayden, on action taken by the Australian Government against South Africa, 19 August 1985.
    Mimeographed.

A/40/592
S/17425

    Policies of <u>apartheid</u> of the Government of South Africa. - Note verbale dated 28 August 1985 from the Permanent Mission of the Union of Soviet Socialist Republics to the United Nations addressed to the Secretary-General. - [New York] : UN, 29 Aug. 1985.
       2 p.
    Mimeographed.

A/40/594
S/17430

    Policies of <u>apartheid</u> of the Government of South Africa. - Letter dated 30 August 1985 from the Permanent Representative of the Union of Soviet Socialist Republics to the United Nations addressed to the Secretary-General. - [New York] : UN, 30 Aug. 1985.
       3 p.
    Transmits statement concerning repression in South Africa.
    Mimeographed.

A/40/651
S/17470

    Policies of <u>apartheid</u> of the Government of South Africa. - Letter dated 17 September 1985 from the Permanent Representative of Canada to the United Nations addressed to the Secretary-General. - [New York] : UN, 17 Sept. 1985.
       7 p.
    Refers to A/40/475-S/17336 and transmits statement on South Africa.
    Mimeographed.

A/40/660
S/17477

Policies of <u>apartheid</u> of the Government of South Africa. - Letter dated
18 September 1985 from the Chairman of the Special Committee against
<u>Apartheid</u> addressed to the Secretary-General.- [New York]: UN, 19 Sept. 1985
    4 p.
    Transmits Declaration adopted by the International Seminar on Racist
    Ideologies, Attitudes and Organizations Hindering Efforts for the
    Elimination of <u>Apartheid</u> and Means to Combat Them.
Mimeographed.

A/40/661
S/17478

Policies of <u>apartheid</u> of the Government of South Africa. - Note verbale
dated 17 September 1985 from the Permanent Representative of the Ukrainian
Soviet Socialist Republic to the United Nations addressed to the
Secretary-General. - [New York] : UN, 19 Sept. 1985.
    3 p.
Mimeographed.

A/40/666

Co-operation between the United Nations and the Organization of African
Unity. - Letter dated 18 September 1985 from the Permanent Representative of
Madagascar addressed to the Secretary-General. - [New York] : UN, 20 Sept.
1985.
    113 p.
    Transmits Annex 1: Declarations and resolutions adopted by the Assembly
    of Heads of State and Government of the Organization of African Unity at
    its twenty-first sess.
    1985 : p. 2-69. - Annex 2: Resolutions adopted by the 42nd OAU Council
    of Ministers, held at Addis Ababa from 10 to 17 July 1985 : p. 70-113.
Mimeographed.

A/40/696
S/17511

Policies of <u>apartheid</u> of the Government of South Africa. - Letter dated
30 September 1985 from the Chairman of the Special Committee against
<u>Apartheid</u> addressed to the Secretary-General. - [New York] :
UN, 2 Oct. 1985.
    5 p.
    Transmits summary report of the Media Workshop on Countering <u>Apartheid</u>
    Propaganda, Marlborough House, London, 20-22 May 1985.
Mimeographed.

A/40/745
S/17563

Policies of <u>apartheid</u> of the Government of South Africa. - Letter dated
10 October 1985 from the Permanent Representative of Japan to the United
Nations addressed to the Secretary-General. - [New York] : UN, 11 Oct. 1985.
 3 p.
 Concerns measures taken by Japan against South Africa, particularly in
 the area of foreign trade.
Mimeographed.

A/40/761
S/17573

Letter dated 14 October 1985 from the Permanent Representative of Togo
to the United Nations addressed to the Secretary-General. - [New York] : UN,
18 Oct. 1985.
 7 p.
 Transmits Regional Conference on Security, Disarmament and Development in
 Africa : Lomé Declaration and Programme of Action.
Mimeographed.

A/40/784
S/17583

Policies of <u>apartheid</u> of the Government of South Africa. - Letter dated
21 October 1985 from the Permanent Representatives of Denmark, Finland,
Iceland, Norway and Sweden to the United Nations addressed to the
Secretary-General. - [New York] : UN, 22 Oct. 1985.
 4 p.
 Transmits Nordic Programme of Action against South Africa adopted at the
 Meeting of Ministers for Foreign Affairs of Nordic Countries, 17-18 Oct.
 1985.
Mimeographed.

A/40/892
S/17632

Policies of <u>apartheid</u> of the Government of South Africa. - Letter dated
14 November 1985 from the Chairman of the Special Committee against
<u>Apartheid</u> to the Secretary-General. - [New York] : UN, 18 Nov. 1985.
 4 p.
 Transmits Declaration adopted by the International Conference of Maritime
 Trade Unions on the Implementation of the United Nations Oil Embargo
 against South Africa.
Mimeographed.

A/41/22

Report of the Special Committee against <u>Apartheid</u>. - New York : UN, 1986.
 vi, 50 p. : tables. - (GAOR, 41st sess., Suppl. no. 22).
Photo-offset.
Price: $US 7.00.

A/41/23 (Part III)
> Report of the Special Committee on the Situation with regard to the Implementation of the Declaration on the Granting of Independence to Colonial Countries and Peoples. - [New York] : UN, 10 Sept. 1986.
>> 26 p.
>> To be issued as GAOR, 41st sess., Suppl. no. 23.
>> Contents: ch. 4. Activities of foreign economic and other interests which are impeding the implementation of the Declaration on the Granting of Independence to Colonial Countries and Peoples in Namibia and in all other territories under colonial domination and efforts to eliminate colonialism, apartheid and racial discrimination in southern Africa - ch. 5. Military activities and arrangements by colonial powers in territories under their administration which might be impeding the implementation of the Declaration on the Granting of Independence to Colonial Countries and Peoples.
> Photo-offset.

A/41/23 (Part IV)
> Report of the Special Committee on the Situation with regard to the Implementation of the Declaration on the Granting of Independence to Colonial Countries and Peoples. - [New York] : UN, 18 Sept. 1986.
>> 38 p.
>> To be issued as GAOR, 41st sess., Suppl. no. 23.
>> Contents: ch. 6. Implementation of the Declaration on the Granting of Independence to Colonial Countries and Peoples by the specialized agencies and international institutions associated with the United Nations - ch. 7. Information from Non-Self-Governing Territories transmitted under article 73 e of the Charter of the United Nations.
> Photo-offset.

A/41/23 (Part IX)
> Report of the Special Committee on the Situation with regard to the Implementation of the Declaration on the Granting of Independence to Colonial Countries and Peoples. - [New York] : UN, 5 Sept. 1986.
>> 18 p.
>> To be issued as GAOR, 41st sess., Suppl. no. 23.
>> Contents: A. Summaries of statements referred to in chapters 4, 5 and 8 - B. Reservations referred to in chapters 4, 5 and 8.
> Photo-offset.

A/41/124
S/17777
> Letter dated 30 January 1986 from the representatives of Sweden and the United Republic of Tanzania to the United Nations addressed to the Secretary-General. - [New York] : UN, 31 Jan. 1986.
>> 8 p.
>> Transmits Delhi statement adopted on 19 January 1986 by the Independent Commission on Disarmament and Security Issues.
> Photo-offset.

A/41/181
E/1986/53
> Policies of <u>apartheid</u> of the Government of South Africa. - Implementation of the Programme of Action for the Second Decade to Combat Racism and Racial Discrimination. - Elimination of all forms of racial discrimination. - Letter dated 19 February 1986 from the Chargé d'affaires a.i. of the Permanent Mission of the Libyan Arab Jamahiriya to the United Nations addressed to the Secretary-General. - [New York] : UN, 26 Feb. 1986.
>> 10 p.
>> Transmits Tripoli Declaration issued by the International Conference in Solidarity with Peoples under Racial Discrimination, 23-27 Nov. 1985.
> Photo-offset.

A/41/361
S/18089
> Policies of <u>apartheid</u> of the Government of South Africa. - Letter dated 22 May 1986 from the Permanent Representative of India to the United Nations addressed to the Secretary-General. - [New York] : UN, 23 May 1986.
>> 3 p.
>> Transmits communiqué adopted by the Co-ordinating Bureau of the Movement of Non-Aligned Countries regarding the situation in South Africa.
> Photo-offset.

A/41/388
S/18121
> Policies of <u>apartheid</u> of the Government of South Africa. - Letter dated 30 May 1986 from the Chairman of the Special Committee against <u>Apartheid</u> addressed to the Secretary-General. - [New York] : UN, 2 June 1986.
>> 9 p.
>> Transmits Final Declaration of the International Seminar on the United Nations Arms Embargo against South Africa, IMO, London, 28-30 May 1986.
> Photo-offset.

A/41/404
S/18141
> Policies of <u>apartheid</u> of the Government of South Africa. - Letter dated 6 June 1986 from the Chairman of the Special Committee against <u>Apartheid</u> addressed to the Secretary-General. - [New York] : UN, 9 June 1986.
>> 7 p.
>> Transmits Declaration adopted by the Seminar on Oil Embargo against South Africa, Oslo, 6 June 1986.
> Photo-offset.

A/41/417
S/18166

Policies of <u>apartheid</u> of the Government of South Africa. - Letter dated 17 June 1986 from the Chargé d'affaires a.i. of the Permanent Mission of Malaysia to the United Nations addressed to the Secretary-General. - [New York] : UN, 17 June 1986.
   2 p.
   Transmits statement of 13 June 1986, by the Prime Minister of Malaysia, on the conclusion of the Commonwealth Eminent Persons Group at the end of its peace initiatives in South Africa.
Photo-offset.

A/41/420
S/18170

Letter dated 18 June 1986 from the Chargé d'affaires a.i. of the Permanent Mission of the Union of Soviet Socialist Republics to the United Nations addressed to the Secretary-General. - [New York] : UN, 18 June 1986.
   3 p.
   Transmits message of 15 June 1986, from the President of the Council of Ministers of the USSR addressed to the participants in the World Conference on Sanctions against Racist South Africa.
Photo-offset.

A/41/428
S/18179

Policies of <u>apartheid</u> of the Government of South Africa. - Question of Namibia. - Letter dated 24 June 1986 from the Chargé d'affaires a.i. of the Permanent Mission of the Philippines to the United Nations addressed to the Secretary-General. - [New York] : UN, 25 June 1986.
   2 p.
   Transmits Declaration of the ASEAN Foreign Ministers on the situation in Southern Africa, 23 June 1986.
Photo-offset.

A/41/430

Letter dated 25 June 1986 from the Chargé d'affaires a.i. of the Permanent Mission of Ethiopia to the United Nations addressed to the Secretary-General. - [New York] : UN, 27 June 1986.
   17 p.
   Transmits declaration and resolutions adopted at the International Seminar on the Struggle for Peace and Progress, Addis Ababa, 7-9 June 1986.
Photo-offset.

A/41/434
S/18185

    Policies of <u>apartheid</u> of the Government of South Africa. - Letter dated
25 June 1986 from the Acting Chairman of the Special Committee against
<u>Apartheid</u> to the Secretary-General. - [New York] : UN, 30 June 1986.
    18 p.
    Transmits Declaration on Sanctions against South Africa adopted by the
  World Conference.
Photo-offset.

A/41/445
S/18204

    Policies of <u>apartheid</u> of the Government of South Africa. - Letter dated
7 July 1986 from the Acting Permanent Representative of Brazil to the United
Nations addressed to the Secretary-General. - [New York] : UN, 7 July 1986.
    2 p.
    Transmits message of 16 June 1986, from the President of Brazil to the
  World Conference against Racist South Africa.
Photo-offset.

A/41/448
S/18211

    Policies of <u>apartheid</u> of the Government of South Africa. - Note verbale
dated 8 July 1986 from the Permanent Representative of Guyana to the United
Nations addressed to the Secretary-General. - [New York] : UN, 9 July 1986.
    3 p.
    Transmits Declaration on Southern Africa, adopted at the 7th Meeting of
  Heads of Government of the Caribbean Community, Georgetown, 3 July 1986.
Photo-offset.

A/41/483

    Policies of <u>apartheid</u> of the Government of South Africa. - Letter dated
23 July 1986 from the Permanent Representative of Zambia to the United
Nations addressed to the Secretary-General. - [New York] : UN, 24 July 1986.
    2 p.
    Transmits statement by the government of Zambia on the situation
in South Africa following statement made by the President of the
United States of America.
Photo-offset.

A/41/506

    Policies of <u>apartheid</u> of the Government of South Africa. - Concerted
international action for the elimination of <u>apartheid</u> : report of the
Secretary-General. - [New York] : UN, 12 Aug. 1986.
    31 p.
    Transmits replies received from Governments.
Photo-offset.

A/41/506/Add.1

    Policies of <u>apartheid</u> of the Government of South Africa. - Concerted international action for the elimination of <u>apartheid</u> : report of the Secretary-General. - [New York] : UN, 16 Sept. 1986.
       3 p.
    Transmits reply received from Greece.
Photo-offset.

A/41/506/Add.2

    Policies of <u>apartheid</u> of the Government of South Africa. - Concerted international action for the elimination of <u>apartheid</u> : report of the Secretary-General. - [New York] : UN, 21 Oct. 1986.
       3 p.
    Transmits reply received from Canada.
Photo-offset.

A/41/506/Add.3

    Policies of <u>apartheid</u> of the Government of South Africa. - Concerted international action for the elimination of <u>apartheid</u> : report of the Secretary-General. - [New York] : UN, 28 Oct. 1986.
       4 p.
    Transmits reply received from Sweden.
Photo-offset.

A/41/550

    Implementation of the Programme of Action for the Second Decade to Combat Racism and Racial Discrimination. - Study on the role of private group action to combat racism and racial discrimination : report of the Secretary-General. - [New York] : UN, 11 Sept. 1986.
       33 p.
Photo-offset.

A/41/609

    Development and international economic co-operation. - Letter dated 15 September 1986 from the Permanent Representative of Yugoslavia to the United Nations addressed to the Secretary-General. - [New York] : UN, 17 Sept. 1986.
       19 p.
    Transmits, on behalf of the Group of 77, Final Documents of the High-Level Meeting of the Group of 77 on Economic Co-operation among Developing Countries, Cairo, 1986.
Photo-offset.

A/41/629
S/18357
Policies of <u>apartheid</u> of the Government of South Africa. - Letter dated
18 September 1986 from the Permanent Representative of the United Kingdom of
Great Britain and Northern Ireland to the United Nations addressed to the
Secretary-General. - [New York] : UN, 19 Sept. 1986.
4 p.
Transmits statement on South Africa by the Foreign Ministers of the
twelve States members of the European Community, 16 Sept. 1986.
Photo-offset.

A/41/633
S/18359
Policies of <u>apartheid</u> of the Government of South Africa. - Letter dated
19 September 1986 from the Permanent Representative of Japan to the United
Nations addressed to the Secretary-General. - [New York] : UN, 22 Sept.
1986.
3 p.
Transmits statement of 19 Sept. 1986, by the Chief Cabinet Secretary of
Japan, Mr. Masaharu Gotoda, on <u>apartheid</u> in the Republic of South Africa.
Photo-offset.

A/41/654
Co-operation between the United Nations and the Organization of African
Unity. - Letter dated 25 September 1986 from the Permanent Representative of
Algeria to the United Nations addressed to the Secretary-General. - [New
York] : UN, 7 oct. 1986.
69 p.
Transmits resolutions adopted by the Council of Ministers of the OAU at
its 44th sess. and declarations, decisions and resolutions adopted by the
Assembly of Heads of State and Government of the OAU at its 22nd sess.
Photo-offset.

A/41/690
Policies of <u>apartheid</u> of the Government of South Africa. - World Conference
on Sanctions against Racist South Africa : report of the Secretary-General.
- [New York] : UN, 8 Oct. 1986.
2 p.
Photo-offset.

A/41/697
S/18392
Letter dated 30 September 1986 from the Permanent Representative of Zimbabwe
to the United Nations addressed to the Secretary-General. - [New York] :
UN, 14 Oct. 1986.
391 p.
Transmits Final Documents of the Eighth Conference of Heads of State or
Government of Non-aligned Countries, Zimbabwe, 1-6 Sept. 1986.
Photo-offset.

A/41/703
S/18395

Note verbale dated 9 October 1986 from the Permanent Mission of Zambia
to the United Nations addressed to the Secretary-General. - [New York] : UN,
13 Oct. 1986.
6 p.
Transmits Final Communiqué of the Meeting of Ministers and Heads of
Delegation of the Non-aligned Countries to the forty-first session of the
UN General Assembly, New York, 2 Oct. 1986.
Photo-offset.

A/41/740
S/18418

Note verbale dated 21 October 1986 from the Permanent Mission of Morocco
to the United Nations addressed to the Secretary-General. - [New York] :
UN, 22 Oct. 1986.
7 p.
Transmits Communiqué of the Co-ordination Meeting of the Ministers of
Foreign Affairs of the Organization of the Islamic Conference, New York,
2 Oct. 1986.
Photo-offset.

A/41/959

Policies of apartheid of the Government of South Africa. - Letter dated
5 Dec. 1986 from the Permanent Representative of Australia to the United
Nations addressed to the Secretary-General. - [New York] : UN, 8 Dec. 1986.
2 p.
Transmits press release on sanctions against South Africa.
Photo-offset.

A/AC.109/660

Military activities and arrangements by colonial powers in territories
under their administration which might be impeding the implementation of the
Declaration on the Granting of Independence to Colonial Countries and
Peoples : working paper prepared by the Secretariat. - New York : UN, 15
June 1981.
15 p. : tables.
Mimeographed.

A/AC.109/673

Question of Namibia : consensus adopted by the Special Committee at its
1195th meeting on 14 August 1981. - New York : UN, 14 Aug. 1981.
5 p.
Mimeographed.

A/AC.109/717

Activities of foreign economic and other interests which are impeding the implementation of the Declaration on the Granting of Independence to Colonial Countries and Peoples in Namibia and in all other Territories under colonial domination and efforts to eliminate colonialism, apartheid and racial discrimination in southern Africa : resolution adopted by the Special Committee at its 1226th meeting on 20 August 1982. - [New York] : UN, 23 Aug. 1982.

    6 p.
Mimeographed.

A/AC.109/755

Activities of foreign economic and other interests which are impeding the implementation of the Declaration on the Granting of Independence to Colonial Countries and Peoples in Namibia and in all other Territories under colonial domination and efforts to eliminate colonialism, apartheid and racial discrimination in southern Africa : resolution adopted by the Special Committee at its 1239th meeting on 1 September 1983. - New York : UN, 1 Sept. 1983.

    6 p.
Mimeographed.

A/AC.109/757

Military activities and arrangements by colonial powers in territories under their administration which might be impeding the implementation of the Declaration on the Granting of Independence to Colonial Countries and Peoples : decision adopted by the Special Committee at its 1240th meeting on 1 September 1983. - New York : UN, 1 Sept. 1983

    4 p.
Mimeographed.

A/AC.109/759

Implementation of the Declaration on the Granting of Independence to Colonial Countries and Peoples by the specialized agencies and the international institutions associated with the United Nations : resolution adopted by the Special Committee at its 1246th meeting on 14 September 1983. - New York : UN, 15 Sept. 1983.

    8 p.
Mimeographed.

A/AC.109/795

Activities of foreign economic and other interests which are impeding the
implementation of the Declaration on the Granting of Independence to
Colonial Countries and Peoples in Namibia and in all other territories under
colonial domination and efforts to eliminate colonialism, apartheid and
racial discrimination in southern Africa : resolution adopted by the
Special Committee on the Situation with regard to the Implementation of the
Declaration on the Granting of Independence to Colonial Countries and
Peoples at its 1263rd meeting on 21 August 1984. - [New York] : UN, 21 Aug.
1984.
    7 p.
Mimeographed.

A/AC.109/830

Extraordinary session of the Special Committee in observance of the 25th
anniversary of the Declaration on the Granting of Independence to Colonial
Countries and Peoples, held at Tunis from 13 to 17 May 1985 : question of
Namibia : consensus adopted by the Special Committee at its 1276th meeting
on 16 May 1985. - [New York] : UN, 31 May 1985.
    8 p.
    "Originally issued in provisional form, under the symbol
    [A/AC.109/]CRP/TUN/9 (16 May 1985)".
Mimeographed.

A/AC.109/840

Activities of foreign economic and other interests which are impeding the
implementation of the Declaration on the Granting of Independence to
Colonial Countries and Peoples in Namibia and in all other territories under
colonial domination and efforts to eliminate colonialism, apartheid and
racial discrimination in southern Africa : resolution adopted by the
Special Committee at its 1282nd meeting on 7 August 1985. - [New York] : UN,
8 Aug. 1985.
    7 p.
Mimeographed.

A/AC.109/841

Military activities and arrangements by colonial powers in territories under
their administration which might be impeding the implementation of the
Declaration on the Granting of Independence to Colonial Countries and
Peoples : decision adopted by the Special Committee at its 1282nd meeting
on 7 August 1985. - [New York] : UN, 12 Aug. 1985.
    4 p.
Mimeographed.

A/AC.109/845

    Twenty-fifth anniversary of the Declaration on the Granting of Independence to Colonial Countries and Peoples : resolution adopted by the Special Committee at its 1293rd meeting on 15 August 1985 : Special Committee on the Situation with regard to the Implementation of the Declaration on the Granting of Independence to Colonial Countries and Peoples. - [New York] : UN, 19 Aug. 1985.
     5 p.
Mimeographed.

A/AC.109/880

    Question of Namibia : decision adopted by the Special Committee at its 1301st meeting on 11 August 1986. - [New York] : UN, 11 Aug. 1986.
     8 p.
Photo-offset.

A/AC.109/881

    Activities of foreign economic and other interests which are impeding the implementation of the Declaration on the Granting of Independence to Colonial Countries and Peoples in Namibia and in all other territories under colonial domination and efforts to eliminate colonialism, apartheid and racial discrimination in southern Africa : resolution adopted by the Special Committee at its 1301st meeting on 11 August 1986. - [New York] : UN, 11 Aug. 1986.
     7 p.
Photo-offset.

A/AC.109/882

    Military activities and arrangements by colonial powers in territories under their administration which might be impeding the implementation of the Declaration on the Granting of Independence to Colonial Countries and Peoples : decision adopted by the Special Committee at its 1301st meeting on 11 August 1986. - [New York] : UN, 11 Aug. 1986.
     4 p.
Photo-offset.

A/AC.109/884

    Implementation of the Declaration on the Granting of Independence to Colonial Countries and Peoples by the specialized agencies and the international institutions associated with the United Nations : resolution adopted by the Special Committee at its 1309th meeting on 15 August 1986. - [New York] : UN, 15 Aug. 1986.
     8 p.
Photo-offset.

A/AC.115/L.533

   Review of the work of the Special Committee. - New York : UN, 5 Feb. 1981.
      [16] p., including annex.
   Mimeographed.
   Distribution: Limited (not for deposit).

A/AC.115/L.538

   Oil tankers to South Africa : replies received from Member States, issued in
   accordance with the decision taken by the Special Committee at its 468th
   meeting held on 12 March 1981. - New York : UN, 3 Apr. 1981.
      12 p.
   Mimeographed.
   Distribution: Limited (not for deposit).

A/AC.115/L.538/Add.1

   Oil tankers to South Africa : replies received from Member States. - [New
   York] : UN, 1 May 1981.
      2 p.
      "Issued in accordance with the decision taken by the Special Committee at
      its 468th meeting held on 12 March 1981".
   Mimeographed.
   Distribution: Limited (not for deposit).

A/AC.115/L.538/Add.2

   Oil tankers to South Africa : replies received from Member States. - New
   York : UN, 2 Jun. 1981.
      11 p.
      "Issued in accordance with the decision taken by the Special Committee at
      its 468th meeting held on 12 March 1981".
   Mimeographed.
   Distribution: Limited (not for deposit).

A/AC.115/L.538/Add.3

   Oil tankers to South Africa : replies received from Member States. - New
   York : UN, 23 Jul. 1981.
      4 p.
      "Issued in accordance with the decision taken by the Special Committee at
      its 468th meeting held on 12 March 1981".
   Mimeographed.
   Distribution Limited (not for deposit).

A/AC.115/L.541

    Second session of the International Commission of Inquiry into the Crimes of
the Racist and <u>Apartheid</u> regimes in Southern Africa, Luanda, 30 January –
3 February 1981: Issued in accordance with the decision taken by the Special
Committee at its 468th meeting held on 12 March 1981. – New York : UN,
3 Apr. 1981.

      [11] p., including annex.

Mimeographed.

Distribution: Limited (not for deposit).

A/AC.115/L.547

    International Seminar on the Implementation and Reinforcement of the Arms
Embargo against South Africa, London, 1-3 April 1981 : report of the World
Campaign against Military and Nuclear Collaboration with South Africa
(issued in accordance with the decision taken by the Special Committee at
its 475th meeting, held on 8 May 1981). – New York : UN, 8 May 1981.

      [36] p., including annexes.

Mimeographed.

Distribution: Limited (not for deposit).

A/AC.115/L.548

    International Seminar on Loans to South Africa, Zurich, 5-7 April 1981 :
report of the Task Force on Churches and Corporate Responsibility, Toronto.
– New York : UN, 8 May 1981.

      [48] p., including annexes.

Mimeographed.

Distribution: Limited (not for deposit).

A/AC.115/L.552

    Declaration of the Conference on Building Forces against United States
Support for South Africa, held on 8 June 1981 in Washington, D.C. – New York
: UN, 1 Jul. 1981.

      5 p.

Mimeographed.

Distribution: Limited (not for deposit).

A/AC.115/L.568

    Declaration of the Conference "Southern Africa – Time to Choose", London,
11-13 March 1982. – New York : UN, 25 Mar. 1982.

      5 p.

Mimeographed.

Distribution: Limited (not for deposit).

A/AC.115/L.587

   Report of the Conference of West European Parliamentarians on Sanctions
   against South Africa, held at The Hague, 26-27 November 1982. - New York :
   UN, 28 Jan. 1983.
       44 p.
       Issued in accordance with the decision taken by the Special Committee at
       its 512th meeting, 13 Jan. 1983.
   Mimeographed.
   Distribution: Limited (not for deposit).

A/AC.115/L.593

   Interim report of the Mission of the Special Committee against Apartheid to
   Front-line States. - New York : UN, 25 May 1983.
       25 p.
   Mimeographed.
   Distribution: Limited (not for deposit).

A/AC.115/L.594

   Report of the International Conference on Sanctions against Apartheid Sport,
   held in London from 27 to 29 June 1983. - New York : UN, 28 July 1983.
       31 p.
       Issued in accordance with the decision taken by the Special Committee at
       its 524th meeting, 27 July 1983.
   Mimeographed.
   Distribution: Limited (not for deposit).

A/AC.115/L.604

   Letter dated 21 October 1983 from the Director-General of IAEA concerning a
   resolution adopted by the General Conference of IAEA. - [New York] : UN,
   10 Nov. 1983.
       3 p.
       Concerns South Africa's nuclear capabilities.
   Mimeographed.
   Distribution: Limited (not for deposit).

A/AC.115/L.606

   Appeal by the Special Committee against Apartheid to the cities of the
   world. - [New York] : UN, 4 Apr. 1984.
       3 p.
   Mimeographed.
   Distribution: Limited (not for deposit).

A/AC.115/L.608
   Resolutions adopted by the fortieth ordinary session of OAU Council of
Ministers,
   Addis Ababa, Ethiopia, 27 February-5 March 1984. - [New York]
   : UN, 26 Apr. 1984.
      7 p.
   Mimeographed.
   Distribution: Limited (not for deposit).

A/AC.115/L.609
   Letters relating to the English Rugby Football Union's proposed tour to
   South Africa. - [New York] : UN, 25 June 1984.
      4 p.
      Consists of letter dated 26 Mar. 1984 from the Chairman of the Special
      Committee against Apartheid to the United Kingdom, and reply from the
      United Kingdom.
   Mimeographed.
   Distribution: Limited (not for deposit).

A/AC.115/L.613
   Statement adopted by consultation of anti-apartheid and solidarity
   movements, London, 25-26 June 1984. - Geneva : UN, 25 July 1984.
      3 p.
      Concerns the pledge of increased support for the national liberation
      movements of Namibia and South Africa.
   Mimeographed.
   Distribution: Limited (not for deposit).

A/AC.115/L.614
   Report of the North American Regional Conference for Action against
   Apartheid, United Nations Headquarters, New York, 18-21 June 1984. - [New
   York] : 29 Aug. 1984.
      77 p.
   Mimeographed.
   Distribution: Limited (not for deposit).

A/AC.115/L.615
   Report of the Conference of Arab Solidarity with the Struggle for Liberation
   in Southern Africa, Tunisia, 7-9 August 1984 : organized by the Special
   Committee against Apartheid in co-operation with the League of Arab States.
   - [New York] : UN, 9 Nov. 1984.
      61 p.
      "Issued in accordance with the decision taken by the Special Committee
      against Apartheid at its 550th meeting held on 18 September 1984".
   Mimeographed.
   Distribution: Limited (not for deposit).

A/AC.115/L.616

Report of the Seminar on the Legal Status of the Apartheid Regime in South
Africa and Other Legal Aspects of the Struggle against Apartheid, Lagos,
13-16 August 1984. - [New York] : UN, 27 Sept. 1984.
  50 p.
  "Organized by the Special Committee against Apartheid in co-operation
  with the Government of Nigeria".
Mimeographed.
Distribution: Limited (not for deposit).

A/AC.115/L.623

Report of the International Conference on Women and Children under
Apartheid, Arusha, United Republic of Tanzania, 7-10 May 1985. - [New York]
: UN, 18 June 1985.
  34 p.
  "Issued in accordance with the decision taken by the Working Group of the
  Special Committee against Apartheid held on Friday, 7 June 1985".
Mimeographed.
Distribution: Limited (not for deposit).

A/AC.115/L.624

Report of the International Conference on Sports Boycott against South
Africa, UNESCO House, Paris, 16-18 May 1985. - [New York] : UN, 15 July
1985.
  36 p.
  "Issued in accordance with the decision taken by the Special Committee at
  its 570th meeting held on 5 July 1985".
Mimeographed.
Distribution: Limited (not for deposit).

A/AC.115/L.627

Statement adopted by the Special Committee against Apartheid at its 571st
meeting, on 24 July 1985. - [New York] : UN, 29 July 1985.
  3 p.
  "Issued in accordance with the decision taken by the Special Committee at
  its 571st meeting, on 24 July 1985". - Concerns the situation in South
  Africa.
Mimeographed.
Distribution: Limited (not for deposit).

A/AC.115/L.634
    Report of the International Seminar on Racist Ideologies, Attitudes and
    Organizations Hindering Efforts for the Elimination of Apartheid and Means
    to Combat Them, Siofok, Hungary, 9-11 September 1985. [New York] : UN,
    31 Jan. 1986.
        23 p.
        "Issued in accordance with the decision taken by the Special Committee
      at its 574th meeting, held in October 1985".
    Photo-offset.

A/AC.115/L.636
    Report of the United Nations Seminar on an Oil Embargo against South Africa,
    Oslo, 4-6 June 1986. - [New York] : UN, 15 Aug. 1986.
        7 p.
    Photo-offset.
    Distribution: Limited (not for deposit).

A/AC.131/114
    Political developments related to Namibia : report of Standing Committee II.
    - [New York] : UN, 24 Apr. 1984.
        23 p.
        Includes bibliographical references.
    Mimeographed.

A/AC.131/132
    Report of the Mission of Consultation of the United Nations Council for
    Namibia to Trinidad and Tobago and Argentina. - [New York] : UN, 6 July
    1984.
        13 p.
    Mimeographed.

A/AC.131/135
    Conclusions and recommendations of the participants in the Seminar on the
    Efforts of the International Community to End South Africa's Illegal
    Occupation of Namibia, held at Montreal from 23 to 27 July 1984. - [New
    York] : UN, 8 Aug. 1984.
        6 p.
    Mimeographed.

A/AC.131/138
    Conclusions and recommendations of the participants in the Regional
    Symposium on International Efforts to Implement Decree No. 1 for the
    Protection of the Natural Resources of Namibia, held at Geneva from 27 to
    31 August 1984. - [New York] : UN, 19 Sept. 1984.
        4 p.
    Mimeographed.

A/AC.131/142
  An appeal for action, by the participants in the Symposium on "A Century of
  Heroic Struggle by the Namibian People against Colonialism", held at United
  Nations Headquarters from 31 October to 2 November 1984. - [New York] : UN,
  12 Nov. 1984.
    5 p.
    Includes bibliographical references.
  Mimeographed.

A/AC.131/161
  Report of the delegation of the Council to the 13th session of the Committee
  on the Elimination of Racial Discrimination, held at Geneva from 6 to
  24 August 1984 : United Nations Council for Namibia. - [New York] : UN,
  4 Apr. 1985.
    8 p.
    "Resolution 1 (XXX) of the Committee on the Elimination of Racial
    Discrimination on the initial report of Namibia": p. 7.
  Mimeographed.

A/AC.131/164
  Conclusions and recommendations of the participants in the Seminar on the
  Intensification of International Action for the Immediate Independence of
  Namibia, held at Brazzaville from 25 to 29 March 1985. - [New York] : UN,
  7 May 1985.
    5 p.
  Mimeographed.

A/AC.131/165
  An appeal for action by the participants in the Symposium on the
  Strengthening of International Solidarity with the Heroic Struggle of the
  Namibian People Led by Their Sole and Authentic Representative, the South
  West Africa People's Organization (SWAPO), held at Sofia from 22 to 26 April
  1985. - [New York] : UN, 8 May 1985.
    5 p.
  Mimeographed.

A/AC.131/174
  Symposium on the Immediate Independence of Namibia - a Common
  Responsibility, held at Singapore from 6 to 10 May 1985 : conclusions and
  recommendations of the participants in the Symposium on the Immediate
  Independence of Namibia - a Common Responsibility. - [New York] : UN,
  14 June 1985.
    8 p.
  Mimeographed.

A/AC.131/176
   Report of the delegation of the Council to the Symposium on South Africa's
   Illegal Occupation of Namibia : the Threat to International Peace and
   Security, held at Arusha, United Republic of Tanzania, from 2 to 5 April
   1984. - [New York] : UN, 25 July 1985.
      36 p. - Includes bibliographical references.
   Mimeographed.

A/AC.131/180
   Report on the Seminar on the Efforts of the International Community to End
   South Africa's Illegal Occupation of Namibia, held at Montreal from
   23 to 27 July 1984. - [New York] : UN, 22 Aug. 1985.
      27 p.
   Mimeographed.

A/AC.131/191
   Plan for the intensification of international action for the independence of
   Namibia, adopted at the conclusion of the Conference held at United Nations
   Headquarters from 11 to 13 September 1985. - [New York] : UN, 9 Oct. 1985.
      8 p. - Includes bibliographical references.
      Adopted at the Conference on the Intensification of International Action
      for the Independence of Namibia.
   Mimeographed.

A/AC.131/193
   Report of the delegation of the United Nations Council for Namibia to the
   Atlantic Seminar on Namibia and Apartheid, held at Washington, D.C., on
   22 and 23 May 1985. - [New York] : UN, 18 Oct. 1985.
      6 p.
   Mimeographed.

A/AC.131/195
   Report of the Symposium on the Strengthening of International Solidarity
   with the Heroic Struggle of the Namibian People, Led by Their Sole and
   Authentic Representative, the South West Africa People's Organization, held
   at Sofia from 22 to 26 April 1985. - [New York] : UN, 3 Jan. 1986.
      19 p.- Includes bibliographical references.
   Mimeographed.

A/AC.131/216
   Final communiqué of the Seminar on World Action for the Immediate
   Independence of Namibia, held at Valetta from 19 to 23 May 1986. - [New
   York] : UN, 18 June 1986.
      8 p.
   Mimeographed.

A/AC.131/217
　　Report of the Mission of Consultation of the United Nations Council for
　　Namibia to Finland, Sweden, Denmark and Norway, from 20 to 30 May 1985. -
　　[New York] : UN, 25 July 1986.
　　　　20 p.
　　Photo-offset.

A/AC.131/218
　　Report of the delegation of the United Nations Council for Namibia to the
　　43rd ordinary session of the Council of Ministers of the Organization of
　　African Unity, held at Addis Ababa from 25 February to 4 March 1986. - [New
　　York] : UN, 27 Aug. 1986.
　　　　5 p.
　　Photo-offset.

A/AC.131/222
　　Report of the delegation of the United Nations Council for Namibia to the
　　Swedish People's Parliament against Apartheid, held at Stockholm from 21 to
　　23 February 1986. - [New York] : UN, 22 Sept. 1986.
　　　　5 p.
　　Photo-offset.

A/AC.131/225
　　Report of the delegation of the United Nations Council for Namibia to the
　　International Atomic Energy Agency at its twenty-ninth regular session,
　　held at Vienna from 23 to 27 September 1985. - [New York] : UN, 9 Oct. 1986.
　　　　3 p.
　　Photo-offset.

A/AC.131/226
　　Report on contacts between Member States and South Africa since the adoption
　　of General Assembly resolution 38/36 A of 1 December 1983 : report of
　　Standing Committee II. - [New York] : UN, 6 Nov. 1986.
　　　　29 p. : tables.
　　Photo-offset.

A/AC.131/227
　　Report of the delegation of the United Nations Council for Namibia to the
　　Ministerial Meeting of the Co-ordinating Bureau of the Movement of
　　Non-aligned Countries, held at New Delhi from 16 to 19 April 1986. - [New
　　York] : UN, 3 Dec. 1986.
　　　　4 p.
　　Photo-offset.

A/AC.131/228
   Reports of delegations of the United Nations Council for Namibia to meetings
   of the Organization of African Unity. - [New York] : UN, 5 Dec. 1986.
      6 p.
   Photo-offset.

A/AC.131/230
   Report of the Mission of Consultation of the United Nations Council for
   Namibia to Belgium and the Netherlands from 5 to 8 May 1986. - [New York] :
   UN, 11 Dec. 1986.
      13 p.
   Photo-offset.

A/CONF.107/1
   The effect on Botswana, Lesotho, Swaziland and Mozambique of sanctions
   imposed against South Africa : report submitted by the Economic Commission
   for Africa. - New York : UN, 26 Mar. 1981.
      13 p.
   Mimeographed.

A/CONF.107/2
   Nuclear South Africa / by Dr. Frank Barnaby, Director, Stockholm Inter-
   national Peace Research Institute. - New York : UN, 17 Apr. 1981.
      [18] p., including annex.
   Mimeographed.

A/CONF.107/3
   Developments in South Africa since the uprising of 1976 : report submitted
   by the Research Department of the International Defence and Aid Fund for
   Southern Africa (IDAF). - New York : UN, 20 Apr. 1981.
      [56] p., including annex.
   Mimeographed.

A/CONF.107/4
   Consideration of all aspects of sanctions against South Africa : report
   submitted by the Organization of African Unity. - New York : UN, 23 Apr.
   1981.
      [108] p., including annexes : tables.
   Mimeographed.

A/CONF.107/4/Corr.1
   Consideration of all aspects of sanctions against South Africa : corrigen-
   dum. - New York : UN, 7 May 1981
      1 p.
      Corrects text.
   Mimeographed.

A/CONF.107/5
    Measures taken by Member States and intergovernmental organizations in the
    light of United Nations resolutions on apartheid. - New York : UN, 5 May
    1981.
        [56] p.
    Mimeographed.

A/CONF.107/5/Add.1
    Measures taken by Member States and intergovernmental organizations in the
    light of United Nations resolutions on apartheid. - New York : UN, 11 May
    1981.
        [11] p.
    Mimeographed.

A/CONF.107/5/Add.2
    Measures taken by Member States and intergovernmental organizations in the
    light of United Nations resolutions on apartheid. - New York : UN, 14 May
    1981.
        4 p.
    Mimeographed.

A/CONF.107/5/Add.4
    Measures taken by Member States and intergovernmental organizations in the
    light of United Nations resolutions on apartheid. - New York : UN, 12 Jun.
    1981.
        8 p.
    Mimeographed.

A/CONF.107/6
    South Africa's oil supply : its importance, how it is obtained, and how the
    existing embargo could be made more effective, by Bernard Rivers and Martin
    Bailey. - New York : UN, 5 May 1981.
        [35] p.
    Mimeographed.

A/CONF.107/7
    The role of foreign banks in South Africa : economic support for apartheid,
    by Timothy Smith, Executive Director, Interfaith Centre on Corporate
    Responsibility, New York. - New York : UN, 11 May 1981.
        12 p.
    Mimeographed.

A/CONF.107/8
   Report of the International Conference on Sanctions against South Africa,
   Paris, 20-27 May 1981. - New York : UN, 1981.
      vi, 143 p.
   Photo-offset.

A/CONF.119/4
   General introductory paper prepared by the Secretary-General. - Geneva :
   UN, 5 May 1983.
      v, 60 p.
   Mimeographed.

A/CONF.119/9
   Report submitted by the World Intellectual Property Organization. - Geneva :
   UN, 14 Apr. 1983.
      2 p.
      Concerns WIPO activities to combat racism and racial discrimination.
   Mimeographed.

A/CONF.119/13
   Specific measures to be taken with a view to ending all forms of commercial,
   financial and technological assistance to the economy of South Africa :
   study prepared in accordance with paragraph 18 of General Assembly
   resolution 34/24. - Geneva : UN, 21 June 1983.
      iv, 42 p.
   Mimeographed.

A/CONF.119/15 (Part I)
   Compilation of United Nations resolutions and decisions relevant to the
   struggle against racism, racial discrimination and apartheid : Security
   Council resolutions. - Geneva : UN, 8 July 1983
      42 p.
   Mimeographed.

A/CONF.119/15 (Part II)
   Compilation of United Nations resolutions and decisions relevant to the
   struggle against racism, racial discrimination and apartheid : General
   Assembly resolutions (1946-1978). - Geneva : UN, 28 June 1983.
      200 p.
   Printed.

A/CONF.119/15 (Part III)
    Compilation of United Nations resolutions and decisions relevant to the
    struggle against racism, racial discrimination and apartheid : Geneva
    resolutions (1979-1982). - Geneva : UN, 28 June 1983.
        196 p.
    Mimeographed.

A/CONF.119/15 (Part IV)
    Compilation of United Nations resolutions and decisions relevant to the
    struggle against racism, racial discrimination and apartheid : Economic
    and Social Council resolutions. - Geneva : UN, 29 July 1983.
        71 p.
    Mimeographed.

A/CONF.119/15 (Part V)
    Compilation of United Nations resolutions and decisions relevant to the
    struggle against racism, racial discrimination and apartheid : Commission
    on Human Rights resolutions. - Geneva : UN, 21 July 1983.
        113 p.
    Mimeographed.

A/CONF.119/19
    Paper submitted by the Special Committee against Apartheid. - Geneva : UN,
    3 Aug. 1983.
        21 p.
    Mimeographed.

A/CONF.119/26
    Report of the Second World Conference to Combat Racism and Racial
    Discrimination, Geneva, 1-12 August 1983. - New York : UN, 1983.
        iv, 132 p.
    Photo-offset.
    Sales No. E.83.XIV.4
    Price: $US 15.00

A/CONF.119/26/Corr.1
    Report of the Second World Conference to Combat Racism and Racial
    Discrimination, Geneva, 1-12 August 1983 : corrigendum. -   New York :
    UN, 4 Nov. 1983.
        [1] p.
        Corrects text.
    Photo-offset.
    Sales No. E.83.XIV.4/ Corrigendum

A/CONF.120/3
A/AC.131/91
    The military situation in and relating to Namibia : report of the United
Nations Council for Namibia. - New York : UN, 28 Mar. 1983.
        27 p. : map.
        Includes UN map no. 3168 : Military map of Namibia, May 1982.
    Mimeographed.

A/CONF.120/4
A/AC.131/92
    Activities of foreign economic interests operating in Namibia : report of
the United Nations Council for Namibia. - New York : UN, 16 Mar. 1983
        33 p. : map, tables
        Includes map of Namibia showing mining areas.
    Mimeographed.

A/CONF.120/13
    Report of the International Conference in Support of the Struggle of the
Namibian People for Independence, Paris, 25-29 April 1983. - New York : UN,
1983.
        ix, 171 p.
    Photo-offset.

A/CONF.137/5
    Report of the World Conference on Sanctions against Racist South Africa,
Paris, 16-20 June 1986. - New York : UN, 1986.
        v, 79 p.
        Includes Declaration adopted by the Conference.
    Photo-offset.
    Sales No.: E.86.I.23.

A/CONF.137/BP.1
    Divestment action by State and local authorities, by the American Committee
on Africa. - [New York] : UN, 29 Apr. 1986.
        16 p.
    Photo-offset.
    Distribution: Limited (not for deposit).

A/CONF.137/BP.2
    Analytical compendium of actions taken by Governments with respect to
sanctions on South Africa, by Paul Conlon. - [New York] : UN, 12 May 1986.
        20 p.
        Includes bibliographical references.
    Photo-offset.
    Distribution: Limited (not for deposit).

A/CONF.137/BP.3
   The cost of <u>apartheid</u>, by Judith Kim. - [New York] : UN, 14 May 1986.
      18 p.
   Photo-offset.
   Distribution: Limited (not for deposit).

A/CONF.137/BP.4
   South Africa : the case for mandatory economic sanctions. - [New York] : UN,
   15 May 1986.
      21 p.
      "Prepared at the request of the Special Committee against <u>Apartheid</u>".
   Photo-offset.
   Distribution: Limited (not for deposit).

A/CONF.137/BP.5
   Bank loans to South Africa from mid-1982 to December 1984, by Eva Militz
   [New York] : UN, 29 Apr. 1986.
      134 p. - includes bibliographical references.
      "Published at the request of the Special Committee against <u>Apartheid</u>".
   Photo-offset.

A/CONF.137/PC/1
   Provisional guidelines for the World Conference on Sanctions against Racist
   South Africa, to be held at Unesco House, Paris, from 16 to 20 June 1986. -
   [New York] : UN, 17 Mar. 1986.
      11 p.
   Photo-offset.

A/CONF.137/Ref.1
   Sanctions against South Africa : a selective bibliography, 1981-1985 =
   Sanctions contre l'Afrique du Sud : bibliographie sélective, 1981-1985. -
   [New York] : UN, 7 May 1986.
      ii, 91 p.
      Prepared by the Dag Hammarskjöld Library at the request of the United
      Nations Centre against <u>Apartheid</u>. - Consists of original language
      entries.
   Photo-offset.
   Distribution: Limited (not for deposit).

A/CONF.137/Ref.2
   Arms embargo against South Africa : a bibliography of United Nations
   resolutions, documents and other publications. - [New York] : UN, 29 Apr.
   1986.
      18 p.
   Photo-offset.
   Distribution: Limited (not for deposit).

A/CONF.137/Ref.4
  International Convention against Apartheid in Sports. - |New York] : UN,
  29 Apr. 1986.
     8 p.
  Photo-offset.
  Distribution: Limited (not for deposit).

A/CONF.137/Ref.7
  Register of entertainers, actors and others who have performed in apartheid
  South Africa. - |New York] : UN, 29 Apr. 1986.
     18 p.
     "This 3rd register... is published at the request of the United Nations
     Special Committee against Apartheid".
  Photo-offset.
  Distribution: Limited (not for deposit).

A/CONF.137/Ref.8
  Bishop Desmond Tutu calls upon the international community to apply punitive
  sanctions against the apartheid régime. - |New York] : UN, 29 Apr. 1986.
     6 p.
     "Contains the text of a statement... on 2 April 1986 at a press
     conference held at Johannesburg, South Africa".
  Photo-offset.
  Distribution: Limited (not for deposit).

A/CONF.137/Ref.9
  Declarations and resolutions on South Africa adopted by the Non-aligned
  Countries in March 1983 and the Organization of African Unity in November
  1984. - |New York] : UN, 29 Apr. 1986.
     15 p.
  Photo-offset.
  Distribution: Limited (not for deposit).

A/CONF.137/Ref.10/Add.1
  Declarations of conferences and seminars organized or co-sponsored by the
  United Nations Special Committee against Apartheid, 1981-1985. - |New York]
  : UN, 12 May 1986.
     6 p.
     Contents: Statement adopted by the Special Committee against Apartheid at
     the conclusion of its consultations with non-governmental anti-apartheid
     organizations, held at United Nations Headquarters from 25 to 26 November
     1985.
  Photo-offset.
  Distribution: Limited (not for deposit).

A/CONF.137/Ref.11
    Communiqué issued by the Heads of State and Government of the Front-Line
    States at their meeting held at Luanda on 8 April 1986. - [New York] : UN,
    14 May 1986.
        4 p.
    Photo-offset.
    Distribution: Limited (not for deposit).

A/CONF.137/Ref.13
    Activities of transnational corporations in South Africa and Namibia and
    follow-up to the report of the Panel of Eminent Persons Established to
    Conduct the Public Hearings on the Activities of Transnational Corporations
    in South Africa and Namibia. - [New York] : UN, 4 June 1986.
        4 p.
    Includes Economic and Social Council resolution 1986/1.
    Photo-offset.
    Distribution: Limited (not for deposit).

A/CONF.138/4
A/AC.131/179/Add.1
    Military situation in and relating to Namibia : report of Standing Committee
    II. - [New York] : UN, 3 Apr. 1986.
        17 p. : map.
    Includes UN map no. 3169/Rev. 1: military map of Namibia (July 1983). -
    Includes bibliographical references.
    Photo-offset.

A/CONF.138/5
    Political developments related to Namibia : report of Standing Committee II
    : International Conference for the Immediate Independence of Namibia. - [New
    York] : UN, 30 Apr. 1986.
        25 p.
    Includes bibliographical references.
    Photo-offset.

A/CONF.138/11
    Report of the International Conference for the Immediate Independence of
    Namibia, Vienna, 7-11 July 1986. - New York : UN, 1986.
        vi, 99 p.
    Photo-offset.
    Sales No. E.86.I.16.
    Price: $US 11.00.

A/DEC/38/419

Military activities and arrangements by colonial powers in territories under their administration which might be impeding the implementation of the Declaration on the Granting of Independence to Colonial Countries and Peoples.

Adopted at the 86th plenary meeting, 7 Dec. 1983.

In: A/38/47 (GAOR, 38th sess., Suppl. no. 47). - 1984. - pp. 293-295.
Photo-offset.

A/DEC/40/415

Military activities and arrangements by colonial powers in territories under their administration which might be impeding the implementation of the Declaration on the Granting of Independence to Colonial Countries and Peoples.

Adopted at the 99th plenary meeting, 2 Dec. 1985.

In: A/40/53 (GAOR, 40th sess., Suppl. no. 53). - pp. 343-344.
Photo-offset.

A/RES/35/227

Question of Namibia.

Adopted at the 111th plenary meeting, 6 Mar. 1981.

In: A/35/48 (GAOR, 35th sess., Suppl. no. 48). - pp. 40-51.
Photo-offset.

A/RES/36/9

Importance of the universal realization of the right of peoples to self-determination and of the speedy granting of independence to colonial countries and peoples for the effective guarantee and observance of human rights.

Adopted at the 42nd plenary meeting, 28 Oct. 1981.

In: A/36/51 (GAOR, 36th sess., Suppl. no. 51). - pp. 160-161.
Photo-offset.

A/RES/36/51

Activities of foreign economic and other interests which are impeding the implementation of the Declaration on the Granting of Independence to Colonial Countries and Peoples in Namibia and in all other territories under colonial domination and efforts to eliminate colonialism, apartheid and racial discrimination in southern Africa.

Adopted at the 70th plenary meeting, 24 Nov. 1981.

In: A/36/51 (GAOR, 36th sess., Suppl. no.51). - pp. 201-203.
Photo-offset.

A/RES/36/52
Implementation of the Declaration on the Granting of Independence to
Colonial Countries and Peoples by the specialized agencies and the
international institutions associated with the United Nations.
    Adopted at the 70th plenary meeting, 24 Nov. 1981.
    In: A/36/51 (GAOR, 36th sess., Suppl. no. 51). - pp. 203-206.
Photo-offset.

A/RES/36/86
Implementation of the Declaration on the Denuclearization of Africa.
    Adopted at the 91st plenary meeting, 9 Dec. 1981.
    In: A/36/51 (GAOR, 36th sess., Suppl. no. 51). - pp. 56-57.
Photo-offset.

A/RES/36/121
Question of Namibia.
    Adopted at the 93rd plenary meeting, 10 Dec. 1981.
    In: A/36/51 (GAOR, 36th sess., Suppl. no. 51). - pp. 29-38.
Photo-offset.

A/RES/36/172
Policies of apartheid of the Government of South Africa.
    Adopted at the 102nd plenary meeting, 17 Dec. 1981.
    In: A/36/51 (GAOR, 36th sess., Suppl. no. 51). - pp. 38-47.
Photo-offset.

A/RES/37/2
South Africa's application for credit from the International Monetary Fund.
    Adopted at the 40th plenary meeting, 21 Oct. 1982.
    In: A/37/51 (GAOR, 37th sess., Suppl. no. 51). - p. 14.
Photo-offset.

A/RES/37/31
Activities of foreign economic and other interests which are impeding the
implementation of the Declaration on the Granting of Independence to
Colonial Countries and Peoples in Namibia and in all other territories under
colonial domination and efforts to eliminate colonialism, apartheid and
racial discrimination in southern Africa.
    Adopted at the 77th plenary meeting, 23 Nov. 1982.
    In: A/37/51 (GAOR, 37th sess., Suppl. no. 51). - pp. 228-230.
Photo-offset.

A/RES/37/32
   Implementation of the Declaration on the Granting of Independence to
   Colonial Countries and Peoples by the specialized agencies and the
   international institutions associated with the United Nations.
      Adopted at the 77th plenary meeting, 23 Nov. 1982.
      In: A/37/51 (GAOR, 37th sess., Suppl. no. 51). - pp. 230-233.
   Photo-offset.

A/RES/37/39
   Adverse consequences for the enjoyment of human rights of political,
   military, economic and other forms of assistance given to the racist and
   colonialist régime of South Africa.
      Adopted at the 90th plenary meeting, 3 Dec. 1982.
      In: A/37/51 (GAOR, 37th sess., Suppl. no. 51). - pp. 172-174.
   Photo-offset.

A/RES/37/43
   Importance of the universal realization of the right of peoples to
   self-determination and of the speedy granting of independence to colonial
   countries and peoples for the effective guarantee and observance of human
   rights.
      Adopted at the 90th plenary meeting, 3 Dec. 1982.
      In: A/37/51 (GAOR, 37th sess., Suppl. no. 51). - pp. 177-179.
   Photo-offset.

A/RES/37/69
   Policies of apartheid of the Government of South Africa.
      Adopted at the 97th plenary meeting, 9 Dec. 1982.
      In: A/37/51 (GAOR, 37th sess., Suppl. no. 51). - pp. 28-34.
   Photo-offset.

A/RES/37/74
   Implementation of the Declaration on the Denuclearization of Africa.
      Adopted at the 98th plenary meeting, 9 Dec. 1982.
      In: A/37/51 (GAOR, 37th sess., Suppl. no. 51). - pp. 55-56.
   Photo-offset.

A/RES/37/233
   Question of Namibia.
      Adopted at the 113th plenary meeting, 20 Dec. 1982.
      In: A/37/51 (GAOR, 37th sess., Suppl. no. 51). - pp. 40-48.
   Photo-offset.

A/RES/38/17

Importance of the universal realization of the right of peoples to self-determination and of the speedy granting of independence to colonial countries and peoples for the effective guarantee and observance of human rights.
Adopted at the 66th plenary meeting, 22 Nov. 1983.
In: A/38/47 (GAOR, 38th sess., Suppl. no. 47). - pp. 185-187.
Photo-offset.

A/RES/38/36

Question of Namibia.
Adopted at the 79th plenary meeting, 1 Dec. 1983.
In: A/38/47 (GAOR, 38th sess., Suppl. no. 47). - pp. 25-36.
Photo-offset.

A/RES/38/39

Policies of apartheid of the Government of South Africa.
Adopted at the 83rd plenary meeting, 5 Dec. 1983.
In: A/38/47 (GAOR, 38th sess., Suppl. no. 47). - pp. 36-42.
Photo-offset.

A/RES/38/50

Activities of foreign economic and other interests which are impeding the implementation of the Declaration on the Granting of Independence to Colonial Countries and Peoples in Namibia and in all other territories under colonial domination and efforts to eliminate colonialism, apartheid and racial discrimination in southern Africa.
Adopted at the 86th plenary meeting, 7 Dec. 1983.
In: A/38/47 (GAOR, 38th sess., Suppl. no. 47). - pp. 230-233.
Photo-offset.

A/RES/38/51

Implementation of the Declaration on the Granting of Independence to Colonial Countries and Peoples by the specialized agencies and the international institutions associated with the United Nations.
Adopted at the 86th plenary meeting, 7 Dec. 1983.
In: A/38/47 (GAOR, 36th sess., Suppl. no. 47). - pp. 233-235.
Photo-offset.

A/RES/38/181

Implementation of the Declaration on the Denuclearization of Africa.
Adopted at the 103rd plenary meeting, 20 Dec. 1983.
In: A/38/47 (GAOR, 38th sess., Suppl. no. 47). - pp. 70-71.
Photo-offset.

A/RES/39/15
Adverse consequences for the enjoyment of human rights of political,
military, economic and other forms of assistance given to the racist and
colonialist régime of South Africa.
Adopted at the 71st plenary meeting, 23 Nov. 1984.
In: A/39/51 (GAOR, 39th sess., Suppl. no. 51). - pp. 184-186.
Photo-offset.

A/RES/39/17
Importance of the universal realization of the right of peoples to
self-determination and of the speedy granting of independence to colonial
countries and peoples for the effective guarantee and observance of human
rights.
Adopted at the 71st plenary meeting, 23 Nov. 1984.
In: A/39/51 (GAOR, 39th sess., Suppl. no. 51). - pp. 187-189.
Photo-offset.

A/RES/39/42
Activities of foreign economic and other interests which are impeding the
implementation of the Declaration on the Granting of Independence to
Colonial Countries and Peoples in Namibia and in all other territories under
colonial domination and efforts to eliminate colonialism, apartheid and
racial discrimination in southern Africa.
Adopted at the 87th plenary meeting, 5 Dec. 1984.
In: A/39/51 (GAOR, 39th sess., Suppl. no. 51). - pp. 248-250.
Photo-offset.

A/RES/39/43
Implementation of the Declaration on the Granting of Independence to
Colonial Countries and Peoples by the specialized agencies and the
international institutions associated with the United Nations.
Adopted at the 87th plenary meeting, 5 Dec. 1984.
In: A/39/51 (GAOR, 39th sess., Suppl. no. 51). - pp. 250-254.
Photo-offset.

A/RES/39/50
Question of Namibia.
Adopted at the 97th plenary meeting, 12 Dec. 1984.
In: A/39/51 (GAOR, 39th sess., Suppl. no. 51). - pp. 28-39.
Photo-offset.

A/RES/39/61
Implementation of the Declaration on the Denuclearization of Africa.
Adopted at the 97th plenary meeting, 12 Dec. 1984.
In: A/39/51 (GAOR, 39th sess., Suppl. no. 51). - pp. 64-66.
Photo-offset.

A/RES/39/72
  Policies of _apartheid_ of the Government of South Africa.
    Adopted at the 99th plenary meeting, 13 Dec. 1984.
    In: A/39/51 (GAOR, 39th sess., Suppl. no. 51). - pp. 40-45.
  Photo-offset.

A/RES/40/25
  Importance of the universal realization of the right of peoples to
  self-determination and of the speedy granting of independence to colonial
  countries and peoples for the effective guarantee and observance of human
  rights.
    Adopted at the 96th plenary meeting, 29 Nov. 1985.
    In: A/40/53 (GAOR, 40th sess., Suppl. no. 53). - pp. 196-199.
  Photo-offset.

A/RES/40/27
  Status of the International Convention on the Suppression and Punishment of
  the Crime of _Apartheid_.
    Adopted at the 96th plenary meeting, 29 Nov. 1985.
    In: A/40/53 (GAOR, 40th sess., Suppl. no. 53). - pp. 199-200.
  Photo-offset.

A/RES/40/52
  Activities of foreign economic and other interests which are impeding the
  implementation of the Declaration on the Granting of Independence to
  Colonial Countries and Peoples in Namibia and in all other Territories under
  colonial domination and efforts to eliminate colonialism, _apartheid_ and
  racial discrimination in southern Africa.
    Adopted at the 99th plenary meeting, 2 Dec. 1985.
    In: A/40/53 (GAOR, 40th sess., Suppl. no. 53). - pp. 269-272.
  Photo-offset.

A/RES/40/53
  Implementation of the Declaration on the Granting of Independence to
  Colonial Countries and Peoples by the specialized agencies and the
  international institutions associated with the United Nations.
    Adopted at the 99th plenary meeting, 2 Dec. 1985.
    In: A/40/53 (GAOR, 40th sess., Suppl. no. 53). - pp. 272-275.
  Photo-offset.

A/RES/40/56
  Twenty-fifth anniversary of the Declaration on the Granting of Independence
  to Colonial Countries and Peoples.
    Adopted at the 99th plenary meeting, 2 Dec. 1986.
    In: A/40/53 (GAOR, 40th sess., Suppl. no. 53). - pp.26-28.
  Photo-offset.

A/RES/40/64
    Policies of apartheid of the Government of South Africa.
        Adopted at the 111th plenary meeting, 10 Dec. 1985.
        In: A/40/53 (GAOR, 40th sess., Suppl. no. 53). - pp. 32-41.
        Includes text of International Convention against Apartheid in Sports.
    Photo-offset.

A/RES/40/89
    Implementation of the Declaration on the Denuclearization of Africa.
        Adopted at the 113th plenary meeting, 12 Dec. 1985.
        In: A/40/53 (GAOR, 40th sess., Suppl. no. 53). - pp. 74-75.
    Photo-offset.

A/RES/40/97
    Question of Namibia.
        Adopted at the 115th plenary meeting, 13 Dec. 1985.
        In: A/40/53 (GAOR, 40th sess., Suppl. no. 53). - pp. 44-57.
    Photo-offset.

A/RES/41/14
    Activities of foreign economic and other interests which are impeding the
    implementation of the Declaration on the Granting of Independence to
    Colonial Countries and Peoples in Namibia and in all other territories under
    colonial domination and efforts to eliminate colonialism, apartheid and
    racial discrimination in Southern Africa.
        Adopted at the 52nd plenary meeting, 31 Oct. 1986.
        In: A/41/53 (GAOR, 41st sess., Suppl. no. 53).
    Photo-offset.

A/RES/41/15
    Implementation of the Declaration on the Granting of Independence to
    Colonial Countries and Peoples by the specialized agencies and the
    international institutions associated with the United Nations.
        Adopted at the 52nd plenary meeting, 31 Oct. 1986.
        In: A/41/53 (GAOR, 41st sess., Suppl. no. 53).
    Photo-offset.

A/RES/41/35
    Policies of apartheid of the Government of South Africa.
        Adopted at the 64th plenary meeting, 10 Nov. 1986.
        In: A/41/53 (GAOR, 41st sess., Suppl. no. 53).
    Photo-offset.

A/RES/41/55
   Implementation of the Declaration on the Denuclearization of Africa.
      Adopted at the 94th plenary meeting, 3 Dec. 1986.
         In: A/41/53 (GAOR, 41st sess., Suppl. no. 53).
      Photo-offset.

A/RES/ES-8/2
   Question of Namibia.
      Adopted at the 12th plenary meeting, 14 Sep. 1981.
         In: A/ES-8/13 (GAOR, 8th emergency special sess., Suppl. no. 1). -
      pp. 3-4.
      Photo-offset.

A/RES/S-14/1
   Question of Namibia.
      Adopted at the 7th plenary meeting, 20 Sept. 1986.
         In: A/S-14/10 (GAOR, 14th special sess., Suppl. no. 1).
      Photo-offset.

E/1981/25
E/CN.4/1475
   Commission on Human Rights: report on the thirty-seventh session, 2
   February-13 March 1981. - New York : UN, 1981.
      xv, 302 p., including annexes. - (ESCOR, 1981, Suppl. no. 5).
   Photo-offset.
   Includes resolutions 1981/5 and 8.

E/1981/49
E/C.10/92
   Commission on Transnational Corporations: report on the seventh session,
   31 August-11 September 1981. New York : UN, 1981.
      iii, 43 p., including index (ESCOR, 1981, Suppl. no. 9).
   Photo-offset.

E/1982/12
E/CN.4/1982/30
   Commission on Human Rights : report on the thirty-eighth session, 1 February
   -12 March 1982. - New York : UN, 1982.
      [xv, 220] p., including annexes : tables (ESCOR, 1982, Suppl. no. 2).
      Includes resolutions 1982/12 and 20.
   Photo-offset.

E/1982/18
E/C.10/1982/19
   Commission on Transnational Corporations: report on the eighth session,
   30 August-10 September 1982. - New York : UN, 1982.
      iii, 50 p. (ESCOR, 1982, Suppl. no. 8).
   Photo-offset.

E/1983/9
   Decade for Action to Combat Racism and Racial Discrimination. - Report of
   the Preparatory Sub-Committee for the second World Conference to Combat
   Racism and Racial Discrimination on its second session, New York, 21-25
   March 1983. - [New York] : UN, 31 March 1983.
      36 p.
   Mimeographed.

E/1983/13
E/CN.4/1983/60
   Commission on Human Rights : report on the thirty-ninth session,
   31 January-11 March 1983. - New York : UN, 1983
      xv, 261 p. - (ESCOR, 1983, Suppl. no. 3).
      Includes resolutions 1983/4 and 11.
   Photo-offset.

E/1983/18/Rev.1
E/C.10/1983/15
   Commission on Transnational Corporations : report on the ninth session,
20-30
   June 1983. - New York : UN, 1983.
      iv, 53 p. - (ESCOR, 1983, Suppl. no. 7A).
   Photo-offset.

E/1984/14
E/CN.4/1984/77
   Commission on Human Rights : report on the fortieth session, 6 February-
   16 March 1984. - New York : UN, 1984.
      xiv, 260 p. : tables. - (ESCOR, 1984, Suppl. no. 4).
      Includes resolutions 1984/6, 14 and 40.
   Photo-offset.

E/1984/18
E/C.10/1984/20
   Commission on Transnational Corporations : report on the tenth session,
   17-27 April 1984. - New York : UN, 1984.
      iv, 53 p. : table. - (ESCOR, 1984, Suppl. no. 8).
   Photo-offset.

E/1985/22
E/CN.4/1985/66
    Commission on Human Rights : report on the forty-first session,
    4 February-15 March 1985. - New York : UN, 1985.
       xii, 294 p. - (ESCOR, 1985, Suppl. no. 2).
    Photo-offset.
    Includes resolutions 1985/6 and 9.

E/1985/28
E/C.10/1985/19
    Commission on Transnational Corporations : report on the eleventh session,
    10-19 April 1985. - New York : UN, 1985.
       iv, 53 p. - (ESCOR, 1985, Suppl. no. 8).
    Photo-offset.

E/1986/14
    Implementation of the Programme of Action for the Second Decade to Combat
    Racism and Racial Discrimination. - Report of the Secretary-General,
    prepared in accordance with paragraph 10 of General Assembly resolution
    39/16. - [New York] : UN, 18 Feb. 1986.
       13 p.
    Transmits summary of reports submitted by Governments.
    Photo-offset.

E/1986/22
E/CN.4/1986/65
    Commission on Human Rights : report on the forty-second session, 3 February-
    14 March 1986. - New York : UN, 1986.
       xiv, 360 p. (ESCOR, 1986, Suppl. no. 2).
    Photo-offset.
    Includes resolutions 1986/4-7.

E/1986/27
E/C.10/1986/19
    Commission on Transnational Corporations : report of the twelfth session,
    9-18 April 1986. - New York : UN, 1986.
       iv, 54 p. - (ESCOR, 1986, Suppl. no. 7).
    Photo-offset.

E/1986/37
    Human rights. - Allegations regarding infringement of trade-union rights in
    South Africa : note by the Secretary-General. - [New York] : UN, 24 Mar.
    1986.
       12 p.
    Transmits extract from the report of the Ad Hoc Working Group of Experts
      on Southern Africa (E/CN.4/1986/9).
    Photo-offset.

E/1986/114
    Implementation of the Declaration on the Granting of Independence to
    Colonial Countries and Peoples by the specialized agencies and the
    international institutions associated with the United Nations. - Report of
    the President of the [Economic and Social] Council on consultations held
    with the Acting Chairman of the Special Committee on the Situation with
    regard to the Implementation of the Declaration on the Granting of
    Independence to Colonial Countries and Peoples and the Acting Chairman of
    the Special Committee against Apartheid. - [New York] : UN, 17 June 1986.
        9 p.
    Mimeographed.

E/C.10/83/Rev.1
    Transnational corporations in southern Africa : update on financial
    activities and employment practices. - New York : UN, 1982.
        iii, 44 p., including annex : tables
    Photo-offset.
    Sales No. 82.II.A.12

E/C.10/1982/11
    Studies on the effects of the operations and practices of transnational
    corporations.- Activities of transnational corporations in southern Africa
    and their collaboration with the racist minority régime in that area. -
    Measures taken pursuant to the resolution recommended by the Commission on
    Transnational Corporations at its seventh session and adopted by the
    Economic and Social Council : report of the Secretariat. - New York : UN,
    25 Jun. 1982
        18 p.
    Mimeographed.

E/C.10/1983/10/Rev.1
    Policies and practices of transnational corporations regarding their
    activities in South Africa and Namibia. - New York : UN, 1984.
        iv, 55 p. : tables.
        At head of title: United Nations Centre on Transnational Corporations. -
        Includes bibliographical references. - "List of transnational
        corporations which operate in strategic sections of the southern African
        economy, and of those that have taken measures to terminate their
        activities in such sectors": pp. 30-43.
    Photo-offset.
    Sales No. E.84.II.A.5.

E/C.10/1984/10

Policy analysis and research. - Activities of transnational corporations in South Africa and Namibia and their collaboration with the racist minority régime in that area. - Activities of transnational corporations and measures being taken by Governments to prohibit investments in South Africa and Namibia : report of the Secretary-General. - [New York] : UN, 30 Jan. 1984

12 p. : tables
Includes bibliographical references.
Mimeographed.

E/C.10/1984/19

Responsibilities of home countries with respect to the transnational corporations operating in South Africa and Namibia in violation of the relevant resolutions and decisions of the United Nations : report of the Secretariat. - [New York] : UN, 10 Feb. 1984.

24 p.
Mimeographed.

E/C.10/1984/19/Add.1

Responsibilities of home countries with respect to the transnational corporations operating in South Africa and Namibia in violation of the relevant resolutions and decisions of the United Nations. - [New York] : UN, 28 Mar. 1984.

4 p.
Summarises replies received from Governments.
Mimeographed.

E/C.10/1985/7

Transnational corporations in South Africa and Namibia. - Activities of transnational corporations in South Africa and Namibia and their collaboration with the racist minority régime in that area : report of the Secretary-General. - [New York] : UN, 30 Jan. 1985.

67 p. : tables.
Annex: List of transnational corporations that operate in South Africa and Namibia and of those that have taken measures to terminate their activities. - Includes bibliographical references.
Mimeographed.

E/C.10/1985/7/Corr.1

Transnational corporations in South Africa and Namibia. - Activities of transnational corporations in South Africa and Namibia and their collaboration with the racist minority régime in that area : report of the Secretary-General : corrigendum.
[New York] : UN, 12 Feb. 1985

1 p.
Corrects text.
Mimeographed.

E/C.10/1985/8

    Organization of public hearings on the activities of transnational corporations in South Africa and Namibia : report of the <u>Ad Hoc</u> Committee on the Preparations for the Public Hearings on the Activities of Transnational Corporations in South Africa and Namibia. - [New York] : UN, 28 Feb. 1985.
      28 p.
    Mimeographed.

E/C.10/1985/9

    Transnational corporations in South Africa and Namibia. - Responsibilities of home countries with respect to transnational corporations operating in South Africa and Namibia in violation of the relevant resolutions and decisions of the United Nations : report of the Secretariat. - [New York] : UN, 11 Feb. 1985.
      40 p. : table.
    Includes bibliographical references.
    Mimeographed.

E/C.10/1986/10

    Transnational corporations in South Africa and Namibia. - Responsibilities of home countries with respect to the transnational corporations operating in South Africa and Namibia in violation of the relevant resolutions and decisions of the United Nations : report of the Secretary-General. - [New York] : UN, 4 Feb. 1986.
      17 p.
    Includes bibliographical references.
    Photo-offset.

E/CN.4/1512
E/CN.4/Sub.2/495

    Report of the Sub-Commission on Prevention of Discrimination and Protection of Minorities on its twenty-fourth session, Geneva, 17 August-11 September 1981. - Geneva : UN, 28 Sept. 1981.
      [122] p., including annexes.
    Mimeographed.

E/CN.4/1983/4
E/CN.4/Sub.2/1982/43

    Report of the Sub-Commission on Prevention of Discrimination and Protection of Minorities on its thirty-fifth session, Geneva, 16 August-10 September 1982. - Geneva : UN, 29 Sept. 1982.
      x, 136 p., including annexes.
    Mimeographed.

E/CN.4/1984/3
E/CN.4/Sub.2/1983/43
   Report of the Sub-Commission on Prevention of Discrimination and Protection
of Minorities on its thirty-sixth session, Geneva, 15 August-9 September 1983.
Geneva : UN, 20 Oct. 1983.
     viii, 112, [26] p.
Mimeographed.

E/CN.4/1985/3
E/CN.4/Sub.2/1984/43
   Report of the Sub-Commission on Prevention of Discrimination and Protection
of Minorities on its thirty-seventh session, Geneva, 6-31 August 1984.
Geneva : UN, 19 Oct. 1984.
     ix, 116, [27] p. : tables.
Mimeographed.

E/CN.4/1985/28
   Implementation of the Programme of Action for the Second Decade to Combat
Racism and Racial Discrimination. - Annual report on racial discrimination
submitted by ILO in accordance with Economic and Social Council resolution
1588 (L) and General Assembly resolution 2785 (XXVI). - Geneva : UN, 8 Jan.
1985.
     4 p.
Mimeographed.

E/CN.4/1986/5
E/CN.4/Sub.2/1985/57
   Report of the Sub-Commission on Prevention of Discrimination and Protection
of Minorities on its thirty-eight session, Geneva, 5-30 August 1985. - Geneva
: UN, 4 Nov. 1985.
     ix, 123, [47] p. : tables
Mimeographed.

E/CN.4/1986/9
   Violations of human rights in Southern Africa : report of the Ad Hoc Working
Group of Experts. - Progress report prepared by the Ad Hoc Working Group
of Experts in accordance with Commission on Human Rights resolutions 1985/7
and 8 and Economic and Social Council resolution 1985/43. - Geneva :
UN, 28 Jan. 1986.
     iv, 104 p.
Mimeographed.

E/CN.4/1986/30

   Implementation of the International Convention on the Suppression and
   Punishment of the Crime of <u>Apartheid</u>. - Report of the Group of Three
   Established under the Convention - Geneva : UN, 31 Jan. 1986.
      10 p.
   Mimeographed.

E/CN.4/1986/31

   Implementation of the Programme of Action for the Second Decade to Combat
   Racism and Racial Discrimination. - Annual report on racial discrimination
   submitted by ILO in accordance with Economic and Social Council resolution
   1588 (L) and General Assembly resolution 2785 (XXVI). - Geneva : UN, 20 Jan.
   1986.
      4 p.
   Mimeographed.

E/CN.4/1987/27

   Implementation of the International Convention on the Suppression and
   Punishment of the Crime of <u>Apartheid</u> : views and information submitted by
   States parties in accordance with Commission resolution
   1986/7 : note by the Secretary-General. - Geneva : UN, 15 Oct. 1986.
      10 p.
   Mimeographed.

E/CN.4/1987/27/Add.1

   Implementation of the International Convention on the Suppression and
   Punishment of the Crime of <u>Apartheid</u> : views and information submitted by
   States parties in accordance with Commission resolution
   1986/7 : note by the Secretary-General. - Geneva : UN, 24 Dec. 1986.
      5 p.
   Mimeographed.

E/CN.4/Sub.2/469

   Adverse consequences for the enjoyment of human rights of political,
   military, economic and other forms of assistance given to colonial and
   racist régimes in southern Africa : updated report prepared by Mr. Ahmed
   Khalifa, Special Rapporteur, in pursuance of Economic and Social Council
   decision 1981/141. - Geneva : UN, 31 Jul. 1981.
      [38] p., including annexes.
   Mimeographed.

E/CN.4/Sub.2/469/Add.1
   Adverse consequences for the enjoyment of human rights of political,
   military, economic and other forms of assistance given to colonial and
   racist régimes in southern Africa :   updated report prepared by Mr. Ahmed
   Khalifa, Special Rapporteur, in pursuance of Economic and Social Council
   decision 1981/141. - Geneva : UN, 6 Nov. 1981.
      2 p.
   Mimeographed.

E/CN.4/Sub.2/1982/10
   Adverse consequences for the enjoyment of human rights of political,
   military, economic and other forms of assistance given to colonial and
   racist régimes in southern Africa : report prepared by Mr. Ahmed Khalifa,
   Special Rapporteur. - Geneva : UN, 30 Jun. 1982.
      ii, [37] p., including annexes : tables
   Mimeographed.

E/CN.4/Sub.2/1983/6
   Adverse consequences for the enjoyment of human rights of political,
   military, economic and other forms of assistance given to colonial and
   racist régimes in southern Africa : updated report prepared by Ahmed M.
   Khalifa, Special Rapporteur. - Geneva : UN, 20 July 1983.
      17 p.
   Transmits list of documents concerning assistance to South Africa.
   Mimeographed.

E/CN.4/Sub.2/1984/6/Add.1
   Review of further developments in fields with which the Sub-Commission
   has been concerned. - Memorandum submitted by the International Labour Office.
   - Geneva : UN, 15 June 1984.
      5 p.
   Mimeographed.

E/CN.4/Sub.2/1984/8/Rev.1
   Adverse consequences for the enjoyment of human rights of political,
   military, economic and other forms of assistance given to the racist and
   colonialist régime of South Africa / by Ahmed M. Khalifa, Special
   Rapporteur (of the Sub-Commission on Prevention of Discrimination and
   Protection of Minorities). - New York : UN, 1985.
      1 v. (various pagings) : tables.
   Mimeographed.
   Sales No. E.85.XIV.4.

E/CN.4/Sub.2/1985/7
   Elimination of racial discrimination. - Measures to combat racism and
   racial discrimination and the role of the Sub-Commission. - Study on the
   achievements made and obstacles encountered during the first Decade to
   Combat Racism and Racial Discrimination. - 1st part, Description. - Report
   by Asbjorn Eide, Special Rapporteur. - Geneva : UN, 31 July 1985.
      32 p.- Includes bibliographical references.
   Mimeographed.

E/CN.4/Sub.2/1985/8
   Adverse consequences for the enjoyment of human rights of political,
   military, economic and other forms of assistance given to the racist and
   colonialist régime of South Africa : updated report prepared by Ahmed M.
   Khalifa, Special Rapporteur. - Geneva : UN, 16 July 1985.
      23 p.
   Mimeographed.

E/RES/1981/54
   Implementation of the Declaration on the Granting of Independence to
   Colonial Countries and Peoples and assistance to the oppressed people of
   South Africa and their national liberation movement by the specialized
   agencies and the international institutions associated with the United
   Nations.
      Adopted at the 39th plenary meeting, 22 July 1981.
      In: E/1981/81/Add.1 (ESCOR, 1981, Suppl. no. 1A). - pp. 8-10.
   Printed.

E/RES/1981/86
   Activities of transnational corporations in southern Africa and their
   collaboration with the racist minority régime in that area.
      Adopted at the 43rd plenary meeting, 2 Nov. 1981.
      In: E/1981/81/Add.2 (ESCOR, 1981, Suppl. no. 1B). - pp. 4-5.
   Photo-offset.

E/RES/1982/47
   Implementation of the Declaration on the Granting of Independence to
   Colonial Countries and Peoples by the specialized agencies and the
   international institutions associated with the United Nations and
   assistance to the oppressed people of South Africa and their national
   liberation movement by agencies and institutions within the United Nations
   system.
      Adopted at the 48th plenary meeting, 27 July 1982.
      In: E/1982/82/Add.1 (ESCOR, 1982, Suppl. no. 1A). - pp. 8-10.
   Printed.

E/RES/1982/69

   Activities of transnational corporations in southern Africa and their
   collaboration with the racist minority régime in that area.
      Adopted at the 54th plenary meeting, 27 Oct. 1982.
      In: E/1982/82/Add.2 (ESCOR, 1982, Suppl. no. 1B). - pp. 5-6.
   Photo-offset.

E/RES/1982/70

   Public hearings on the activities of transnational corporations in South
   Africa and Namiba.
      Adopted at the 54th plenary meeting, 27 Oct. 1982.
      In: E/1982/82/Add.2 (ESCOR, 1982, Suppl. no. 1B). - p. 6.
   Photo-offset.

E/RES/1983/42

   Implementation of the Declaration on the Granting of Independence to
   Colonial Countries and Peoples by the specialized agencies and the
   international institutions associated with the United Nations and assistance
   to the oppressed people of South Africa and their national liberation
   movements by agencies and institutions within the United Nations system.
      Adopted at the 39th plenary meeting, 25 July 1983.
      In: E/1983/83/Add.1 (ESCOR, 1983, Suppl. no. 1A). - pp. 5-7.
   Photo-offset.

E/RES/1983/74

   Activities of transnational corporations in South Africa and Namibia and
   collaboration of such corporations with the racist minority régime in South
   Africa.
      Adopted at the 41st plenary meeting, 29 July 1983.
      In: E/1983/83/Add.1 (ESCOR, 1983, Suppl. no. 1A). - pp. 29-31.
   Photo-offset.

E/RES/1984/53

   Activities of transnational corporations in South Africa and Namibia and
   their collaboration with the racist minority régime in South Africa.
      Adopted at the 28th plenary meeting, 26th July 1984.
      In: E/1984/84/Add.1 (ESCOR, 1984, Suppl. no. 1A). - pp. 8-11.
   Photo-offset.

E/RES/1984/55

   Implementation of the Declaration on the Granting of Independence to
   Colonial Countries and Peoples by the specialized agencies and the
   international institutions associated with the United Nations.
      Adopted at the 48th plenary meeting, 25 July 1984.
      In: E/1984/84/Add.1 (ESCOR, 1984, Suppl. no. 1A). - pp. 7-9.
   Photo-offset.

E/RES/1985/59
   Implementation of the Declaration on the Granting of Independence to
   Colonial Countries and Peoples by the specialized agencies and the
   international institutions associated with the United Nations.
      Adopted at the 52nd plenary meeting, 26 July 1985.
      In: E/1985/85/Add.1 (ESCOR, 1985, Suppl. no. 1A). - pp. 13-15.
   Photo-offset.

E/RES/1985/72
   Activities of transnational corporations in South Africa and Namibia and
   their collaboration with the racist minority régime of South Africa.
      Adopted at the 52nd plenary meeting, 26 July 1985.
      In: E/1985/85/Add.1 (ESCOR, 1985. Suppl. no. 1A). - pp. 21-22.
   Photo-offset.

E/RES/1986/1
   Activities of transnational corporations in South Africa and Namibia and
   follow-up to the report of the Panel of Eminent Persons Established to
   Conduct the Public Hearings on the Activities of Transnational Corporations
   in South Africa and Namibia.
      Adopted at the 15th plenary meeting, 19 May 1986.
      In: E/1986/86 (ESCOR, 1986, Suppl. no. 1).
   Photo-offset.

E/RES/1986/22
   Women and children under apartheid.
      Adopted at the 19th plenary meeting, 23 May 1986.
      In: E/1986/86 (ESCOR, 1986, Suppl. no. 1).
   Photo-offset.

E/RES/1986/48
   Implementation of the Declaration on the Granting of Independence to
   Colonial Countries and Peoples by the specialized agencies and the
   international institutions associated with the United Nations.
      Adopted at the 38th plenary meeting, 22 July 1986.
      In: E/1986/86/Add. 1 (ESCOR, 1986, Suppl. no. 1A). - pp. 7-9.
   Photo-offset.

S/14329
   Note by the Secretary-General. - New York : UN, 16 Jan. 1981.
      1 p.
      Includes paragraphs 5 and 7 of General Assembly resolution 35/146A
      and paragraph 5 of resolution 35/146B.
   Mimeographed.

S/14359

    Note by the Secretary-General. - New York : UN, 4 Feb. 1981.
      3 p.
      Includes paragraphs of General Assembly resolutions 35/206 A-Q calling
      for action by the Security Council.
    Mimeographed.

S/14423

    Note by the Secretary-General. - New York : UN, 1 Apr. 1981.
      2 p.
      Includes paragraphs of General Assembly resolutions 35/227 A-J relating
      the Namibia question.
    Mimeographed.

S/14486

    Note by the President of the Security Council.
    New York : UN, 25 May 1981.
      2 p.
      Concerns apartheid.
    Mimeographed.

S/14700

    Note by the Secretary-General. - New York : UN, 18 Sep. 1981.
      1 p.
      Includes paragraph 12 of General Assembly resolution ES-8/2 concerning
      the Namibia question.
    Mimeographed.

S/14765

    Note by the Secretary-General. - New York : UN, 23 Nov. 1981.
      1 p.
      Concerns sanctions against South Africa.
    Mimeographed.

S/14794

    Note by the President of the Security Council.
    New York : UN, 15 Dec. 1981.
      1 p.
      Concerns proclamation by South Africa of independence of Ciskei.
    Mimeographed.

S/14867

    Note by the Secretary-General. - New York : UN, 12 Feb. 1982.
      1 p.
      Concerns the Namibia question. - Transmits General Assembly resolu-
      tion 36/121.
    Mimeographed.

S/15062

    Note verbale dated 5 May 1982 from the Permanent Representative of Denmark to the United Nations addressed to the Secretary-General. - New York : UN, 10 May 1982.

      2 p.

    Concerns arms embargo against South Africa.

    Mimeographed.

S/15080

    Letter dated 14 May 1982 from the Permanent Representative of Romania to the United Nations addressed to the President of the Security Council. - New York : UN, 14 May 1982.

      2 p.

    Concerns arms embargo against South Africa.

    Mimeographed.

S/15247

    Letter dated 15 June 1982 from the Acting Chairman of the Special Committee against Apartheid addressed to the Secretary-General. - New York : UN, 22 Jun. 1982.

      2 p.

    Transmits statement adopted on 14 Jun. 1982 for the attention of the General Assembly (12th spec. sess.).

    Mimeographed.

S/15580

    Note by the Secretary-General. - New York : UN, 1 Feb. 1983.

      1 p.

    Includes paragraph 5 of General Assembly resolution 37/39 requesting the Council to consider mandatory sanctions against South Africa.

    Mimeographed.

S/15581

    Note by the Secretary-General. - New York : UN, 1 Feb. 1983.

      1 p.

    Includes paragraph 8 of General Assembly resolution 37/40 requesting the Council to consider mandatory sanctions against South Africa.

    Mimeographed.

S/16050

    Letter dated 17 October 1983 from the Chairman of the Special Committee on the Situation with regard to the Implementation of the Declaration on the Granting of Independence to Colonial Countries and Peoples addressed to the President of the Security Council. - New York : UN, 18 Oct. 1983.

      2 p.

    Transmits decision on the question of Namibia.

    Mimeographed.

S/16266

    Report of the Secretary-General concerning the implementation of Security Council resolution 546 (1984) relating to a complaint by Angola against South Africa. - New York : UN, 10 Jan. 1984.
      3 p.
    Includes text of Security Council resolution 546 (1984).
Mimeographed.

S/16320

    Note by the Secretary-General. - |New York] : UN, 6 Feb. 1984.
      1 p.
    Includes paragraph 3 of General Assembly resolution 38/14 requesting the Council to consider mandatory sanctions against South Africa.
Mimeographed.

S/16324

    Note by the Secretary-General. - |New York] : UN, 7 Feb. 1984.
      1 p.
    Includes paragraphs 5-6 of General Assembly resolution 38/181 on implementation of the Declaration on the Denuclearization of Africa.
Mimeographed.

S/16860

    Letter dated 13 December 1984 from the Chairman of the Security Council Committee Established by Resolution 421 (1977) concerning the Question of South Africa addressed to the President of the Security Council. - |New York] : UN, 13 Dec. 1984.
      2 p.
    Transmits a recommendation adopted at the Committee's 63rd meeting, 13 Dec. 1984.
Mimeographed.

S/17142

    Letter dated 26 April 1985 from the Chairman of the Special Committee against Apartheid addressed to the Secretary-General. - |New York] : UN, 3 May 1985.
      5 p.
    Transmits: Declaration adopted on 28 March 1985 by the Special Committee against Apartheid at the conclusion of its special session in commemoration of the 25th anniversary of the Sharpeville massacre.
Mimeographed.

S/17899

    Note by the Secretary-General. - |New York] : UN, 28 Feb. 1986.
      |1] p.
    Includes paragraph 20 of General Assembly resolution 40/56 on the 25th anniversary of the Declaration on the Granting of Independence to Colonial Countries and Peoples.
Photo-offset.

S/18160
>   Note by the President of the Security Council. - New York : UN,
> 16 June 1986.
>   2 p.
>   Tranmsmits message from the President of the Security Council to the
> World Conference on Sanctions against Racist South Africa.
> Mimeographed.

S/18272
>   Letter dated 13 August 1986 from the Acting Chairman of the Special
> Committee
> on the Situation with regard to the Implementation of the Declaration on the
> Granting of Independence to Colonial Countries and Peoples addressed to the
> President of the Security Council. - [New York] : UN, 14 Aug. 1986.
>   2 p.
>   Concerns consensus on the question of Namibia adopted by the Committee on
>   11 Aug. 1986.
> Photo-offset.

S/18278
>   Letter dated 13 August 1986 from the Acting Chairman of the Special
> Committee
> on the Situation with regard to the Implementation of the Declaration on the
> Granting of Independence to Colonial Countries and Peoples addressed to the
> President of the Security Council. - [New York] : UN, 15 Aug. 1986.
>   2 p.
>   Concerns decision adopted by the Committee at its 1301st meeting, 11 Aug.
>   1986, on military activities and arrangements by colonial powers in
>   territories under their administration which might be impeding the
>   implementation of the Declaration on the Granting of Independence to
>   Colonial Countries and Peoples.
> Photo-offset.

S/18288
>   Note by the President of the Security Council. - [New York] : UN, 20 Aug.
> 1986.
>   5 p.
>   Transmits report on the Seminar on the Arms Embargo against South Africa,
>   28-20 May 1986, by the Chairman of the Security Council Committee
>   Established by Resolution 421 (1977) concerning the Question of South
>   Africa.
> Photo-offset.

S/18314
>   Note verbale dated 29 August 1986 from the Permanent Mission of Denmark to
> the
> United Nations addressed to the Secretary-General. - [New York] : UN,
> 4 Sept. 1986.
>   2 p.
>   Transmits Decree of Amendment of the Decree of Certain Measures against
>   South Africa.
> Photo-offset.

S/18435

Note by the Secretary-General. - [New York] : UN, 30 Oct. 1986.
[1] p.
Includes paragraphs 15 and 19 of General Assembly resolution S-14/1
on the question of Namibia.
Photo-offset.

S/18474

Letter dated 24 November 1986 from the Chairman of the Security Council
Committee Established by Resolution 421 (1977) concerning the Question of
South Africa addressed to the President of the Security Council. - [New
York] : UN, 24 Nov. 1986.
3 p.
Concerns arms embargo against South Africa.
Photo-offset.

S/AC.20/32

Letter dated 15 May 1981 from the Permanent Representative of Spain to the
United Nations addressed to the Chairman of the Security Council Committee
Established by Resolution 421 (1977) concerning the question of South
Africa. - New York : UN, 18 May 1981.
1 p.
Concerns arms embargo against South Africa.
Mimeographed.

S/AC.20/33

Note verbale dated 6 November 1981 from the Permanent Representative of
Denmark to the United Nations addressed to the Chairman of the Security
Council Committee established by resolution 421 (1977) concerning the
question of South Africa. - New York : UN, 9 Nov. 1981.
2 p.
Concerns arms embargo against South Africa.
Mimeographed.

S/AC.20/34

Note verbale dated 29 January 1983 from the Acting Permanent Representative
of the United Kingdom of Great Britain and Northern Ireland to the United
Nations addressed to the Chairman of the Security Council Committee
Established by Resolution 421 (1977) concerning the Question of South
Africa. - New York : UN, 31 Jan. 1983.
2 p.
Concerns arms embargo against South Africa.
Mimeographed.

S/AC.20/35

    Note verbale dated 17 February 1983 from the Permanent Representative of Denmark to the United Nations addressed to the Chairman of the Security Council Committee Established by Resolution 421 (1977) concerning the Question of South Africa. - New York : UN, 18 Feb. 1983.

      2 p.

    Concerns arms embargo against South Africa.

    Mimeographed.

S/AC.20/36

    Note verbale dated 9 May 1983 from the Permanent Representative of the United Kingdom of Great Britain and Northern Ireland to the United Nations addressed to the Chairman of the Security Council Committee Established by Resolution 421 (1977) concerning the Question of South Africa. - New York : UN, 12 May 1983.

      1 p.

    Mimeographed.

S/AC.20/37

    Note verbale dated 15 January 1985 from the Permanent Representative of Denmark to the United Nations addressed to the Chairman of the Security Council Committee Established by Resolution 421 (1977) concerning the Question of South Africa. - [New York] : UN, 16 Jan. 1985.

      1 p.

    Concerns arms embargo against South Africa.

    Mimeographed.

S/AC.20/38

    Report of the Secretary-General on the implementation of Security Council resolution 558 (1984). - [New York] : UN, 20 Dec. 1985.

      41 p. : tables.

      Includes Security Council resolution 558 (1984) and transmits replies received from States.

    Mimeographed.

S/AC.20/38/Add.1

    Report of the Secretary-General on the implementation of Security Council resolution 558 (1984). - [New York] : UN, 31 Dec. 1985.

      2 p.

    Transmits reply received from Netherlands.

    Mimeographed.

S/AC.20/38/Add.2

    Report of the Secretary-General on the implementation of Security Council resolution 558 (1984). - [New York] : UN, 24 Jan. 1986.

      2 p.

    Transmits replies received from States.

    Mimeographed.

S/AC.20/38/Add.3
   Report of the Secretary-General on the implementation of Security Council
   resolution 558 (1984). - [New York] : UN, 14 Feb. 1986.
      2 p.
      Transmits replies received from States.
   Mimeographed.

S/AC.20/38/Add.4
   Report of the Secretary-General on the implementation of Security Council
   resolution 558 (1984). - [New York] : UN, 14 Mar. 1986.
      2 p.
      Transmits reply received from New Zealand.
   Photo-offset.

S/AC.20/38/Add.5
   Report of the Secretary-General on the implementation of Security Council
   resolution 558 (1984). - [New York] : UN, 29 May 1986.
      2 p.
      Transmits reply received from Ireland.
   Photo-offset.

S/AC.20/38/Add.6
   Report of the Secretary-General on the implementation of Security Council
   resolution 558 (1984). - [New York] : UN, 10 July 1986.
      2 p.
      Transmits reply received from Norway.
   Photo-offset.

S/RES/546(1984)
   Complaint by Angola against South Africa : resolution 546 (1984).
      Adopted at the 2511th meeting, 6 Jan. 1984.
      In: S/INF/40 (SCOR, 39th year, 1984). - pp. 1-2.
   Photo-offset.

S/RES/558(1984)
   The question of South Africa : resolution 558 (1984).
      Adopted at the 2564th meeting, 13 Dec. 1984.
      In: S/INF/40 (SCOR, 39th year, 1984). - p. 5.
   Photo-offset.

S/RES/566(1985)
   The situation in Namibia : resolution 566 (1985).
      Adopted at the 2595th meeting, 19 June 1985.
      In: S/INF/41 (SCOR, 40th year, 1985). - pp. 11-12.
   Photo-offset.

S/RES/569(1985)
   The question of South Africa : resolution 569 (1985).
      Adopted at the 2602nd meeting, 26 July 1985.
         In: S/INF/41 (SCOR, 40th year, 1985). - pp. 8-9.
   Photo-offset.

S/RES/571(1985)
   Complaint by Angola against South Africa : resolution 571 (1985).
      Adopted at the 2607th meeting, 20 Sept. 1985.
         In: S/INF/41 (SCOR, 40th year, 1985). - pp. 16-17.
   Photo-offset.

S/RES/574(1985)
   Complaint by Angola against South Africa : resolution 574 (1985).
      Adopted at the 2617th meeting, 7 Oct. 1985.
         In: S/INF/41 (SCOR, 40th year, 1985). - p. 18.
   Photo-offset.

S/RES/591(1986)
   The question of South Africa : resolution 591 (1986).
      Adopted at the 2723rd meeting, 28 Nov. 1986.
         In: S/INF/42 (SCOR, 41st year, 1986). - pp. 17-18.
   Photo-offset.

ST/CTC/68
   Transnational corporations in South Africa and Namibia : United Nations
   public hearings. Volume 1, Reports of the Panel of Eminent Persons and of
   the Secretary-General. - New York : UN, 1986.
      xvi, 242 p. : tables.
      Bibliography: pp. 169-242.
   Photo-offset.
   Sales No. E.86.II.A.6.
   Price: $US 65.00.

ST/CTC/68
   Transnational corporations in South Africa and Namibia : United Nations
   public hearings. Volume 2, Verbatim records. - New York : UN, 1986.
      x, 282 p.
      "Annex I: Members of the Panel": p. 274 (1st group) - "Annex II: Terms of
      reference of the Panel": p. 275 (2nd group) - "Annex III: List of
      participants": pp. 276-278 (3rd group).
   Photo-offset.
   Sales No. E.86.II.A.7.
   Price: $US 200.00 (4 v. set).

ST/CTC/84
    Activities of transnational corporations in South Africa and Namibia and the
    responsibilities of home countries with respect to their operations in this
    area. - New York : UN, 1986.
        iii, 59 p. : tables.
        Includes bibliographical references.
    Photo-offset.
    Sales No. E.85.II.A.16.
    Price: $US 7.00.

ST/HR/SER.A/9
    Seminar on Effective Measures to Prevent Transnational Corporations and
    Other Established Interests from Collaborating with the Racist Régime of
    South Africa, Geneva, 29 June-3 July 1981. - New York : UN, 1981.
        ii, [50] p., including annexes.
    Printed.

ST/LIB/SER.B/32
    Sanctions against South Africa : a selective bibliography. - New York : UN,
    1981.
        vii, 28 p. - (Bibliographical series ; no. 32).
    Photo-offset.
    Price: $US 4.00.

كيفية الحصول على منشورات الأمم المتحدة

يمكن الحصول على منشورات الأمم المتحدة من المكتبات ودور التوزيع في جميع أنحاء العالم . استعلم عنها من المكتبة التي تتعامل معها أو اكتب إلى : الأمم المتحدة ، قسم البيع في نيويورك أو في جنيف .

如何购取联合国出版物

联合国出版物在全世界各地的书店和经售处均有发售。请向书店询问或写信到纽约或日内瓦的 联合国销售组。

HOW TO OBTAIN UNITED NATIONS PUBLICATIONS

United Nations publications may be obtained from bookstores and distributors throughout the world. Consult your bookstore or write to: United Nations, Sales Section, New York or Geneva.

COMMENT SE PROCURER LES PUBLICATIONS DES NATIONS UNIES

Les publications des Nations Unies sont en vente dans les librairies et les agences dépositaires du monde entier. Informez-vous auprès de votre libraire ou adressez-vous à : Nations Unies, Section des ventes, New York ou Genève.

КАК ПОЛУЧИТЬ ИЗДАНИЯ ОРГАНИЗАЦИИ ОБЪЕДИНЕННЫХ НАЦИЙ

Издания Организации Объединенных Наций можно купить в книжных магазинах и агентствах во всех рснах мира. Наводите справки об изданиях в вашем книжном магазине или пишите по адресу: Организация Объединенных Наций, Секция по продаже изданий, Нью-Йорк или Женева.

COMO CONSEGUIR PUBLICACIONES DE LAS NACIONES UNIDAS

Las publicaciones de las Naciones Unidas están en venta en librerías y casas distribuidoras en todas partes del mundo. Consulte a su librero o diríjase a: Naciones Unidas, Sección de Ventas, Nueva York o Ginebra.

Litho in United Nations, New York   02900   United Nations publication
02327—March 1988—1,825   ISBN 92-1-100324-5   Sales No. E.88.I.5

HOW TO OBTAIN UNITED NATIONS PUBLICATIONS

United Nations publications may be obtained from bookstores and
distributors throughout the world. Consult your bookstore or
write to: United Nations, Sales Section, New York or Geneva.

Printed in U.S.A.   02900   United Nations publication
88-40119—March 1988—1,825   Sales No. E.88.I.5
                                                       ISBN 92-1-100324-5